Authors In Depth

· · · ·

PLATINUM LEVEL

PRENTICE HALL
Upper Saddle River, New Jersey
Glenview, Illinois
Needham, Massachusetts

ISBN 013-050403-3

2 3 4 5 6 7 8 9 10   03 02 01 00

PRENTICE HALL

Acknowledgments

Grateful acknowledgment is made to the following for permission to reprint copyrighted material:

Arte Público Press
From *Communion* by Pat Mora, Copyright © 1991 by Pat Mora: "Still Life," "Desert Pilgrimage," *"Sueños/*Dreams," "Fences," *"Tigua* Elder," and *"Tejedora maya,"* "Silence Like Cool Sand." From *Borders* by Pat Mora, Copyright © 1986 by Pat Mora: "Oral History" and "Secrets." *"Bailando"* from *Chants* by Pat Mora, Copyright © 1985 by Pat Mora.

Beacon Press
From *"Febrero loco/*Crazy February" from *House of Houses* by Pat Mora. Copyright © 1997 by Pat Mora. Reprinted by permission of Beacon Press, Boston.

Blackwell Publishers
"Love is like the wild rose-briar" by Emily Brontë from *Selected Brontës,* Edward Chitham and Tom Winnifrith, © Edward Chitham and Tom Winnifrith 1985.

Gwendolyn Brooks Blakely
From *Selected Poems* by Gwendolyn Brooks (Harper & Row). Copyright 1944, 1945, 1949, 1959, 1960, 1963 by Gwendolyn Brooks Blakely: "In Honor of David Anderson Brooks, My Father," "Of Robert Frost," "Langston Hughes," "The Crazy Woman," and "The Last Quatrain of the Ballad of Emmett Till." From *Beginnings* by Gwendolyn Brooks (Broadside Press). Copyright © by Gwendolyn Brooks Blakely 1975: "Horses Graze" and "When Handed a Lemon, Make Lemonade." From *Annie Allen* by Gwendolyn Brooks (Greenwood Press). Copyright 1945, 1949 by Gwendolyn Brooks Blakely: "IX: truth" and "X." "Speech to the Young. Speech to the Progress-Toward" from *Family Pictures* by Gwendolyn Brooks (Broadside Press). Copyright © 1970 by Gwendolyn Brooks. From *Report From Part One* by Gwendolyn Brooks (Broadside Press). Copyright © 1972 Gwendolyn Brooks Blakely.

Acknowledgments continue on page 198

Contents

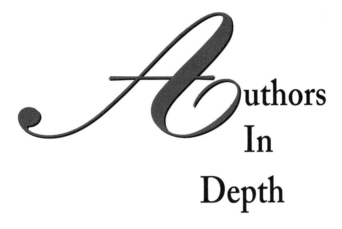

Authors
In
Depth

• • • •

PLATINUM LEVEL

Edgar Allan Poe In Depth

"I know several striking poems by American poets, but I think that Edgar Poe is (taking his poetry and prose together) the most original American genius."

—*Alfred, Lord Tennyson*

EDGAR ALLAN POE's literary legacy is sometimes overshadowed by his personal life. After he died, his enemies published unflattering reports about him concerning the reckless way in which he lived his life. Poe's other, and more important, legacy is the poems, essays, and stories that have influenced writers and other artists throughout the decades. Much of his work is still read and studied today.

Early Tragedy Poe was born in 1809; his parents were actors. Poe's father deserted the family in 1810. In 1811, his mother died in Richmond, Virginia, at the age of 24. Edgar went to live with a guardian.

Edgar's guardian was John Allan, a tobacco exporter. Although he never adopted Edgar legally, Allan gave him the name Edgar Allan. At schools in Virginia and Great Britain, Edgar was considered a scholar and athlete.

Studies and Problems Poe studied at the University of Virginia until, deep in debt, he was forced to leave the university. He ran off to Boston, where he paid to have his first book of poems published. To earn a living, he joined the Army.

When Mrs. Allan died in 1829, Poe and John Allan resumed relations. Poe's next plan was to apply to the U. S. Military Academy at West Point. He entered in 1830, after publishing another collection of his poems. At West Point he again got into trouble with debt and was court-martialed and expelled for disobeying orders. He then published a third collection of poems, which included "To Helen."

Magazine Work In 1831, Poe worked part-time for newspapers and wrote stories for literary magazines. When John Allan died in 1834, Poe was left out of his will. He moved to Richmond in 1835 to work as an editor of a new magazine, the *Southern Literary Messenger*.

The book reviews that Poe wrote for the magazine attracted attention and subscribers. He was often harsh in his criticism but always interesting. He challenged the New England writers who were the literary establishment of his day. In 1836 Poe married a girl named Virginia. By then he had begun writing the stories that he is known for today, but the magazine's owner complained about his depressed moods and fired Poe at the end of 1836.

Fame After a year in New York and the publication of a short novel which did not sell well, Poe moved with his wife to Philadelphia. He held editing jobs there while publishing many of his best-known stories. Some of Poe's work reflected the popular taste of the time for Gothic art, architecture, and literature, with its dark mysteries, ruined castles, horror, and the supernatural. Like other Americans of his era, Poe was interested in the classical ideals of order, light, and rationality, exemplified in the ancient Greeks and Romans.

By 1844, Poe was becoming recognized for his writing, especially when his poem "The Raven" was published in dozens of magazines and newspapers. He began to give public lectures on poetry. In addition, a volume of his stories called *The Raven and Other Poems* was published in 1845.

At the height of his success and fame, Poe also experienced several difficult years as well. No one is certain what caused his troubles. Many observers wrote about Poe's excesses. Recent scholarship, however, suggests too much emphasis may have been placed on Poe's behavior. It may be that Poe's macabre way of writing had more to do with the popular interests of the time than with his personal life.

Nightmare's End Poe's best known characters are fascinating because they seem driven by terrible forces. It would be a mistake, however, to view the author as one of his own creations, because Poe functioned relatively well in his life and was a productive writer. In his later years, however, Poe grieved over Virginia's death, often making him morose.

On a lecture tour in 1849, he was found unconscious on a street in Baltimore. After treatment in a hospital, he fell into a coma and died. The doctor, limited by the medical knowledge of the times, called Poe's condition "congestion of the brain." We will probably never know exactly what caused Poe's death, and it is indeed ironic that one of America's foremost creators of the detective story died in a mysterious way.

◆ Poe's Invention, the Detective Story

While watching detective characters on television or in a movie, we probably do not realize they are frequently offshoots of Edgar Allan Poe's work.

Poe most likely based C. Auguste Dupin, the detective in three of his stories, on the memoirs of a French detective named Vidocq. Many features found in detective stories today are claimed to be inventions of Poe's, including the super-intelligent detective, the police who are stumped by a crime, and the detective's friend who narrates the story. "Sherlock Holmes," the famous detective story by Sir Arthur Conan Doyle, shares all of these characters, as do many others.

A fitting recognition of Poe's literary contribution is the name of the awards given each year by the Mystery Writers of America: the Edgar Awards.

◆ Literary Works

Poetry
"To Science" (1829); **"To Helen"** (1831);
"The Raven" (1845); **"Ulalume"** (1847);
"The Bells" (1848); **"For Annie; Eldorado"** (1849).

Short Stories Poe's short stories were written between 1829–1849.

"Manuscript Found in a Bottle" (1832); **"Hans Phaall"** (1836); **"The Fall of the House of Usher"** (1839); **"The Murders in the Rue Morgue"** (1841); **"The Pit and the Pendulum"** (1842); **"The Mystery of Marie Roget"**; **"The Gold-Bug"**; **"The Tell-Tale Heart"** (1843); **"The Purloined Letter"** (1845); **"Hop-Frog"** (1849).

Criticism Poe published essays providing perspective on his stories and poems, and on writing in general.

"How to Write a Blackwood Article" (1838); **"The Philosophy of Composition"** (1846); **"The Poetic Principle"** (1850).

TIMELINE

Poe's Life		World Events	
1809	Edgar Poe is born in Boston	1804–15	Napoleon is Emperor of France
1811	His mother dies; the Allans provide a home for Edgar and his sister	1808	Beethoven writes Fifth and Sixth Symphonies; Goethe publishes Part One of *Faust*
1815–20	The Allans live in Scotland and England	1812	Grimms' *Fairy Tales* published
1826	Enters and leaves the University of Virginia	1812–15	U. S. at war with Great Britain
1827	Moves to Boston and enlists in Army	1817–25	Thomas Jefferson founds University of Virginia and designs its buildings in Classical style
1829	Mrs. Allan dies; Poe leaves army	1818	*Frankenstein* published
1830	At West Point	1821	Mexican independence
1831	Expelled from West Point; lives with relatives in Baltimore	1822	Liberia founded in West Africa as homeland for freed slaves
1831–34	Begins publishing stories	1827	Photography is invented
1835–36	Works for Southern Literary Messenger	1833	Slavery abolished in British Empire
1836	Marries Virginia Clemm; fired from Messenger	1837	Accession of Queen Victoria; rules Great Britain and the British Empire until her death in 1901
1837–44	Magazine and newspaper work in New York and Philadelphia; publishes many of best-known stories	1838	Telegraph is invented
1845	Publishes "The Raven" and becomes famous; lectures on literature	1839	Dickens's *Oliver Twist* published
		1846	Potato famine in Ireland
		1846–48	War between U. S. and Mexico
1847	Virginia dies	1847	*Jane Eyre* and *Wuthering Heights* are published
1849	After sickness, depression, and irrational episodes, Poe dies in Baltimore and is buried there	1848	Revolutions in Europe; Seneca Falls, New York, meeting for women's rights
		1848–49	Gold Rush

Edgar Allan Poe

The Pit and the Pendulum

Impia tortorum longas hic turba furores
Sanguinis innocui, non satiata, aluit.
Sospite nunc patria, fracto nunc funeris antro,
Mors ubi dira fuit vita salusque patent.[1]
*[Quatrain composed for the gates of a market to be erected
upon the site of the Jacobin Club House at Paris.]*

I was sick—sick unto death with that long agony; and when they at length unbound me, and I was permitted to sit, I felt that my senses were leaving me. The sentence—the dread sentence of death—was the last of distinct accentuation which reached my ears. After that, the sound of the inquisitorial[2] voices seemed merged in one dreamy indeterminate hum. It conveyed to my soul the idea of *revolution*—perhaps from its association in fancy with the burr of a mill-wheel. This only for a brief period; for presently I heard no more. Yet, for a while, I saw; but with how terrible an exaggeration! I saw the lips of the black-robed judges. They appeared to me white—whiter than the sheet upon which I trace these words—and thin even to grotesqueness; thin with the intensity of their expression of firmness—of immovable resolution—of stern contempt of human torture. I saw that the decrees of what to me was Fate, were still issuing from those lips. I saw them writhe with a deadly locution.[3] I saw them fashion the syllables of my name; and I shuddered because no sound succeeded. I saw, too, for a few moments of delirious horror, the soft and nearly imperceptible waving of the sable draperies which enwrapped the walls of the apartment. And then my vision fell upon the seven tall candles upon the table. At first they wore the aspect of charity, and seemed white slender angels who would save me; but then, all at once, there came a most deadly nausea over my spirit, and I felt every fibre in my frame thrill as if I had touched the wire of a galvanic battery, while the angel forms became meaningless spectres, with heads of flame, and I saw that from them there would be no help. And then there stole into my fancy, like a rich musical note, the thought of what sweet rest there must be in the grave. The thought came gently and stealthily, and it seemed long before it attained full appreciation; but just as my spirit came at length properly to feel and entertain it, the figures of the judges

---

1. Here the wicked mob, unappeased, long cherished a hatred of innocent blood. Now that the fatherland is saved, and the cave of death demolished, where grim death has been, life and health appear.
2. inquisitorial: Of the Spanish Inquisition, a court for religious offenses.
3. locution: Word.

vanished, as if magically, from before me; the tall candles sank into nothingness; their flames went out utterly; the blackness of darkness supervened; all sensations appeared swallowed up in a mad rushing descent as of the soul into Hades.[4] Then silence, and stillness, and night were the universe.

I had swooned; but still will not say that all of consciousness was lost. What of it there remained I will not attempt to define, or even to describe; yet all was not lost. In the deepest slumber—no! In delirium—no! In a swoon—no! In death—no! even in the grave all is *not* lost. Else there is no immortality for man. Arousing from the most profound of slumbers, we break the gossamer web of *some* dream. Yet in a second afterward (so frail may that web have been) we remember not that we have dreamed. In the return to life from the swoon there are two stages; first, that of the sense of mental or spiritual; secondly, that of the sense of physical, existence. It seems probable that if, upon reaching the second stage, we could recall the impressions of the first, we should find these impressions eloquent in memories of the gulf beyond. And that gulf is—what? How at least shall we distinguish its shadows from those of the tomb? But if the impressions of what I have termed the first stage, are not, at will, recalled, yet, after long interval, do they not come unbidden, while we marvel whence they come? He who has never swooned, is not he who finds strange palaces and wildly familiar faces in coals that glow; is not he who beholds floating in mid-air the sad visions that the many may not view; is not he who ponders over the perfume of some novel flower—is not he whose brain grows bewildered with the meaning of some musical cadence which has never before arrested his attention.

Amid frequent and thoughtful endeavors to remember; amid earnest struggles to regather some token of the state of seeming nothingness into which my soul had lapsed, there have been moments when I have dreamed of success; there have been brief, very brief periods when I have conjured up remembrances which the lucid reason of a later epoch assures me could have had reference only to that condition of seeming unconsciousness. These shadows of memory tell, indistinctly, of tall figures that lifted and bore me in silence down—down—still down—till a hideous dizziness oppressed me at the mere idea of the interminableness of the descent. They tell also of a vague horror at my heart, on account of that heart's unnatural stillness. Then comes a sense of sudden motionlessness throughout all things; as if those who bore me (a ghastly train!) had outrun, in their descent, the limits of the limitless, and paused from the wearisomeness of their toil.

---

4. **Hades:** Hell.

After this I call to mind flatness and dampness; and then all is *madness*—the madness of a memory which busies itself among forbidden things.

Very suddenly there came back to my soul motion and sound —the tumultuous motion of the heart, and, in my ears, the sound of its beating. Then a pause in which all is blank. Then again sound, and motion, and touch—a tingling sensation pervading my frame. Then the mere consciousness of existence, without thought—a condition which lasted long. Then, very suddenly, *thought*, and shuddering terror, and earnest endeavor to comprehend my true state. Then a strong desire to lapse into insensibility. Then a rushing revival of soul and a successful effort to move. And now a full memory of the trial, of the judges, of the sable draperies, of the sentence, of the sickness, of the swoon. Then entire forgetfulness of all that followed; of all that a later day and much earnestness of endeavor have enabled me vaguely to recall.

So far, I had not opened my eyes. I felt that I lay upon my back, unbound. I reached out my hand, and it fell heavily upon something damp and hard. There I suffered[5] it to remain for many minutes, while I strove to imagine where and *what* I could be. I longed, yet dared not to employ my vision. I dreaded the first glance at objects around me. It was not that I feared to look upon things horrible, but that I grew aghast lest there should be *nothing* to see. At length, with a wild desperation at heart, I quickly unclosed my eyes. My worst thoughts, then, were confirmed. The blackness of eternal night encompassed me. I struggled for breath. The intensity of the darkness seemed to oppress and stifle me. The atmosphere was intolerably close. I still lay quietly, and made effort to exercise my reason. I brought to mind the inquisitorial proceedings, and attempted from that point to deduce my real condition. The sentence had passed; and it appeared to me that a very long interval of time had since elapsed. Yet not for a moment did I suppose myself actually dead. Such a supposition, notwithstanding what we read in fiction, is altogether inconsistent with real existence; —but where and in what state was I? The condemned to death, I knew, perished usually at the *auto-da-fes*[6] and one of these had been held on the very night of the day of my trial. Had I been remanded[7] to my dungeon, to await the next sacrifice, which would not take place for many months? This I at once saw could not be. Victims had been in immediate demand. Moreover, my dungeon, as well as all the condemned cells at Toledo, had stone floors, and light was not altogether excluded.

A fearful idea now suddenly drove the blood in torrents upon

---

5. **Suffered:** Permitted.
6. *auto-da-fes*: Executions.
7. **remanded:** Sent

my heart, and for a brief period, I once more relapsed into insensibility. Upon recovering, I at once started to my feet, trembling convulsively in every fibre. I thrust my arms wildly above and around me in all directions. I felt nothing; yet dreaded to move a step, lest I should be impeded by the walls of a *tomb.* Perspiration burst from every pore, and stood in cold big beads upon my forehead. The agony of suspense, grew at length intolerable, and I cautiously moved forward, with my arms extended, and my eyes straining from their sockets, in the hope of catching some faint ray of light. I proceeded for many paces; but still all was blackness and vacancy. I breathed more freely. It seemed evident that mine was not, at least, the most hideous of fates.

And now, as I still continued to step cautiously onward, there came thronging upon my recollection a thousand vague rumors of the horrors of Toledo. Of the dungeons there had been strange things narrated—fables I had always deemed them—but yet strange, and too ghastly to repeat, save in a whisper. Was I left to perish of starvation in this subterranean world of darkness; or what fate, perhaps even more fearful, awaited me? That the result would be death, and a death of more than customary bitterness, I knew too well the character of my judges to doubt. The mode and the hour were all that occupied or distracted me.

My outstretched hands at length encountered some solid obstruction. It was a wall, seemingly of stone masonry—very smooth, slimy, and cold. I followed it up; stepping with all the careful distrust with which certain antique narratives had inspired me. This process, however, afforded me no means of ascertaining the dimensions of my dungeon; as I might make its circuit, and return to the point whence I set out, without being aware of the fact; so perfectly uniform seemed the wall. I therefore sought the knife which had been in my pocket, when led into the inquisitorial chamber; but it was gone; my clothes had been exchanged for a wrapper of coarse serge. I had thought of forcing the blade in some minute crevice of the masonry, so as to identify my point of departure. The difficulty, nevertheless, was but trivial; although in the disorder of my fancy, it seemed at first insuperable.[8] I tore a part of the hem from the robe and placed the fragment at full length, and at right angles to the wall. In groping my way around the prison, I could not fail to encounter this rag upon completing the circuit. So, at least, I thought: but I had not counted upon the extent of the dungeon, or upon my own weakness. The ground was moist and slippery. I staggered onward for some time, when I stumbled and fell. My excessive fatigue induced me to remain prostrate; and sleep soon overtook me as I lay.

---

8. **insuperable:** Impossible.

Upon awaking, and stretching forth an arm, I found beside me a loaf and a pitcher with water. I was too much exhausted to reflect upon this circumstance, but ate and drank with avidity. Shortly afterward, I resumed my tour around the prison, and with much toil, came at last upon the fragment of the serge. Up to the period when I fell, I had counted fifty-two paces, and, upon resuming my walk, I had counted forty-eight more—when I arrived at the rag. There were in all, then, a hundred paces; and, admitting two paces to the yard, I presumed the dungeon to be fifty yards in circuit. I had met, however, with many angles in the wall, and thus I could form no guess at the shape of the vault; for vault I could not help supposing it to be.

I had little object—certainly no hope—in these researches; but a vague curiosity prompted me to continue them. Quitting the wall, I resolved to cross the area of the enclosure. At first, I proceeded with extreme caution, for the floor, although seemingly of solid material, was treacherous with slime. At length, however, I took courage, and did not hesitate to step firmly—endeavoring to cross in a direct a line as possible. I had advanced some ten or twelve paces in this manner, when the remnant of the torn hem of my robe became entangled between my legs. I stepped on it, and fell violently on my face.

In the confusion attending my fall, I did not immediately apprehend a somewhat startling circumstance, which yet, in a few seconds afterward, and while I still lay prostrate, arrested my attention. It was this: my chin rested upon the floor of the prison, but my lips, and the upper portion of my head, although seemingly at a less elevation than the chin, touched nothing. At the same time, my forehead seemed bathed in a clammy vapor, and the peculiar smell of decayed fungus arose to my nostrils. I put forward my arm, and shuddered to find that I had fallen at the very brink of a circular pit, whose extent, of course, I had no means of ascertaining at the moment. Groping about the masonry just below the margin, I succeeded in dislodging a small fragment, and let it fall into the abyss. For many seconds I listened to its reverberations as it dashed against the sides of the chasm in its descent: at length, there was a sullen plunge into water, succeeded by loud echoes. At the same moment, there came a sound resembling the quick opening, and as rapid closing of a door overhead, while a faint gleam of light flashed suddenly through the gloom, and as suddenly faded away.

I saw clearly the doom which had been prepared for me, and congratulated myself upon the timely accident by which I had escaped. Another step before my fall, and the world had seen me no more. And the death just avoided, was of that very character which I had regarded as fabulous and frivolous in the tales respecting the Inquisition.[9] To the victims of its tyranny, there was the choice of death with its direst physical agonies, or death with its most hideous moral horrors. I had been reserved for the latter. By long suffering my nerves had been unstrung until I trembled at the sound of my own voice, and had become in every respect a fitting subject for the species of torture which awaited me.

Shaking in every limb, I groped my way back to the wall— resolving there to perish rather than risk the terrors of the wells, of which my imagination now pictured many in various positions about the dungeon. In other conditions of mind, I might have had courage to end my misery at once, by a plunge into one of these abysses; but now I was the veriest of cowards. Neither could I forget what I had read of these pits—that the *sudden* extinction of life formed no part of their most horrible plan.

Agitation of spirit kept me awake for many long hours; but at length I again slumbered. Upon arousing, I found by my side, as before, a loaf and a pitcher of water. A burning thirst consumed me, and I emptied the vessel at a draught. It must have been drugged—for scarcely had I drunk, before I became irresistibly drowsy. A deep sleep fell upon me—a sleep like that of death. How long it lasted, of course I know not; but when, once again, I unclosed my eyes, the objects around me were visible. By a wild, sulphurous lustre, the origin of which I could not at first determine, I was enabled to see the extent and aspect of the prison.

In its size I had been greatly mistaken. The whole circuit of its walls did not exceed twenty-five yards. For some minutes this fact occasioned me a world of vain trouble; vain indeed—for what could be of less importance, under the terrible circumstances which environed[10] me, than the mere dimensions of my dungeon? But my soul took a wild interest in trifles, and I busied myself in endeavors to account for the error I had committed in my measurement. The truth at length flashed upon me. In my first attempt at exploration, I had counted fifty-two paces, up to the period when I fell: I must have been within a pace or two of the fragment of serge; in fact, I had nearly performed the circuit of the vault. I then slept—and, upon awaking, I must have returned upon my steps—thus supposing the circuit nearly double what it actually was. My confusion of mind prevented me from observing that I began my tour with the wall to the left, and ended it with the wall to the right.

I had been deceived, too, in respect to the shape of the enclosure. In feeling my way, I had found many angles, and thus deduced an idea of great irregularity; so potent is the effect of total darkness upon one arousing from lethargy or sleep! The

---

9. **Inquisition:** The Spanish Inquisition, a court for religious offenses.
10. **environed:** Surrounded.

angles were simply those of a few slight depressions or niches, at odd intervals. The general shape of the prison was square. What I had taken for masonry, seemed now to be iron, or some other metal, in huge plates, whose sutures or joints occasioned the depression. The entire surface of this metallic enclosure was rudely daubed in all the hideous and repulsive devices to which the charnel[11] superstition of the monks has given rise. The figures of fiends in aspects of menace, with skeleton forms, and other more really fearful images, overspread and disfigured the walls. I observed that the outlines of these monstrosities were sufficiently distinct, but that the colors seemed faded and blurred, as if from the effects of a damp atmosphere. I now noticed the floor, too, which was of stone. In the centre yawned the circular pit from whose jaws I had escaped; but it was the only one in the dungeon.

All this I saw indistinctly and by much effort—for my personal condition had been greatly changed during slumber. I now lay upon my back, and at full length, on a species of low framework of wood. To this I was securely bound by a long strap resembling a surcingle.[12] It passed in many convolutions about my limbs and body, leaving at liberty only my head, and my left arm to such extent, that I could, by dint of much exertion, supply myself with food from an earthen dish which lay by my side on the floor. I saw, to my horror, that the pitcher had been removed. I say, to my horror—for I was consumed with intolerable thirst. This thirst it appeared to be the design of my persecutors to stimulate—for the food in the dish was meat pungently seasoned.

Looking upward, I surveyed the ceiling of my prison. It was some thirty or forty feet overhead, constructed much as the side walls. In one of its panels a very singular figure riveted my whole attention. It was the painted figure of Time as he is commonly represented, save that, in lieu of a scythe, he held what, at a casual glance, I supposed to be the pictured image of a huge pendulum, such as we see on antique clocks. There was something, however, in the appearance of this machine which caused me to regard it more attentively. While I gazed directly upward at it, (for its position was immediately over my own,) I fancied that I saw it in motion. In an instant afterward the fancy was confirmed. Its sweep was brief, and of course slow. I watched it for some minutes, somewhat in fear, but more in wonder. Wearied at length with observing its dull movement, I turned my eyes upon the other objects in the cell.

A slight noise attracted my notice, and, looking to the floor, I saw several enormous rats traversing it. They had issued from

---

11. **charnel:** Concerning death.
12. **surcingle:** Cloth belt or sash.

the well, which lay just within view to my right. Even then, while I gazed, they came up in troops, hurriedly, with ravenous eyes, allured by the scent of the meat. From this it required much effort and attention to scare them away.

It might have been half an hour, perhaps even an hour (for I could take but imperfect note of time), before I again cast my eyes upward. What I then saw, confounded and amazed me. The sweep of the pendulum had increased in extent by nearly a yard. As a natural consequence, its velocity was also much greater. But what mainly disturbed me, was the idea that it had percep-tibly *descended.* I now observed—with what horror it is needless to say – that its nether[13] extremity was formed of a crescent of glittering steel, about a foot in length from horn to horn; the horns upward, and the under edge evidently as keen as that of a razor. Like a razor also, it seemed massy and heavy, tapering from the edge into a solid and broad structure above. It was appended to a weighty rod of brass, and the whole *hissed* as it swung through the air.

I could no longer doubt the doom prepared for me by monk-ish ingenuity in torture. My cognizance[14] of the pit had become known to the inquisitorial agents—*the pit,* whose horrors had been destined for so bold a recusant[15] as myself—*the pit,* typical of hell, and regarded by rumor as the Ultima Thule[16] of all their punishments. The plunge into this pit I had avoided by the mer-est of accidents, and I knew that surprise, or entrapment into torment, formed an important portion of all the grotesquerie of these dungeon deaths. Having failed to fall, it was no part of the demon plan to hurl me into the abyss; and thus (there being no alternative) a different and a milder destruction awaited me. Milder! I half smiled in my agony as I thought of such applica-tion of such a term.

What boots it to tell of the long, long hours of horror more than mortal, during which I counted the rushing oscillations of the steel! Inch by inch—line by line—with a descent only appre-ciable at intervals that seemed ages—down and still down it came! Days passed—it might have been that many days passed—ere it swept so closely over me as to fan me with its acrid breath. The odor of the sharp steel forced itself into my nostrils. I prayed—I wearied heaven with my prayer for its more speedy descent. I grew frantically mad, and struggled to force myself upward against the sweep of the fearful scimitar.[17] And

---

13. **nether:** Lower.
14. **cognizance:** Awareness.
15. **recusant:** Rebel.
16. **Ultima Thule:** Absolute extreme.
17. **scimitar:** Curved blade.

then I fell suddenly calm, and lay smiling at the glittering death, as a child at some rare bauble.

There was another interval of utter insensibility; it was brief; for, upon again lapsing into life, there had been no perceptible descent in the pendulum, But it might have been long—for I knew there were demons who took note of my swoon, and who could have arrested the vibration at pleasure. Upon my recovery, too, I felt very—oh inexpressibly—sick and weak, as if through long inanition.[18] Even amid the agonies of that period, the human nature craved food. With painful effort I outstretched my left arm as far as my bonds permitted, and took possession of the small remnant which had been spared me by the rats. As I put a portion of it within my lips, there rushed to my mind a half-formed thought of joy—of hope? Yet what business had *I* with hope? It was, as I say, a half-formed thought—man has many such, which are never completed. I felt that it was of joy—of hope; but I felt also that it had perished in its formation. In vain I struggled to perfect—to regain it. Long suffering had nearly annihilated all my ordinary powers of mind. I was an imbecile—an idiot.

The vibration of the pendulum was at right angles to my length. I saw that the crescent was designed to cross the region of the heart. It would fray the serge of my robe—it would return and repeat its operations—again—and again. Notwithstanding its terrifically wide sweep (some thirty feet or more) and the hissing vigor of its descent, sufficient to sunder these very walls of iron, still the fraying of my robe would be all that, for several minutes, it would accomplish. And at this thought I paused. I dared not go further than this reflection. I dwelt upon it with a pertinacity[19] of attention—as if, in so dwelling, I could arrest *here* the descent of the steel. I forced myself to ponder upon the sound of the crescent as it should pass across the garment—upon the peculiar thrilling sensation which the friction of cloth produces on the nerves. I pondered upon all this frivolity until my teeth were on edge.

Down—steadily down it crept. I took a frenzied pleasure in contrasting its downward with its lateral velocity. To the right—to the left—far and wide—with the shriek of a damned spirit! to my heart, with the stealthy pace of the tiger! I alternately laughed and howled, as the one or the other idea grew predominant.

Down—certainly relentlessly down! It vibrated within three inches of my bosom! I struggled violently—furiously—to free my left arm. This was free only from the elbow to the hand. I could reach the latter, from the platter beside me, to my mouth, with

---

18. inanition: Exhaustion.
19. pertinacity: Persistence.

great effort, but no farther. Could I have broken the fastenings above the elbow, I would have seized and attempted to arrest the pendulum. I might as well have attempted to arrest an avalanche!

Down—still unceasingly—still inevitably down! I gasped and struggled at each vibration. I shrunk convulsively at its every sweep. My eyes followed its outward or upward whirls with the eagerness of the most unmeaning despair; they closed themselves spasmodically at the descent, although death would have been a relief, oh, how unspeakable! Still I quivered in every nerve to think how slight a sinking of the machinery would precipitate that keen, glistening axe upon my bosom. It was *hope* that prompted the nerve to quiver—the frame to shrink. It was *hope*—the hope that triumphs on the rack[20]—that whispers to the death-condemned even in the dungeons of the Inquisition.

I saw that some ten or twelve vibrations would bring the steel in actual contact with my robe—and with this observation there suddenly came over my spirit all the keen, collected calmness of despair. For the first time during many hours—or perhaps days —I thought. It now occurred to me, that the bandage, or surcingle, which enveloped me, was *unique*. I was tied by no separate cord. The first stroke of the razor-like crescent athwart[21] any portion of the band, would so detach it that it might be unwound from my person by means of my left hand. But how fearful, in that case, the proximity of the steel! The result of the slightest struggle, how deadly! Was it likely, moreover, that the minions[22] of the torturer had not foreseen and provided for this possibility? Was it probable that the bandage crossed my bosom in the track of the pendulum? Dreading to find my faint, and, as it seemed, my last hope frustrated, I so far elevated my head as to obtain a distinct view of my breast. The surcingle enveloped my limbs and body close in all directions—*save in the path of the destroying crescent.*

Scarcely had I dropped my head back into its original position, when there flashed upon my mind what I cannot better describe than as the unformed half of that idea of deliverance to which I have previously alluded, and of which a moiety[23] only floated indeterminately through my brain when I raised food to my burning lips. The whole thought was now present—feeble, scarcely sane, scarcely definite—but still entire. I proceeded at once, with the nervous energy of despair, to attempt its execution.

For many hours the immediate vicinity of the low framework upon which I lay, had been literally swarming with rats. They

---

20. **rack:** A device to torture a victim by stretching his or her body.
21. **athwart:** Across.
22. **minions:** Helpers.
23. **moiety:** Portion.

were wild, bold, ravenous—their red eyes glaring upon me as if they waited but for motionlessness on my part to make me their prey. "To what food," I thought, "have they been accustomed in the well?"

They had devoured, in spite of all my efforts to prevent them, all but a small remnant of the contents of the dish. I had fallen into an habitual see-saw, or wave of the hand about the platter; and, at length, the unconscious uniformity of the movement deprived it of effect. In their voracity, the vermin frequently fastened their sharp fangs in my fingers. With the particles of the oily and spicy viand[24] which now remained, I thoroughly rubbed the bandage wherever I could reach it; then, raising my hand from the floor, I lay breathlessly still.

At first, the ravenous animals were startled and terrified at the change—at the cessation of movement. They shrank alarmedly back; many sought the well. But this was only for a moment. I had not counted in vain upon their voracity. Observing that I remained without motion, one or two of the boldest leaped upon the frame-work, and smelt at the surcingle. This seemed the signal for a general rush. Forth from the well they hurried in fresh troops. They clung to the wood—overran it, and leaped in hundreds upon my person. The measured movement of the pendulum disturbed them not at all. Avoiding its strokes, they busied themselves with the anointed bandage. They pressed —they swarmed upon me in ever accumulating heaps. They writhed upon my throat; their cold lips sought my own; I was half stifled by their thronging pressure; disgust, for which the world has no name, swelled my bosom, and chilled, with a heavy clamminess, my heart. Yet one minute, and I felt that the struggle would be over. Plainly I perceived the loosening of the bandage. I knew that in more than one place it must be already severed. With a more than human resolution I lay *still*.

Nor had I erred in my calculations—nor had I endured in vain. I at length felt that I was *free*. The surcingle hung in ribands[25] from my body. But the stroke of the pendulum already pressed upon my bosom. It had divided the serge of the robe. It had cut through the linen beneath. Twice again it swung, and a sharp sense of pain shot through every nerve. But the moment of escape had arrived. At a wave of my hand my deliverers hurried tumultuously away. With a steady movement—cautious, sidelong, shrinking, and slow—I slid from the embrace of the bandage and beyond the reach of the scimitar. For the moment, at least, *I was free.*

Free!—and in the grasp of the Inquisition! I had scarcely

---

24. **viand:** Piece of food.
25. **ribands:** Strips.

stepped from my wooden bed of horror upon the stone floor of the prison, when the motion of the hellish machine ceased, and I beheld it drawn up, by some invisible force, through the ceiling. This was a lesson which I took desperately to heart. My every motion was undoubtedly watched. Free!—I had but escaped death in one form, of agony, to be delivered unto worse than death in some other. With that thought I rolled my eyes nervously around on the barriers of iron that hemmed me in. Something unusual—some change which, at first, I could not appreciate distinctly—it was obvious, had taken place in the apartment. For many minutes of a dreamy and trembling abstraction, I busied myself in vain, unconnected conjecture. During this period, I became aware, for the first time, of the origin of the sulphurous light which illumined the cell. It proceeded from a fissure, about half an inch in width, extending entirely around the prison at the base of the walls, which thus appeared, and were completely separated from the floor. I endeavored, but of course in vain, to look through the aperture.

As I arose from the attempt, the mystery of the alteration in the chamber broke at once upon my understanding. I have observed that, although the outlines of the figures upon the walls were sufficiently distinct, yet the colors seemed blurred and indefinite. These colors had now assumed, and were momentarily assuming, a startling and most intense brilliancy, that gave to the spectral and fiendish portraitures an aspect that might have thrilled even firmer nerves than my own. Demon eyes, of a wild and ghastly vivacity, glared upon me in a thousand directions, where none had been visible before, and gleamed with the lurid lustre of a fire that I could not force my imagination to regard as unreal.

Unreal! Even while I breathed there came to my nostrils the breath of the vapor of heated iron! A suffocating odor pervaded the prison! A deeper glow settled each moment in the eyes that glared at my agonies! A richer tint of crimson diffused itself over the pictured horrors of blood. I panted! I gasped for breath! There could be no doubt of the design of my tormentors—oh! most unrelenting! oh! most demoniac of men! I shrank from the glowing metal to the centre of the cell. Amid the thought of the fiery destruction that impended,[26] the idea of the coolness of the well came over my soul like balm. I rushed to its deadly brink. I threw my straining vision below. The glare from the enkindled roof illumined its inmost recesses. Yet, for a wild moment, did my spirit refuse to comprehend the meaning of what I saw. At length it forced—it wrestled its way into my soul—it burned itself in upon my shuddering reason. Oh! for a voice to speak!—oh! horror!—oh!

---

26. **impended:** Threatened to take place.

any horror but this! With a shriek, I rushed from the margin, and buried my face in my hands—weeping bitterly.

The heat rapidly increased, and once again I looked up, shuddering as with a fit of the ague.[27] There had been a second change in the cell—and now the change was obviously in the *form.* As before, it was in vain that I at first endeavored to appreciate or understand what was taking place. But not long was I left in doubt. The Inquisitorial vengeance had been hurried by my two-fold escape, and there was to be no more dallying with the King of Terrors.[28] The room had been square. I saw that two of its iron angles were now acute—two, consequently—obtuse. The fearful difference quickly increased with a low rumbling or moaning sound. In an instant the apartment had shifted its form into that of a lozenge. But the alteration stopped not here—I neither hoped nor desired it to stop. I could have clasped the red walls to my bosom as a garment of eternal peace. "Death," I said, "any death but that of the pit!" Fool! might I not have known that *into the pit* it was the object of the burning iron to urge me? Could I resist its glow? or if even that, could I withstand its pressure? And now, flatter and flatter grew the lozenge, with a rapidity that left me no time for contemplation. Its centre, and of course, its greatest width, came just over the yawning gulf. I shrank back—but the closing walls pressed me resistlessly onward. At length for my seared and writhing body there was no longer an inch of foothold on the firm floor of the prison. I struggled no more, but the agony of my soul found vent in one loud, long, and final scream of despair. I felt that I tottered upon the brink—I averted my eyes—

There was a discordant hum of human voices! There was a loud blast as of many trumpets! There was a harsh grating as of a thousand thunders! The fiery walls rushed back! An out-stretched arm caught my own as I fell, fainting, into the abyss. It was that of General Lasalle.[29] The French army had entered Toledo. The Inquisition was in the hands of its enemies.

---

27. **ague:** Fit of shivering.
28 **King of Terrors:** Death.
29 **General Lasalle:** French general who attacked Toledo, Spain, in 1808.

☑ Check Your Comprehension

1. In the first paragraph the narrator speaks about tracing his words on a sheet of paper. What does that suggest about the outcome of the story?

2. After he throws a piece of stone or mortar down the pit, the narrator hears the opening and closing of a door and sees a flash of light. What caused these sounds and the light?

3. What are the two motions of the pendulum?

4. Is the narrator finally able to save himself by his own efforts? Explain.

◆ Critical Thinking

APPLY

1. We do not know the crime for which the narrator was sentenced to death. Is it possible that his crime could justify the punishments imposed on him? Explain your answer. **[Speculate]**

2. Does the narrator seem driven to madness by his ordeal? Why or why not? **[Make a Decision]**

EVALUATE

3. What is the effect of having the story told by a first-person narrator? **[Evaluate]**

4. Is the ending believable? Would you prefer a different ending? Explain. **[Make a Judgment]**

Edgar Allan Poe

Ulalume—A Ballad

The skies they were ashen and sober;
The leaves they were crisped and sere[1]—
The leaves they were withering and sere:
It was night, in the lonesome October
5   Of my most immemorial year:
It was hard by the dim lake of Auber,
In the misty mid region of Weir:—
It was down by the dank tarn[2] of Auber,
In the ghoul-haunted woodland of Weir.

10   Here once, through an alley Titanic,[3]
Of cypress, I roamed with my Soul—
Of cypress, with Psyche[4], my Soul.
These were days when my heart was volcanic
As the scoriac[5] rivers that roll—
15   As the lavas that restlessly roll
Their sulphurous currents down Yaanek,
In the ultimate climes of the Pole—
That groan as they roll down Mount Yaanek,
In the realms of the Boreal Pole.[6]

20   Our talk had been serious and sober,
But our thoughts they were palsied and sere—
Our memories were treacherous and sere;
For we knew not the month was October,
And we marked not the night of the year—
25   (Ah, night of all nights in the year!)
We noted not the dim lake of Auber,
(Though once we had journeyed down here)
We remembered not the dank tarn of Auber,
Nor the ghoul-haunted woodland of Weir.

30   And now, as the night was senescent,[7]
And star-dials pointed to morn—

---

1. **sere:** Withered.
2. **tarn:** Mountain lake.
3. **Titanic:** Huge. The titans were a mythical race of giants.
4. **Psyche:** The soul.
5. **Scoriac:** Made of dark lava.
6. **Boreal Pole:** North Pole, after Boreas, Greek god of the north wind.
7. **senescent:** Growing old.

As the star-dials hinted of morn—
At the end of our path a liquescent
And nebulous lustre was born,
35   Out of which a miraculous crescent
Arose with a duplicate horn—
Astarte's[8] bediamonded crescent,
Distinct with its duplicate horn.

And I said—"She is warmer than Dian;[9]
40   She rolls through an ether of sighs—
She revels in a region of sighs.
She has seen that the tears are not dry on
These cheeks where the worm never dies,
And has come past the stars of the Lion[10]
45   To point us the path to the skies—
To the Lethean[11] peace of the skies—
Come up, in despite of the Lion,
To shine on us with her bright eyes—
Come up, through the lair of the Lion,
50   With love in her luminous eyes."

But Psyche, uplifting her finger,
Said—"Sadly this star I mistrust—
Her pallor I strangely mistrust—
Ah, hasten!—ah, let us not linger!
55   Ah, fly!—let us fly!—for we must."
In terror she spoke; letting sink her
Wings till they trailed in the dust—
In agony sobbed; letting sink her
Plumes till they trailed in the dust—
60   Till they sorrowfully trailed in the dust.

I replied—"This is nothing but dreaming.
Let us on, by this tremulous light!
Let us bathe in this crystalline light!
Its Sibyllic[12] splendor is beaming
65   With Hope and in Beauty to-night—
See!—it flickers up the sky through the night!
Ah, we safely may trust to its gleaming
And be sure it will lead us aright—
We surely may trust to a gleaming
70   That cannot but guide us aright

---

8. **Astarte:** Ancient Phoenician goddess of love and fertility.
9. **Dian:** Diana, goddess of the moon.
10. **Lion:** The constellation Leo.
11. **Lethean:** With the forgetfulness of death.
12. **Sibyllic:** Like a woman who tells the future.

Since it flickers up to Heaven through the night."
Thus I pacified Psyche and kissed her,
And tempted her out of her gloom—
75   And conquered her scruples and gloom;
And we passed to the end of the vista
But were stopped by the door of a tomb—
By the door of a legended tomb:—
And I said—"What is written, sweet sister,
On the door of this legended tomb?"
80   She replied—"Ulalume – Ulalume! –
'T is the vault of thy lost Ulalume!"

Then my heart it grew ashen and sober
As the leaves that were crisped and sere—
As the leaves that were withering and sere—
85   And I cried—"It was surely October,
On *this* very night of last year,
That I journeyed—I journeyed down here!—
That I brought a dread burden down here—
On this night, of all nights in the year,
90   Ah. what demon hath tempted me here?
Well I know, now, this dim lake of Auber—
This misty mid region of Weir:—
Well I know, now, this dank tarn of Auber—
This ghoul-haunted woodland of Weir."

95   Said we, then—the two, then—"Ah, can it
Have been that the woodlandish ghouls—
The pitiful, the merciful ghouls,
To bar up our way and to ban it
From the secret that lies in these wolds[13]—
100   From the thing that lies hidden in these wolds—
Have drawn up the spectre of a planet
From the limbo of lunary[14] souls—
This sinfully scintillant[15] planet
From the Hell of the planetary souls?"

---

13. **wolds:** Fields.
14. **lunary:** Affected by the moon.
15. **scintillant:** Sparkling.

Edgar Allan Poe

Alone

From childhood's hour I have not been
As others were—I have not seen
As others saw—I could not bring
My passions from a common spring—
5   From the same source I have not taken
My sorrow—I could not awaken
My heart to joy at the same tone—
And all I lov'd—I lov'd alone—
Then—in my childhood—in the dawn
10   Of a most stormy life—was drawn
From ev'ry depth of good and ill
The mystery which binds me still—
From the torrent, or the fountain—
From the red cliff of the mountain—
15   From the sun that 'round me roll'd
In its autumn tint of gold—
From the lightning in the sky
As it pass'd me flying by—
From the thunder and the storm—
20   And the cloud that took the form
(When the rest of Heaven was blue)
Of a demon in my view

Sonnet — To Science

Science! true daughter of Old Time thou art!
    Who alterest all things with thy peering eyes.
Why preyest thou thus upon the poet's heart,
    Vulture, whose wings are dull realities?
5   How should he love thee? or how deem thee wise?
    Who wouldst not leave him in his wandering
To seek for treasure in the jeweled skies,
    Albeit he soared with an undaunted wing?
Hast thou not dragged Diana¹ from her car?
10   And driven the Hamadryad² from the wood
To seek a shelter in some happier star?
    Hast thou not torn the Naiad from her flood,
The Elfin from the green grass, and from me
The summer dream beneath the tamarind³ tree?

1. Diana: The Roman goddess of the hunt who was associated with the moon, which serves as her "car."
2. Hamadryad: A wood nymph fabled to pass her entire life in a single tree.
3. tamarind: A tropical tree, the fruit of which is valued as food and medicine.

☑ Check Your Comprehension

1. In "Ulalume", what has the speaker forgotten about this night in October?
2. In ancient mythology, the god Psyche referred to a person's soul. What is suggested by the speaker's relationship with Psyche in "Ulalume"?
3. In what ways does that the speaker of "Alone" feel unlike the "others"?
4. What is the "mystery" of line 12 of "Alone"?
5. In "Sonnet—To Science," why is Science addressed as "Vulture"?
6. In line 7 of "Sonnet—To Science," what is the treasure that the poet seeks in "the jeweled skies"?

◆ Critical Thinking

1. What is the effect of all the repetitions in "Ulalume"? **[Connect]**
2. Does the speaker of "Alone" assume others will feel as he does about the "mystery"? Explain. **[Draw Conclusions]**
3. Is science as negative a force in the world as the poem "Sonnet—To Science" suggests? Why or why not? **[Speculate]**

COMPARE LITERARY WORKS

4. The speaker in each of these poems has a powerful imagination. Which one has the kind of imagination that is closest to yours? **[Relate]**

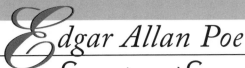

Edgar Allan Poe
Comparing and Connecting the Author's Works

◆ Literary Focus: First-Person Point of View

Stories are told by a narrator. When a narrator tells the story from his or her own point of view, the story is being told from the first-person point of view. (Otherwise, the narrative is told from the third-person point of view.)

The first-person narrator can seem to be the author or a character in the story.

In some of Poe's stories, however, we suspect the narrator of being insane or of having prejudice toward the other characters. The first-person narrator is limited to telling what he or she has either observed or been told.

A work of prose may have a first-person narrator if a specific speaker describes scenes or events.

1. Would "The Pit and the Pendulum" be more or less effective if it were told in the third person? Explain your answer.
2. Of the three poems in this unit, which speaker would seem to be the most like Edgar Allan Poe himself?
3. Which speaker seems to be most strongly effected by his strange experiences?

◆ Drawing Conclusions About Poe's Work

Many of Poe's works include elements of gothic literature. The following chart gives examples of gothic elements from "Ulalume." Draw a similar chart and fill in gothic elements from "The Pit and the Pendulum."

GOTHIC ELEMENTS FROM "ULALUME"	
Mysterious Mood	ashen and sober skies, dim lake
Old, Unfamiliar Words	sere, scoriac
Distant or Long-Ago Setting	lake of Auber, woodland of Weir
Old Building or Ruins	the tomb of Ulalume
Unexplained Events	"Ah, what demon hath tempted me here?"
Horror	ghoul-haunted woodland
Extreme Mental States	Psyche's terror and agony; speaker's ashen and sober heart

◆ Idea Bank

Writing

1. **News Article** Pretend you are a reporter who accompanied General Lasalle's troops as they freed the narrator of "The Pit and the Pendulum." Write a news article about the rescue.
2. **Monologue** Invent an interesting character who would have a unique way of speaking about a subject you know something about. Write 3–4 paragraphs from the character's point of view, speaking about the subject in his or her own voice.
3. **Sounds of Words** For literary effect, a poem like "Ulalume" depends on the sounds of the words that the poet chooses. Words are repeated; rhymes are used many times in a stanza; words begin with the same sounds (alliteration); sounds are repeated within words ("sinfully scintillant planet").

Using a dictionary, an encyclopedia, or a rhyming dictionary, find words with interesting sounds that describe an object or creature. Choose words for categories like the following, describing the subject of "birds." Make a copy of the chart, and write your words in it.

Birds

Words that Rhyme
feather
weather
together

Words Beginning With Same Sound
wings flap in flight
querulous cooing
lustrous liquidity

Words Including Same Sound
iridescence and radiance

Words Having Interesting Sounds
ornithological
grackle
phalarope
blue-gray gnatcatcher

Use your words in a descriptive paragraph or poem. Read over your work to see if you can make it sound more interesting or musical.

Speaking and Listening

4. **Dramatic Reading** Work with other students to find a poem or part of a story by Poe for a dramatic reading. Decide which student or students will read specific lines or sections. Then rehearse to make your reading smooth and dramatic. Present your reading for other students. **[Group Activity; Performing Arts Link]**

Researching and Representing

5. **Further Reading** Find an example of a horror story or novel in the library. Read it and write a report about it from the point of view of one of the main characters. See if you can interest other students in reading the story or novel.

6. **Illustration** Create an illustration for a story or poem by Poe. You could use paints or drawing supplies, or you could prepare a collage or construction. Try to create a visual image that suggests the feelings in Poe's writing. **[Art Link]**

◆ **Further Reading, Listening, and Viewing**

• Video – *Edgar Allan Poe: Terror of the Soul,* PBS video cassette, 1 hour from the American Masters series, 1995. (A comprehensive film biography of Poe with dramatic recreations of important scenes from his life and work)

• Audio –*The Narrative of A. Gordon Pym of Nantucket* (unabridged) books on Tape, 1988, 6 audio cassettes, read by John Chatty

• Audio – *The Poetry of Edgar Allan Poe,* Dove Audio, 1995 1 hour, 1 cassette, His major poetry read by several readers

• Art Books – *Gothic Revivial* by Megan Aldrich, Phaidon Press Ltd. 1997 Fabulous coverage of all aspects of art, architecture, design and furnishings

On the Web:

http://www.phschool.com/atschool/literature
Go to the student edition *Platinum*. Proceed to Unit 1. Then, click Hot Links to find Web sites featuring Edgar Allan Poe.

Pat Mora in Depth

"We earn the poem by following it rather than directing or leading it. . . . It is frightening, of course, not to know where I am going in the mesh of words. On the other hand, a blank piece of paper is a way of giving myself space, to explore what will happen. Poetry is both an act of faith and an act of hope."

—**Pat Mora**

"I live in a doorway / between two rooms . . ." is how Pat Mora describes herself in her poem "Sonrisas". These lines might easily sum up Mora's position as a writer. In twenty books of poetry and prose, this award-winning Mexican American writer has explored the "complications of living in multiple cultures," of crossing borders of identity, language, and heritage.

Crossing the Border Mora was born on January 19, 1942, in El Paso, Texas, near the Mexican border. Her grandparents went across the Rio Grande to escape the Mexican Revolution. Mora's mother, Estela, was born in El Paso a year after Estela's father had previously crossed the river at night.

Mora's father, Raúl, was born in Mexico and came to El Paso with his family when he was three years old. At the age of seven, he was selling newspapers in downtown El Paso. As a young man, he edited a Spanish-language newspaper and then became an optician.

Full House The oldest of four children, Mora grew up in an adobe house located in the desert on the western edge of El Paso. It was a bilingual home full of strong women. Mora's maternal grandmother, Amelia, moved in after she was diagnosed with cancer. Her mother's older half-sister, Aunt Ignacia, also lived with the family, spoiling the children and entertaining them with family stories.

Mora attended Catholic schools and until she was seventeen never considered "being anything other than a nun,"

but by the time she graduated from the all-girls Loretta Academy in 1960, she had decided to become a doctor instead. Mora entered the University of Texas—El Paso as a pre-medical student, but after two years switched majors to English, with a minor in speech.

Teacher, Mother, Poet The summer after she graduated in 1963, Mora married William Burnside and moved out of the desert house she had lived in her entire life. The next ten years were extremely productive: she taught high school English for three years, had three children, and received a master's degree in English from the University of Texas—El Paso (1971). From 1971 to 1981 she taught part-time at El Paso Community College and the University of Texas.

In 1981, Mora entered a new phase of her life; she got divorced and took a job as an administrator and later became a museum director at the University of Texas. She also began writing poetry and published her first collection, *Chants,* in 1984. That same year she married Vern Scarborough, an archeologist. In 1986, she published her second poetry collection, *Borders,* and won a prestigious fellowship to study ways of preserving cultural ties.

Leaving Texas Three years later, severing some of her own cultural ties, Mora and her husband left Texas and moved to Ohio, where she is currently a professor at the University of Cincinnati. Although the Midwest doesn't feel like home, Mora says there's a benefit to having left El Paso: "It helped me see things and say things I might never have said. . . . There's a knowing in leaving."

Since her move in 1989, Mora has been devoting herself full-time to writing and speaking, giving lectures, readings, and poetry workshops. In the last ten years, she has published three more poetry collections: *Communion* (1991), *Agua Santa/Holy Water* (1995), and *Aunt Carmen's Book of Practical Saints* (1997). Mora's poems have appeared in many anthologies, including *Best American Poetry, 1996*, and she has won a poetry fellowship from the National Endowment for the Arts.

New Directions In the last decade, Mora has published thirteen children's books, many of them based on family stories or folklore. Mora has also turned to nonfiction, with *Nepantla: Essays From the Land in the Middle* (1993) and *House of Houses* (1997). She wrote *House of Houses* while living for a year in Santa Fe, New Mexico. A family memoir told in the voices of Mora's ancestors, *House of Houses* begins with her father's sister, Aunt Chole, asking her brother, "How can you still be hungry if you're dead?" According to one reviewer, Mora turns her family's house "into a place where present and past tense are one, a realm where memory and imagination are fused." Another review describes the memoir as almost seamlessly "moving in and out of life and death, English and Spanish, the kitchen and the garden, then and now." Clearly, Mora is a writer who understands this fusion of worlds, this movement across borders.

◆ The Art of Maya Weaving

The majority of people think of the Maya as an ancient civilization that died out a thousand years ago. However, more than a million Maya still live in Chiapas, Mexico, and another five million are spread throughout the rest of Central America. Though they struggle to preserve their culture, there is one art form that remains: the art of weaving and fine embroidery.

Contemporary Maya women and girls (like the weaver in "*Tejedora maya*") weave clothing with designs that are almost identical to those of their ancestors. The most important symbol is the diamond, which represents the universe and the sun. The toad symbolizes the earth's fertility. Other symbols are the vulture, monkey, scorpion, and flower.

According to Maya mythology, the Goddess of the Moon taught women to weave. The designs of each garment are considered sacred because they are revealed to the weaver in dreams, and dreams are believed to be messages sent from the spirit world.

For generations the art of Maya weaving had died out, but in the last century the ancient techniques and symbols have been completely revived.

◆ Literary Works

Poetry Collections
Chants (1984), *Borders* (1986), *Agua Santa/Holy Water* (1995), *Aunt Carmen's Book of Practical Saints* (1997)

Nonfiction
Nepantla: Essays From the Land in the Middle (1993), *House of Houses* (1997)

Selected Children's Books
A Birthday Basket for Tía (1992), *The Race of Toad and Deer* (1995), *Tomás and the Library Lady* (1997), *The Rainbow Tulip* (1999)

T I M E L I N E

Mora's Life		World Events	
1942	Pat Mora born in El Paso, Texas	1941	U.S. enters World War II
1960	Graduates from Loretta Academy	1945	U.S. drops atomic bombs on
1962	Grandmother (Amelia) dies		Japan, ending World War II;
1963	Graduates from University of		United Nations formed; Gabriela
	Texas–El Paso; marries William		Mistral wins Nobel Prize in
	Burnside		Literature
1963–66	Teaches high school English	1950–53	Korean War
1967	Son William born	1954	*Brown v. Board of Education*
1970	Daughter Elizabeth born	1955	Martin Luther King, Jr., organizes
1971	Gets master's degree in English		Montgomery bus boycott
	from University of Texas–El Paso	1957	Congress passes first Civil Rights
1971–78	Teaches English and communica-		Act; Soviets launch *Sputnik I*
	tions at El Paso Community	1962	Cuban missile crisis; John Glenn is
	College		first American to orbit Earth
1973	Daughter Cecilia born	1963	President John F. Kennedy assassi-
1979–81	Teaches English at University of		nated
	Texas–El Paso; Gets divorced	1965	U.S. begins bombing North
1981–89	Works as administrator and		Vietnam; César Chávez begins
	museum director at University of		organizing farm workers;
	Texas–El Paso		Congress passes Bilingual
1983–84	Hosts public radio show, *Voices:*		Education Act
	The Mexican American in	1967	Chicano student movement
	Perspective; *Chants* is published;		begins
	marries Vernon Scarborough	1968	Martin Luther King assassinated
1986	*Borders* is published	1969	First U.S. moon walk, *Apollo 11*
1986–89	Receives Kellogg National fellow-	1972	Rudolfo Anaya's *Bless Me, Ultima* is
	ship		published
1989	Moves to Cincinnati, Ohio	1973	U.S. troops leave Vietnam
1991	*Communion* is published	1974	President Richard M. Nixon
1992	First children's book, *A Birthday*		resigns after Watergate scandal
	Basket for Tía, about Lobo's nineti-	1976	Jimmy Carter elected president
	eth birthday party, is published	1980	Ronald Reagan elected president
1993	Father dies; *Nepantla* is published	1983	Sandra Cisneros' *The House on*
1994–5	National Endowment for the Arts		*Mango Street* is published
	poetry fellowship; spends year in	1988	George Bush elected president
	Santa Fe, New Mexico	1989	Berlin Wall dismantled
1995	*Agua Santa/Holy Water* is published	1990	Octavio Paz wins Nobel Prize for
1996–97	Spends year in Santa Fe		literature
1997	*Aunt Carmen's Book of Practical*	1991	Breakup of Soviet Union; Persian
	Saints and *House of Houses* are		Gulf War
	published; poetry included in *Best*	1992	Bill Clinton elected president
	American Poetry, 1986	1993	Apartheid ends in South Africa
1998	Moves to Covington, Kentucky	1999	Thirtieth anniversary of the first
1999	Thirteenth children's book, *The*		moonwalk
	Rainbow Tulip is published		

Pat Mora

Febrero loco[1] / Crazy February
from House of Houses

I am Patricia Mora, born in El Paso, Texas, daughter of the desert, of the border, of the Río Grande del Norte,[2] daughter of Estela Delgado, who is the great-granddaughter of Anacleta Manquera and Nepomuceno Delgado, granddaughter of Ignacio Delgado y Manquera and María Ignacia Barragán; daughter of the circuit judge, Eduardo Luis Delgado of Cusihuirachic, México, husband of María Dolores Prieto Yrigoyen, father of Eduardo Octavo, who died young, and of the fierce and loving Ignacia Raymunda, of Adelina, Elodia Natalia Zenaida, and Dolores Ester Delgado, all born in México, their father, the maternal grandfather I never knew who below Revolutionary bullets and stars, floated in a carriage with his grown daughters across the dark Río Grande, a widower who married, the orphaned, red-haired Sotero Amelia Landavazo, daughter of the widow Refugio Rochín and the sea captain, Juan Domingo Landavazo of Bilbao, Spain; mother of Juan Domingo Delgado and Eduardo Luis, called Lalo, born in El Paso, as was Amelia's daughter,

my mother, the feisty, articulate, Estela, who married my father, Raúl Antonio Mora, the optician born in Chihuahua, great-grandson of Elena Meléndez and Damian Monárrez, mayor of Boca de Avino, Durango; grandson of Simona Porras and Gregorio Mora, grandson of the tiny Tomasa Monárrez and Brígido Pérez, son of the teary Natividad Pérez of Boca de Avino, Durango, and the tailor Lázaro Mora of Jiménez, whose first three sons, Lázaro, Manuel and Saúl, all died young, who brought Raúl, brother of Soledad, Salvador Saúl, Concepción, Julieta, Aurora and Edermida Mora, at three years of age, brought Raúl across the Río Grande to live in El Paso, father of Patricia Estella, Cecilia Teresa, Stella Anne, and Roy Antonio Mora, always the crossing of that brown river of sorrows to that city of our births, mine, my mother's, my children's, William Roy, Elizabeth Anne and Cecilia Anne Burnside.

El Paso. Skies wider than oceans, a bare mountain that talks to itself; hard, sandy mesas; fossils who murmur the time of great waters; hawks and snakes; yucca and agave;[3] roots and

---

1. ***Febrero loco*** (fe brā´ rō lō´ kō)
2. ***del Norte*** (del nôr´ tā): of the North.
3. ***agave*** (ä gä´ vā)

branches thorny for survival; the smell of fear, fear of dryness and fangs, human fangs and coilings; the clashings carried on currents of water and wind, of music and silence; music of old women dancing to melodies that come from their own mouths; silence of sunsets and moon risings; storms, whirlings and gustings; the grace of children who spin with the wind, deaf to our fears and forebodings, *el río*,[4] the river, the listening river, the whispering river, the river of rumors, the river of tears, the river of hope, the river of stories slipping by on a hot afternoon, and in the breeze, the green, wet scent of herbs, *manzanilla* and *hierbabuena*,[5] the gifts of wrinkled hands, the blessings, strummings and strokings, the gift of light, of sun, moon, stars, and the gift, the gift of naming.

Voices weave through bare branches. I write what I hear, my inheritance a luxury, the generation with time to record the musings of turtles, the poetics of cactus, the stoicism[6] of stones, the voices from the interior of this family house, *la casa de casas*.[7] The garden like the stark desert in which it hovers has its moods, its storms, its seasons.

---

4. *el río* (el rē′ ō)
5. *manzanilla* and *hierbabuena* (män sä nē′ ä yär bä bwä′ nä)
6. **stoicism** (stō′ i siz′m) *n.*: Indifference to pain or pleasure.
7. *la casa de casas* (lä kä′ sä dä kä säs): The house of houses.

Pat Mora

Remembering Lobo

We called her *Lobo*.[1] The word means "wolf" in Spanish, an odd name for a generous and loving aunt. Like all names it became synonymous with her, and to this day returns me to my childself. Although the name seemed perfectly natural to us and to our friends, it did cause frowns from strangers throughout the years. I particularly remember one hot afternoon when on a crowded streetcar between the border cities of El Paso and Juárez,[2] I momentarily lost sight of her. "Lobo! Lobo!" I cried in panic. Annoyed faces peered at me, disappointed at such disrespect to a white-haired woman.

Actually the fault was hers. She lived with us for years, and when she arrived home from work in the evening, she'd knock on our front door and ask, *"¿Dónde están mis lobitos?"*[3] "Where are my little wolves?"

Gradually she became our lobo, a spinster aunt who gathered the four of us around her, tying us to her for life by giving us all she had. Sometimes to tease her we would call her by her real name. *"¿Dónde está Ignacia?"*[4] we would ask. Lobo would laugh and say, "She is a ghost."

To all of us in nuclear families today, the notion of an extended family under one roof seems archaic,[5] complicated. We treasure our private space. I will always marvel at the generosity of my parents, who opened their door to both my grandmother and Lobo. No doubt I am drawn to the elderly because I grew up with two entirely different white-haired women who worried about me, tucked me in at night, made me tomato soup or hot *hierbabuena* [6] (mint tea) when I was ill.

Lobo grew up in Mexico, the daughter of a curcuit judge, my grandfather. She was a wonderful storyteller and over and over told us about the night her father, a widower, brought his grown daughters on a flatbed truck across the Rio Grande at the time of the Mexican Revolution. All their possessions were left in Mexico. Lobo had not been wealthy, but she had probably never expected to have to find a job and learn English.

---

1. **Lobo** (lō´ bō)
2. **Juárez** (hwä´ rās)
3. **¿Dónde están mis lobitos?** (dōn´ dä es tän´ mēs lō bē´ tōs)
4. **¿Dónde está Ignacia?** (dōn´ dä es tä´ ēg nä´ sē ä)
5. **archaic** (är kā´ ik) *adj.*: Belonging to another era; old-fashioned.
6. *hierbabuena* (yār bä bwä´ nä)

When she lived with us, she worked in the linens section of a local department store. Her area was called "piece goods and bedding." Lobo never sewed, but she would talk about materials she sold, using words I never completely understood, such as *pique*[7] and *broadcloth*. Sometimes I still whisper such words just to remind myself of her. I'll always savor the way she would order "sweet milk" at restaurants. The precision of a speaker new to the language.

Lobo saved her money to take us out to dinner and a movie, to take us to Los Angeles in the summer, to buy us shiny black shoes for Christmas. Though she never married and never bore children, Lobo taught me much about one of our greatest challenges as human beings: loving well. I don't think she ever discussed the subject with me, but through the years she lived her love, and I was privileged to watch.

She died at ninety-four. She was no sweet, docile Mexican woman dying with perfect resignation. Some of her last words before drifting into semiconsciousness were loud words of annoyance at the incompetence of nurses and doctors.

"*No sirven.*"[8] "They're worthless," she'd say to me in Spanish. "They don't know what they're doing. My throat is hurting and they're taking X-rays. Tell them to take care of my throat first."

I was busy striving for my cherished middle-class politeness. "Shh, shh," I'd say. "They're doing the best they can."

"Well, it's not good enough," she'd say, sitting up in anger.

Lobo was a woman of fierce feelings, of strong opinions. She was a woman who literally whistled while she worked. The best way to cheer her when she'd visit my young children was to ask for her help. Ask her to make a bed, fold laundry, set the table or dry dishes, and the whistling would begin as she moved about her task. Like all of us, she loved being needed. Understandable, then, that she muttered in annoyance when her body began to fail her. She was a woman who found self-definition and joy in visibly showing her family her love for us by bringing us *te´ de canela*[9] (cinnamon tea) in the middle of the night to ease a cough, by bringing us comics and candy whenever she returned home. A life of giving.

One of my last memories of her is a visit I made to her on November 2, *El Día de los Muertos*,[10] or All Souls' Day. She was sitting in her rocking chair, smiling wistfully. The source of the smile may seem a bit bizarre to a U.S. audience. She was

---

7. **pique** (pē kā´) *n.*: Tightly woven ribbed fabric.
8. **No sirven** (nō sēr´ ven)
9. **té de canela** (tā dā kä nä´ lä)
10. **El Día de los Muertos** (el dē´ä dā lōs mwāer´tōs)

fondly remembering past visits to the local cemetery on this religious feast day.

"What a silly old woman I have become," she said. "Here I sit in my rocking chair on All Souls' Day, sitting when I should be out there. At the cemetery. Taking good care of *mis muertos*,[11] my dead ones.

"What a time I used to have. I'd wake while it was still dark outside. I'd hear the first morning birds, and my fingers would almost itch to begin. By six I'd be having a hot bath, dressing carefully in black, wanting *mis muertos* to be proud of me, proud to have me looking respectable and proud to have their graves taken care of. I'd have my black coffee and plenty of toast. You know the way I like it. Well browned and well buttered. I wanted to be ready to work hard.

"The bus ride to the other side of town was a long one, but I'd say a rosary[12] and plan my day. I'd hope that my perfume wasn't too strong and yet would remind others that I was a lady.

"The air at the cemetery gates was full of chrysanthemums: that strong, sharp, fall smell. I'd buy tin cans full of the gold and wine flowers. How I liked seeing aunts and uncles who were also there to care for the graves of their loved ones. We'd hug. Happy together.

"Then it was time to begin. The smell of chrysanthemums was like a whiff of pure energy. I'd pull the heavy hose and wash the gravestones over and over, listening to the water pelting away the desert sand. I always brought newspaper. I'd kneel on the few patches of grass, and I'd scrub and scrub, shining the gray stones, leaning back on my knees to rest for a bit and then scrubbing again. Finally a relative from nearby would say, '*Ya, ya, Nacha*,'[13] and laugh. Enough. I'd stop, blink my eyes to return from my trance. Slightly dazed, I'd stand slowly, place a can of chrysanthemums before each grave.

"Sometimes I would just stand there in the desert sun and listen. I'd hear the quiet crying of people visiting new graves; I'd hear families exchanging gossip while they worked.

"One time I heard my aunt scolding her dead husband. She'd sweep his gravestone and say, '*¿Porque?*[14] Why did you do this, you thoughtless man? Why did you go and leave me like this? You know I don't like to be alone. Why did you stop living?'

---

11. *mis muertos* (mēs mwār´ tōs)
12. rosary (rō´ sər ē) *n.*: Roman Catholic prayer said in a certain pattern and counted out in sets using rosary beads.
13. '*Ya, ya, Nacha*' (yä yä nä´chä): 'Yes, yes, Nacha' (short for "Ignacia").
14. *¿Porqué?* (pôr kā´)

Such a sight to see my aunt with her proper black hat and her fine dress and her carefully polished shoes muttering away for all to hear.

"To stifle my laughter, I had to cover my mouth with my hands."

I see Lobo in that afternoon sun, and I wonder if the sharp smell of chrysanthemums on her fingertips startled her. Surely she wanted to save it, to save the day, to horde the pleasure of using the love trapped inside all year long. I imagine how she must have enjoyed the feeling of strength in her arms as she scrubbed those graves, loving the notion that her relatives' markers would be the cleanest in the cemetery. They would sparkle.

Bizarre? Bizarre to find happiness in a cemetery? Perhaps, but understanding that attitude toward death—and love—is a key to understanding the growing U.S. Latino population. Family ties are so strong that not even death can sever them. Although Emily Dickinson writes of "sweeping up the Heart / and putting love away / We shall not want to use again / Until Eternity," Mexicans don't always do this. Such tidiness eludes us.

Explanations for such attitudes abound: Indian beliefs of life and death as a continuum, the strong influence of the Catholic Church with its tenets about the soul and afterlife. Somehow we continue to want to openly demonstrate our love. Lobo's annual cemetery excursions were, yes, a testimony to family pride, but also a testimony to her enduring love for family members.

I wonder if, as she sat before me that last November 2, her arms ached as love pushed against the inside of her skin, trying to find a way out. Her emotional pain at her trapped love, at no longer being able to use her body to help her loved ones—living and dead—was probably as distressing as the physical pain of arthritis. Such capacity for love is as startling as the scent of chrysanthemums.

I have no desire to put my love for Lobo away. Quite the contrary, I don't want to forget: I want to remember. My tribute to her won't be in annual pilgrimages to a cemetery. I was born in these United States and am very much influenced by this culture. But I do want to polish, polish my writing tools to preserve images of women like Lobo, unsung women whose fierce family love deserves our respect. Lobo has been dead almost ten years now. I will always miss her physical presence in my life, her laughter. She's not one to stay out of my life, though. She manages to slip into every book of poetry I write. Her poem for poetry book four is already written, and my first children's book is about her ninetieth birthday party. She danced.

"Bailando"[1]

from Remembering Lobo

I will remember you dancing,
spinning round and round
a young girl in Mexico,
your long, black hair free in the wind,
spinning round and round
a young woman at village dances
your long, blue dress swaying
to the beat of *La Varsoviana*[2]
smiling into the eyes of your parents,
years later smiling into my eyes
when I'd reach up to dance with you
my dear aunt, who years later
danced with my children,
you, white-haired but still young
waltzing on your ninetieth birthday,
more beautiful than the orchid
pinned on your shoulder,
tottering now when you walk
but saying to me, *"Estoy bailando,"*[3]
and laughing.

---

1. *Bailando* (bī län´dō): Dancing.
2. *La Varsoviana* (lä vär´sō vē än´ ä) *n.*: Slow, mazurka-like dance, popular
in Central America, that originated in France during the 1850's.
3. *"Estoy bailando"* (es toi´ bī län´dō): "I'm dancing."

Pat Mora

Oral History

You're dead but your voice spins
out from tape cassettes, reels me
back to my child-bed, storytelling
in the dark. While my teenagers bend
5   to kiss me good-night, I'm lullaby-
rocked by your rhythms,
like a mother's heartbeat, familiar,
comforting old friends, stories
with names wearing high collars
10   like Nepomuceno and Anacleta[1]
who walk in genteel shoes on the dirt
streets of tongue-twister towns

Cuauhtemoc and Cusihuirachic.[2]
You're dead but you walk
15   and talk in my dreams
night after night we're together
you're savoring the taste of your stories
your face lively with life
not the gray, boney silhouette
20   breathing loudly in that pale
hospital room where I'd whisper
             stop   stop
No. You're my grand wolf again
Lobo, as you dubbed yourself
25   when you claimed four of us
as your *lobitos,*[3] little wolves
who even now curl round the memory
of you and rest peacefully
in your warmth.

---

1. **Nepomuceno and Anacleta** (nā pō mōō sā´; nō ä nä klā´ tä)
2. **Cuauhtemoc and Cusihuirachic** (kwou tā´ mōk; kōō´ sē wēr ä´ chēk)
3. *lobitos* (lō bē´ tōs)

Secrets

His feet could read mountains,
dark, hard, bare feet, beating
a rhythm in the canyons,
season by season, feeling paths
5   no one else saw, leading
the weary judge up rock slopes,
senses bare to the whisper of smoke,
the scent of crushed herb,
classic guide to that mystery
10   world devoid of books, people,
my usual clues.

Felipe, the Tarahumara,[1] guiding
my great-grandfather, pointing:
to the man hushing horses with hay,
15   to the machete dark, dark in the sun,
to his wife scrubbing blood stains
in the arroyo[2]

The old tale buzzes round
my head till I wish
20   for such a guide, a woman,
teaching me the art of bending
close to the land,
silent, listening, feeling the path.

---

1. Tarahumara (tä rä o͞o mä´ rä) *n.*: Native American tribe in northern
Mexico.
2. arroyo (ä roi´ ō) *n.*: Gully cut by a stream.

Pat Mora

Desert Pilgrimage

A few more steps, old feet.
Tonight I'll simmer dandelions
picked early this morning.
In pale tea I'll see
5   me with her, tasting wild grapes
at dawn, tasting dew
on tender leaves, another year.

I'll see us picking berries
to sprinkle in our soup,
10   all day harvesting desert herbs
her hands still guiding me,
at sunset grinding seeds
to thicken our stew.

I'll see us sitting
15   two boulders in the dark
listening   listening
watching stars tumble onto the sand
scattering white glowing
midnight blooms, a scent
20   I dream for months.

Tomorrow I'll store
creosote[1] leaves to soothe
sore throats, and golden
pollen crystals, incense
25   I burn all year to hear her voice.

---

1. creosote (krē´ ə sōt) *n.*: A strong-smelling evergreen shrub found in the Southwest and Mexico.

☑ Check Your Comprehension

1. In *"Febrero loco / Crazy February,"* what exactly is the "luxury" that Mora says her generation possesses?
2. In "Remembering Lobo," why is Lobo able to find "happiness in a cemetery"?
3. In "Oral History," what is the speaker comforted by "night after night"?
4. In "Secrets," what is Felipe able to do that the speaker cannot do?
5. List details in "Desert Pilgrimage" that evoke each of the five senses: sight, sound, taste, smell, and touch/feeling.

◆ Critical Thinking

INTERPRET

1. In *"Febrero loco,"* why do you think Mora summarizes her family history in the form of a single enormous sentence? **[Interpret]**
2. (a) In "Remembering Lobo," how is Mora like her aunt? (b) How is she different from Lobo? **[Analyze]**

3. In "Oral History," what do you think the speaker is telling Lobo to "stop" doing (line 22)? **[Interpret]**

4. Why do you think the speaker in "Secrets" wishes she had a guide like Felipe? In other words, what "secrets" does she want to learn?

5. In "Desert Pilgrimage," find two images that appeal to two different senses at the same time—that talk about one type of sensation as if it were another.

COMPARE LITERARY WORKS

6. How are the voices that "weave through bare branches" in *"Febrero loco"* similar to the tale that "buzzes round" (lines 18–19) the speaker's head in "Secrets"? **[Compare]**

7. How is the unnamed woman in "Desert Pilgrimage" like Felipe in "Secrets"? **[Compare]**

Pat Mora

Tigua[1] Elder

How do I tell my children:
there is worse than pain.

I bury pills.
Let my stomach burn.
5   I bury them in the sand by the window,
under the limp cactus.
Maybe it slipped into a long sleep instead of me.
I speak to my grandchildren in our language,
but they hear only television, radio
10   in every room, all day, all night.
They do not understand.

How do I tell my children:
forgetting is worse than pain, forgetting
stories old as the moon; owl, coyote,
15   snake weaving through the night like smoke,
forgetting the word for the Spirit,
waida, waida,[2] the sound I hear in shells
and damp caves, forgetting the wind,
the necessary bending to her spring tantrums.

20   Afternoons I limp like a wounded horse
to the shade of the willow and wait for sunset,
for wind's breath, familiar, cool.
She eases this fire.

There is worse than pain.
25   There is forgetting
those are my eyes in the mirror.
There is forgetting my own true name.

---

1. *Tigua* (tē´ gwä) n.: Native American tribe in the Southwest.
2. **waida** (wĭ´ dä)

Tejedora maya[1]

You too know the persistent buzz
of white space, stubborn as a fly,
the itch. My white is paper,
yours is cotton cloth you smooth
5   with rough palms in the shade of the old tree,
feel designs alive,
a braile[2] we can't see,
butterflies, scorpions, snakes
darting and tumbling in your dreams
10   brushing the backs of your eyes
slither to your fingertips, dart
into red and black threads
      your hands, your mother's hands
      your grandmother's hands
15   unleash frogs and flowers
older than your bones.

---

1. *Tejedora maya* (tä hä dōʹrä): Maya weaver. The Mayas are a native people who live in southern Mexico and other Central American countries.
2. braile (braille) (brāl) *n.*: System of writing and printing for the blind that
uses a pattern of raised dots to represent letters and numbers (invented by
Louis Braille).

Pat Mora

Still Life

Still hearing dawn
alive with birds
stirring the morning breeze.

Still warming my fingers
5   round a cup, *café*[1] I made
in the quiet
before the world fills the air.

Still opening these doors
heavier now
10   with my own hands,
weathered brown on brown.

Still holding soles and hammer
mending leather stubborn as my palms
gently drumming
15   gently drumming.

Still sweeping slowly as the sun
sets before I walk to the *plaza*[2]
to watch the stars come out,
to watch the girls.

20   Spring again.

---

1. *café* (kä fã´) *n.*: Coffee.
2. *plaza* (plä´ zä) *n.*: A public square or open marketplace in a town or city.

Sueños: / Dreams

She dreams her hands are feathered.
On the dirt floor, curled between
Coke crates, cardboard boxes,
and her clay menagerie,[1] under the green
5   bananas hanging on a line away from
dogs, rats, and brothers,
as clouds seep into the adobe[2] bricks,
stroke her ankles caked with mud,
her patched clothes, tangled hair,
10   she dreams the clay birds and butterflies
still wet in her hands, stir, flutter, lift
their wings like petals opening
on a hot afternoon, and she too
rises into the sun
15   light as a dandelion plume,
in silent laughter tumbles, glides.

---

1. **menagerie** (mə naj´ ər ē) *n.*: Collection of animals, often kept for show.
2. **adobe** (ə dō bē) *n:* Sun-dried mixture of clay and straw.

☑ Check Your Comprehension

1. (a) In "*Tigua* Elder," what does the speaker believe is worse than pain? (b) What is his "own true name" (line 27)?
2. In "*Tejedora maya,*" what is the weaver's "white space" (line 2)?
3. Which of the five senses do most of the images in this poem appeal to?
4. (a) What is the setting in "*Sueños:* Dreams"? (b) What details do we learn about the unnamed person the speaker is describing?
5. Who is the speaker in "Still Life"?

◆ Critical Thinking

INTERPRET

1. (a) Why do you think the speaker in "*Tigua* Elder" is burying pills? (b) What do the pills represent to him? **[Interpret]**

2. (a) In "*Tejedora maya,*" what connection does the speaker see between the weaver and herself? (b) What is "the itch" she refers to in line 3? **[Analyze]**

3. Maya weavers believe that the inspiration for their designs comes to them in their dreams as messages from their ancestors. Why do you think the speaker describes the weaver's designs as "a braile we can't see" (line 7)? **[Infer]**

4. In "*Sueños:* Dreams," how does the dreamer's setting contrast with her dreams? **[Connect]**

COMPARE LITERARY WORKS

5. How is the weaver in "*Tejedora maya*" like the dreamer in "*Sueños:* Dreams"? **[Compare]**

6. (a) How are the speakers in "*Tigua* Elder" and "Still Life" similar? (b) In what key way are they different? **[Compare/Contrast]**

*P*at Mora

Fences

Mouths full of laughter,
the *turistas*[1] come to the tall hotel
with suitcases full of dollars.

Every morning my brother makes
5   the cool beach sand new for them.
With a wooden board he smooths
away all footprints.

I peek through the cactus fence
and watch the women rub oil
10   sweeter than honey into their arms and legs
while their children jump waves
or sip drinks from long straws,
coconut white, mango yellow.

Once my little sister
15   ran barefoot across the hot sand
for a taste.

My mother roared like the ocean,
"No. No. It's their beach.
It's their beach."

---

1. *turistas* (to͞o rēs´ täs) *n.*: Tourists.

Silence Like Cool Sand

First lie in it.
Close your eyes.
Let it move through you.
Rock your shoulders back and forth.
5   Dig your heels in.
Slow your breath.

Curl forward and wash
your hands with it.
Pour it slowly on your legs.
10   Rub your heels deeper
into the damp.
Bury your toes.
Roll back, eyes shut.
Disappear into it.
15   Listen to the scratchings, then listen,
listen to the roar.

☑ Check Your Comprehension

1. Who is the speaker in "Fences"?

2. Why does her brother make "the cool beach sand new" (lines 4–5) every morning?

3. (a) Why does the speaker's sister run across the sand? (b) Why does her mother yell at her?

4. In "Silence Like Cool Sand," which of the five senses do most of the images appeal to?

◆ Critical Thinking

INTERPRET

1. What can we infer about the speaker's family in "Fences"? **[Infer]**

2. (a) Why is her mother's attitude toward the beach **ironic,** or the opposite of what we would expect? (b) In what way is it also completely logical? **[Analyze]**

3. What do you think the title of this poem refers to? **[Interpret]**

4. In "Silence Like Cool Sand," what does "it" refer to? (Is there more than one possible interpretation?) **[Interpret]**

5. How do you interpret the last two lines of the poem? In other words, what are the "scratchings" and the "roar," and how do they relate to the poem's title? **[Interpret]**

COMPARE LITERARY WORKS

6. Compare and contrast the images of sand in "Fences" and "Silence Like Cool Sand." **[Compare/Contrast]**

Pat Mora
Comparing and Connecting the Author's Works

◆ Literary Focus: Figures of Speech

A **figure of speech** makes an imaginative comparison between two things that seem different from one another. A **simile** compares two unlike things by using a connecting word such as *like, as,* or *than.* The speaker in "*Tigua* Elder" uses a simile when he says, "I limp like a wounded horse" (line 20). A **metaphor** compares two unlike things by referring to one as if it were the other. The speaker in "Desert Pilgrimage" uses a metaphor when she describes people as "two boulders in the dark" (line 15).

1. Some metaphors are directly stated, but others are implied (suggested). Explain the **implied metaphor** in this line from "Remembering Lobo": "But I do want to polish, polish my writing tools to preserve images of women like Lobo . . . ."
2. (b) What metaphors do "taste" (line 17) and "curl round" (26) imply?
3. In "Secrets," what metaphors do "read" (line 1) and "buzzes" (18) imply?
4. In "*Tejedora maya,*" what connection does the speaker make between her paper and the weaver's cloth? (b) Why does she compare both to a fly?
5. What would you say is the central metaphor in "*Sueños:* Dreams"?
6. Sometimes a writer extends a metaphor over several lines or throughout an entire poem. Explain the extended metaphor in "Silence Like Cool Sand."

◆ Drawing Conclusions About Mora's Work

Mora told a newspaper reporter who profiled her in 1999:

"One of the realities of the border for me was realizing I could have been born on the other side. I could have had a very different kind of experience, and so I always have to be listening to that. It's a part of my heritage. . . ."

Write a brief essay discussing how this quote applies to three of the selections you have read. Where does Mora seem to be looking over a border, listening to an experience that is different from her own but that she nevertheless sees as part of her own heritage?

◆ Idea Bank

Writing

1. **Children's Book** Pat Mora has written more than a dozen children's books, many of them based on family stories. For example, her latest book, *The Rainbow Tulip,* is about an experience her mother had as a child. Using poetry or prose, write the text for a simple picture book about someone in your family. If you know more than one language, try creating a bilingual children's book.
2. **Poem** Using Mora's poetry as a model, write a poem that describes a person who is different from you but who does something you admire and wish you could learn. You might title your poem "Secrets" or "Dreams."
3. **Compare and Contrast Poems** Write an essay analyzing the similarities and differences between two of Mora's poems. Before you begin writing, make a Venn diagram like the one at the top of the next page to organize your ideas. Write similarities—in subject matter, imagery, figures of speech, tone, theme or another element—in the space where the ovals

overlap. Write differences in the outer regions of the ovals.

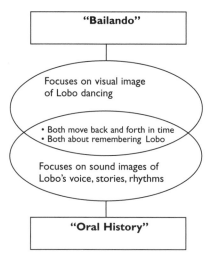

"Bailando"

Focuses on visual image of Lobo dancing

• Both move back and forth in time
• Both about remembering Lobo

Focuses on sound images of Lobo's voice, stories, rhythms

"Oral History"

Speaking and Listening

4. Oral Interpretation Choose your favorite Mora poem and practice reading it aloud. Think about your tone of voice, pacing (how fast you read), and phrasing. Where will you pause? What words will you emphasize? Present your interpretation to a small group or your whole class. **[Performing Arts Link]**

Researching and Representing

5. Oral History Using audiotape or videotape, record a relative telling a family or personal story. Before you begin, decide on your own role: will you be a silent recorder of the story or a participating interviewer asking questions and pulling out more of the tale? Present your oral history to the class. You might also combine your work with that of your classmates to create a longer work .**[Social Studies Link; Group Activity]**

6. Research Report The Mexican Day of the Dead *(El Día de los Muertos),* or All Souls Day, figures prominently in "Remembering Lobo" and is the imaginative framework for Mora's *House of Houses.* Do a research report on this holiday or on your own culture's ritual for honoring the dead. Be sure to use Web resources. **[Social Studies Link]**

◆ Further Reading, Listening, and Viewing

- *This Is About Visions: Interviews with Southwestern Writers,* edited by William Balassi, et al. (1990). Includes an interview with Mora.

- Victor Montejo, *The Bird Who Cleans the World and Other Mayan Fables* (1991). Folktales told by a Guatemalan Mayan.

- Americanos: *Latino Life in the United States / La Vida Latina en los Estados Unidos,* edited by Edward James Olmos and Lea Ybarra, introduction by Carlos Fuentes (1999). Gorgeous photos and bilingual text.

- *The Desert Is No Lady: Women Artists and Writers of the Southwest* (1995). Film documenting the impact of the Southwest landscape on nine artists and writers, including Mora.

On the Web:

http://www.phschool.com/atschool/literature
Go to the student edition *Platinum.* Proceed to Unit 2. Then, click Hot Links to find Web sites featuring Pat Mora.

Langston Hughes In Depth

> "Modestly, like a relay runner, Langston Hughes picks up the folk tradition and carries it on toward the goal of social change in the real world."
>
> *—Susan L. Blake*

JAMES MERCER LANGSTON HUGHES was born in Joplin, Missouri, on February 1, 1902, but called many places home. While growing up, he lived, alternately with his parents and with his grandmother in Ohio, Illinois, Kansas, and even Mexico. As a young man, he traveled to Africa and France and began a career as a versatile and prolific writer. His work included poetry, novels, plays, essays, journalism, and two autobiographies. Hughes settled at last in New York City and became one of the major figures of the Harlem Renaissance.

Student Years At his graduation from elementary school in Lincoln, Illinois, in 1915, the young Hughes recited his first poem. He wrote his first short story during high school in Cleveland, Ohio. Hughes's early work drew the attention of W.E.B. Du Bois, an influential writer and teacher. The African American literary magazine *The Crisis*, edited by Du Bois, became one of the first to publish Hughes's poetry.

In 1921, Hughes moved to New York City and started college. He attended Columbia University, which is located near Harlem, a predominantly African American neighborhood in upper Manhattan. After one year, however, Hughes dropped out of Columbia and began to travel again. He pursued a series of odd jobs—including working on merchant ships that journeyed to Europe and Africa—that gave him time to write.

Early Success When still in his early twenties, Hughes began to win accolades for his poetry. At this time he also became acquainted with members of the Harlem Renaissance movement—a flowering of the arts partially fueled by the great number of African Americans who moved north in the early twentieth century. By 1926, when Hughes published his first book of poems, *The Weary Blues*, he had joined these talented ranks.

Shortly thereafter, however, Hughes was on the move again. He had earned a scholarship to Lincoln University in Pennsylvania. While enrolled at Lincoln, Hughes toured the southern U.S. with fellow African American writer Zora Neale Hurston. Their goal was to collect traditional African American folktales, a genre that would influence the later works of both writers. In 1929, Hughes received his B.A. degree.

Maturity During the 1930's, Hughes continued to write and travel. He collaborated with Hurston on the play *Mule Bone*, an African American folk comedy. In addition, Hughes published a novel, a short story collection, two books of verse, and three more plays. He visited Haiti and Russia and went to Spain as a correspondent, covering the Spanish Civil War. Hughes also began to speak out publicly against poverty and racial discrimination.

This pattern of creative diversity would continue for the rest of Hughes's life. When he wasn't writing fiction, traveling, or teaching, he pursued new challenges. In the 1940's, he published *The Big Sea*, an autobiography that recounts his experiences up to age twenty-eight, and he wrote the lyrics for

Street Scene, a new opera by the prestigious German-born playwright and composer Kurt Weill (1900–1950). With Arna Bontemps, he also edited *The Poetry of the Negro, 1746–1949.* In the 1950's, Hughes translated *Gypsy Ballads,* a work by the revered Spanish poet and playwright Federico García Lorca. Other literary endeavors of this period include books for children and a second volume of autobiography.

His Final Years By the end of the 1950's, Hughes—nicknamed "Shakespeare in Harlem"— had long been an internationally renowned writer. Despite occasional financial difficulties, he purchased a home in Harlem that became an oasis for other creative artists. In 1960, Hughes was awarded the Springarn Medal from the National Association for the Advancement of Colored People (NAACP). In 1961, he was elected to the National Institute of Arts and Letters, and in 1963, he received an honorary doctorate from Howard University.

Hughes continued to write until he died on May 22, 1967, in his beloved New York City. At his memorial service, friends read from his poems, and jazz musicians performed a blues song. Hughes's final collection of poems, *The Panther and the Lash,* was published posthumously.

◆ The Harlem Renaissance

During the 1920's and 1930's, Harlem was the U.S. capital of African American culture. It was home to myriad theaters, clubs, newspapers, and magazines owned and managed by African Americans. Among the talents of the movement were Jean Toomer, author of *Cane* (1923); Claude McKay, who became the first African American best-selling author with his novel *Home to Harlem* (1928); poet Countee Cullen; Zora Neal Hurston, author of the 1937 classic *Their Eyes Were Watching God;* James Weldon Johnson, who helped found the NAACP; Arna Bontemps, librarian and historian of African American culture; and novelist and short story writer Nella Larsen. Although the movement dwindled after the Great Depression, its achievements continue to influence writers and artists today.

◆ Literary Works

Greatest Books Hughes's works are known both for their down-to-earth language and their variations on the theme of freedom. Much of his poetry also reflects the rhythms, moods, and improvisations of jazz, the blues, and be-bop—musical forms that had been part of the popular Harlem nightlife.

Hughes's most acclaimed works include the following:

The Weary Blues (1926), poems
The Big Sea (1940), autobiography
Montage of a Dream Deferred (1951), poem sequence

Other Publications These additional works are only a sampling of Hughes's enormous creative output.

Not Without Laughter (1930), Hughes's first novel
The Dream Keeper (1932), poems
The Ways of White Folks (1934), short stories
Troubled Island (1936), play
Shakespeare in Harlem (1942), poems
I Wonder as I Wander (1956), autobiography
Tambourines to Glory (1958), novel
Something in Common and Other Stories (1963),
The Prodigal Son (1965), play

TIMELINE

Hughes's Life		World Events	
1902	James Mercer Langston Hughes born February 1 in Joplin, Missouri	1901	Booker T. Washington's autobiography, *Up from Slavery*, published
1921	Moves to New York City; enters Columbia University	1910	Founding of the NAACP
1926	*The Weary Blues* published; wins scholarship to Lincoln University	1914–18	World War I
		1914–19	The Great Migration: 500,000 African Americans move north
1929	Receives B.A. from Lincoln University	1920	Paul Robeson opens in Eugene O'Neill's play *The Emperor Jones*
1930	*Not Without Laughter* published; the play *Mule Bone* opens	1922	*Book of Negro Poetry* published, edited by James Weldon Johnson
1934	Hughes's father dies	1927	Duke Ellington and his orchestra open at the Cotton Club in Harlem
1935	Success of his Broadway play *Mulatto*		
1937	Hired as correspondent to cover Spanish Civil War; his mother dies	1929	Stock market crashes
		1939	African American singer Marian Anderson performs at the Lincoln Memorial
1938	Founds the Harlem Suitcase Theater		
1940	*The Big Sea* published	1940	Richard Wright's *Native Son* published
1942	Moves to Harlem; founds Skyloft Players	1941	U.S. enters World War II
1943	Begins writing column for *Chicago Defender*	1947	Jackie Robinson becomes first African American major-league baseball player
1947	Teaches writing at Atlanta University	1948	President Truman ends segregation in U.S. Armed Forces
1948	Writes lyrics for Kurt Weill's *Street Scene*	1950–53	The Korean War
1956	*I Wonder as I Wander* published	1954	*Brown v. Board of Education* ends school segregation
1960	Receives the Springarn Medal from the NAACP	1963	250,000 people gather to hear Martin Luther King, Jr., in Washington, D.C.
1961	Elected to the National Institute of Arts and Letters	1964	Civil Rights Act passed
1967	Dies in New York City	1968	Assassination of Martin Luther King, Jr.

Langston Hughes

Stars

O, sweep of stars over Harlem streets,
O, little breath of oblivion[1] that is night.
  A city building
  To a mother's song.
5 A city dreaming
  To a lullaby.
Reach up your hand, dark boy, and take a star.
Out of the little breath of oblivion[1]
  That is night,
10 Take just
  One star.

---

1. **oblivion:** Total forgetfulness.

Juke Box Love Song

I could take the Harlem night
and wrap around you,
Take the neon lights and make a crown,
Take the Lenox Avenue buses,
5 Taxis, subways,
And for your love song tone their rumble down.
Take Harlem's heartbeat,
Make a drumbeat,
Put it on a record, let it whirl,
10 And while we listen to it play,
Dance with you till day—
Dance with you, my sweet brown Harlem girl.

Langston Hughes

Good Morning

Good morning, daddy!
I was born here, he said,
watched Harlem grow
until colored folks spread
5   from river to river
across the middle of Manhattan
out of Penn Station[1]
dark tenth of a nation,
planes from Puerto Rico,
10   and holds of boats, chico,
up from Cuba Haiti Jamaica,
in buses marked New York
from Georgia Florida Louisiana
to Harlem Brooklyn the Bronx[2]
15   but most of all to Harlem
dusky sash across Manhattan
I've seen them come dark
    wondering
    wide-eyed
20   dreaming
out of Penn Station—
but the trains are late.
The gates open—
    Yet there're bars
25   at each gate.

    What happens
    to a dream deferred?

    Daddy, ain't you heard?

---

1. Penn Station: Pennsylvania Station is one of New York City's main train stations.
2. Harlem Brooklyn the Bronx: Brooklyn and the Bronx are boroughs (counties) of New York City. Harlem is a neighborhood in the New York borough of Manhattan.

Boogie: 1 a.m.

Good evening, daddy!
I know you've heard
The boogie-woogie rumble
Of a dream deferred
5   Trilling the treble
And twining the bass
Into midnight ruffles
Of cat-gut lace.[1]

---

1. **cat-gut:** Musical instrument strings are made of catgut.

☑ Check Your Comprehension

1. In "Stars," what does the narrator command the boy to do?
2. In "Juke Box Love Song," what does the poem suggest using for a drumbeat?
3. (a) From what places are people departing to come to Harlem in "Good Morning"? (b) By what four modes of transportation do they arrive?
4. To what does the phrase "cat-gut lace" refer at the end of the poem "Boogie: 1 a.m."?

◆ Critical Thinking

1. (a) In "Stars," what might the star represent? (b) What do you think the boy is supposed to forget during "the little breath of oblivion that is night"? **[Interpret]**
2. In "Good Morning," what might be the meaning of the statement that "the gates open—Yet there're bars at each gate"? **[Infer]**
3. What do you think Hughes means by the phrase "a dream deferred" in "Good Morning" and "Boogie: 1 a.m."? **[Draw Conclusions]**

COMPARE LITERARY WORKS

4. To which of the five senses do the poems "Stars," "Juke Box Love Song," and "Boogie: 1 a.m." most often appeal? Note at least five examples to support your opinion. **[Connect]**

Langston Hughes

Me and My Song

Black
As the gentle night
Black
As the kind and quiet night
5   Black
As the deep productive earth
Body
Out of Africa
Strong and black
10   As iron
First smelted[1] in
Africa
Song
Out of Africa
15   Deep and mellow song
Rich
As the black earth
Strong
As black iron
20   Kind
As the black night
My song
From the dark lips
Of Africa
25   Deep
As the rich earth
Beautiful
As the black night
Strong
30   As the first iron
Black
Out of Africa
Me and my
Song

---

1. smelted: Separated by melting or fusing.

Afro-American Fragment

So long,
So far away
Is Africa.
Not even memories alive
5 Save those that history books create,
Save those that songs
Beat back into the blood—
Beat out of blood with words sad-sung
In strange un-Negro tongue—
10 So long,
So far away
Is Africa.

Subdued and time-lost
Are the drums—and yet
15 Through some vast mist of race
There comes this song
I do not understand
This song of atavistic¹ land,
Of bitter yearnings lost
20 Without a place—
So long,
So far away
Is Africa's
Dark face.

---

1. atavistic: Relating to a reappearance after a period of absence,
here relating to the reappearance of ancestral feelings of Africa.

Langston Hughes

Bouquet

Gather quickly
Out of darkness
All the Songs you know
And throw them at the sun
5   Before they melt
Like snow.

My People

The night is beautiful,
So the faces of my people.

The stars are beautiful,
so the eyes of my people.

5   Beautiful, also, is the sun.
Beautiful, also, are the souls of my people.

☑ Check Your Comprehension

1. In "Me and My Song," to what does the narrator compare himself and his song?
2. In your own words, describe the meaning of the poem "Afro-American Fragment."
3. What does the poet request the reader to gather in the poem "Bouquet"?

◆ Critical Thinking

1. How does this repetition add to the meaning of "Me and My Song"? **[Analyze]**

2. In your opinion, why might Hughes have decided to call the last poem, "Afro-American Fragment," a "fragment"?
3. In "My People," why is the sun an appropriate metaphor for a person's soul? **[Interpret]**

COMPARE LITERARY WORKS
4. In what ways are the poems "Me and My Song," "My People," and "Afro-American Fragment" similar? Give examples to support your opinions. **[Connect]**

We're All in the Telephone Book

We're all in the telephone book,
Folks from everywhere on earth—
Anderson to Zabowski,
It's a record of America's worth.

5   We're all in the telephone book.
There's no priority—
A millionaire like Rockefeller
Is likely to be behind me.

For generations men have dreamed
10   Of nations united as one.
Just look in your telephone book
To see where that dream's begun.

When Washington crossed the Delaware
And the pillars of tyranny shook,[1]
15   He started the list of democracy
That's America's telephone book.

---

1. the pillars of tyranny shook: Early in the American Revolution, General George Washington's forces defeated the British after crossing the Delaware River.

Langston Hughes

Luck

Sometimes a crumb falls
From the tables of joy,
Sometimes a bone
Is flung.

5   To some people
Love is given,
To others
Only heaven.

I Dream a World

I dream a world where man
No other man will scorn,
Where love will bless the earth
And peace its paths adorn.
5   I dream a world where all
Will know sweet freedom's way,
Where greed no longer saps the soul
Nor avarice[1] blights our day.
A world I dream where black or white,
10   Whatever race you be,
Will share the bounties of the earth
And every man is free,
Where wretchedness will hang its head
And joy, like a pearl,
15   Attends the needs of all mankind—
Of such I dream, my world!

---

1. **avarice:** An excessive desire for wealth; greed.

☑ Check Your Comprehension

1. In "We're All in the Telephone Book," what does the narrator mean by "There's no priority"?

2. In the same poem, why is "America's telephone book" different from those of other countries?

3. What do you think the poem "Luck" is about?

4. In "I Dream a World," what do you think the poet means when he writes that greed "saps the soul"?

◆ Critical Thinking

1. How does the choice of the two names "Anderson" and "Zabowski" emphasize the meaning of the poem? **[Analyze]**

2. In "Luck," what does the narrator imply by contrasting "love" and "heaven"? **[Infer]**

3. Do you think that a world like the one described in "I Dream a World" is possible? Explain your opinion. **[Apply]**

COMPARE LITERARY WORKS

4. Compare the themes explored in "We're All in the Telephone Book," "Luck," and "I Dream a World." **[Connect]**

Langston Hughes
Comparing and Connecting the Author's Works

◆ Literary Focus: Rhythm

Rhythm in spoken and written language is an arrangement of beats, similar to the beats found in music. A poet creates a beat by combining stressed and unstressed syllables. For example, in the opening lines of his poem "I Dream a World," Hughes repeatedly alternates stressed and unstressed syllables.

> Ĭ dréam ă wórld whĕre mán
>
> Nŏ óthĕr mán wĭll scórn….

This creates a regular rhythmical pattern. Traditional poetry often follows a rhythmical pattern, which is also called the meter of the poem.

Most of Hughes's poems, however, do not employ a predictable pattern. Consider these lines from "We're All in the Telephone Book."

> We're áll ĭn thĕ télĕphŏne bóok,
>
> Fólks frŏm évĕrywhĕre ŏn eárth….

This unpredictable arrangement of stressed and unstressed syllables creates an irregular rhythm. Poetry that does not have a regular rhythmical pattern, or meter, is called free verse.

Main Features of Rhythm

- It is an arrangement of beats.
- The beats are made up of stressed and unstressed syllables.
- Rhythm can be regular or irregular.

1. What kind of tone might a poem written in free verse convey? How might this tone compare to the tone of a poem written with a regular rhythmical pattern?
2. Why do you think Hughes chose to write most often in free verse?

◆ Drawing Conclusions About Hughes's Work

In the introduction to his collection of poems *Montage of a Dream Deferred*, Hughes wrote:

[T]his poem on contemporary Harlem, like be-bop, is marked by conflicting changes, sudden nuances, sharp and impudent interjections, broken rhythms, and passages punctuated by the riffs, runs, breaks, and distortions of a community in transition.

Another form of music that greatly influenced Hughes's writing is the blues. A blues song is usually a solo. It often expresses sadness or worry. Hughes described blues as "songs folks made up when their hearts hurt." Hughes's poetry uses other characteristics of popular music, such as repetition and improvisation.

The following chart shows the use of various musical devices in Hughes's poem "Afro-American Fragment." Create a chart to identify similar elements in his poems. Summarize your findings in a report you share with your class.

Musical Device	"Afro-American Fragment"
solo voice	"I do not understand"
interjections	rhymed lines (stanza 1, lines 8—9)
broken rhythms	doesn't have a regular rhythm
repetition	"So long, / So far away / Is Africa"

◆ Idea Bank

Writing

1. **Poem** In the poem "Good Morning," Hughes asks "What happens to a dream deferred?" Create an original poem that offers one possible answer to this question. In your work, you may decide to include some of the devices Hughes repeatedly uses in his own writing.

2. **Compare and Contrast** Write a paragraph or two comparing and contrasting two of Hughes's poems. You might analyze aspects such as form, structure, tone, voice, and setting. Before you begin organize your findings in a chart like the following one that compares "My People" and "Boogie: 1 a.m."

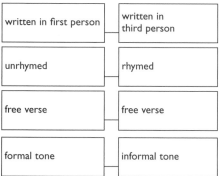

"My People"	"Boogie: 1 a.m."
written in first person	written in third person
unrhymed	rhymed
free verse	free verse
formal tone	informal tone

3. **Autobiographical Essay** Hughes wrote, "My best poems were all written when I felt the worst. When I was happy, I didn't write anything." Write about creative activities you pursue when you are happy, sad, or in another mood. Explain why you turn to these activities at such times.

Speaking and Listening

4. **Musical Interpretation** Choose a piece of music that complements one of Hughes's poems. Read aloud the poem while playing a recording of your chosen music in the background. If you like, you may create original music for the occasion. Explain why you believe the music suits the poem. **[Music Link]**

5. **Oral Report** Research the life and literary contribution of some other figure of the Harlem Renaissance, such as Countee Cullen, Zora Neale Hurston, James Weldon Johnson, Claude McKay, Nella Larsen, Arna Bontemps, or Jean Toomer. Present your findings to the class.

6. **Researching and Representing Civil Rights Time Line** Explore the history of the U.S. Civil Rights Movement. What were its major events? When did they happen? Who were the most influential individuals? Work with others to create an illustrated time line for display in a public area of your school. **[Social Studies Link]**

◆ Further Reading, Listening, and Viewing

- *Langston Hughes: The Dream Keeper* (South Carolina Educational TV Network, 1988) Video relating the life and career of Hughes

- Langston Hughes, editor, *A Pictorial History of African Americans* (1956; revised 1995)

- *Against the Odds: The Artists of the Harlem Renaissance* (PBS Home Video)

- *Langston Hughes: Rhythms of the World* (Smithsonian Folkways Recording) Audio CD

On the Web:

http://www.phschool.com/atschool/literature
Go to the student edition *Platinum*. Proceed to Unit 3. Then, click Hot Links to find Web sites featuring Langston Hughes.

Emily Brontë In Depth

"Under an unsophisticated culture, inartificial tastes, and an unpretending outside, lay a secret power and fire that might have informed the brain and kindled the veins of a hero . . ."

—Charlotte Brontë, Biographical Notice of Ellis and Acton Bell written for the 1850 edition of Emily Brontë's Wuthering Heights

EMILY BRONTË published only one novel. The daughter of a Yorkshire clergyman, Brontë was a reclusive Victorian gentlewoman who left home only three times in the course of her thirty years. Yet *Wuthering Heights,* along with her poetry and the novels and poems of her sisters Charlotte and Anne, is part of the most extraordinary legacy any one family has contributed to English literature.

Yorkshire Emily Brontë was born on July 30, 1818, at Thornton, Yorkshire. In 1820, the family moved to Haworth, where Patrick Brontë remained curate for the rest of his life. In 1821, Emily's mother, Maria Branwell Brontë, died of cancer. Her sister Elizabeth Branwell came to help raise the six children. They turned inward for entertainment, and were raised as readers—at one time, the family received five newspapers. By 1826, Branwell, Charlotte, Emily, and Anne were creating 'great plays' starring Branwell's toy soldiers.

School Years, Gondal, and Angria Because of ill health, the Brontës had difficulty remaining in school. After a stint at the Cowan Bridge School, the two eldest sisters, Maria and Elizabeth, fell ill and died of tuberculosis. Charlotte and Emily were brought home. Emily grew ill and returned home after only a few months at the Roe Head School as a pupil, and later had to leave her position as a teacher at the Law Hill School.

At home in Haworth, however, the Brontës flourished; their collective imaginative life centered around the chronicles of the make-believe cities of Gondal and Angria. These tales, in verse, dialogue, and prose, were written in minuscule script in more than 100 tiny (2 1/4 x 1 1/4 inches) booklets. The Brontës' creative energy was absorbed by these stories for more than a decade.

Plans and Poems In 1842, Emily and Charlotte journeyed to Brussels to study languages. Their plan was to establish a school at Haworth. Within six months, however, Aunt Branwell died, and the Brontës returned to Haworth. Emily, who had been writing poems since 1836, began copying them into two notebooks, "Gondal Poems"—related to the city and its imaginary inhabitants—and "E.J.B."

Private to Public In 1845, the sisters had leaflets printed describing the school's program, but gave up the scheme due to lack of inquiries. During this period, Charlotte accidentally discovered Emily's notebooks in her lap desk. Despite Emily's anger, Charlotte persuaded her to try publishing a collection of the poetry of all three sisters. *Poems: by Currer, Ellis, and Acton Bell,* was published in 1846 at the Brontës' own expense. Despite the male pen names, it received scant critical attention. Undiscouraged, the sisters continued the projects all three had begun: novels, marketed with little success while still works in progress.

1847 The year 1847 marked a spate of publishing for the three "Bell brothers."

In July, T.C. Newby accepted Emily's *Wuthering Heights* and Anne's *Agnes Grey* for publication, though the publisher rejected Charlotte's *The Professor.* However, Smith, Elder & Co. accepted Charlotte's *Jane Eyre,* and all three novels were published by year's end. *Jane Eyre* met with immediate success. The reviews of the more intense, darker *Wuthering Heights* were mixed. By 1853, the Brontë sisters had brought an astonishing seven books before the English reading public.

Lives Cut Short The Brontës did not enjoy their success for long. Branwell died on September 24, 1848. Emily, with a tubercular condition brought on by catching cold at his funeral, fell into a decline and died on December 19, at the age of thirty. Anne died five months later, at twenty-nine. Emily Brontë is buried with her siblings at the rebuilt Haworth church in Yorkshire.

For the Record Female authors commonly used male pseudonyms during this period ("George Eliot" was Mary Ann Evans) as a way of attracting an unprejudiced readership. In 1848, Smith, Elder informed the "Bells" that their novels were being offered to an American publisher as the work of one male author. Charlotte and Anne had to go to London to prove their separate identities and gender. Confusion persisted about the question of authorship. Charlotte reissued an edited version of *Wuthering Heights* in 1850 with an "Editor's Preface" and a "Biographical Notice," which settles the question once and for all.

◆ Tuberculosis and Early Death

That Emily Brontë should have died so young and experienced so much death while she lived seems remarkable. Yet life expectancy during the period was generally low: In the Whitehall district of London, for example, in 1840, a gentleman was expected to live 45 years, a tradesman 27 years, and a laborer 22 years. These figures were even lower for women.

Tuberculosis, a highly contagious respiratory disease known at the time as consumption, was the leading cause of death. At mid-century, it caused half of all deaths in women between the ages of fifteen and thirty-five and accounted for the higher death rate for women than for men. Women were more susceptible because of poorer nutrition and poor ventilation in homes and enclosed workplaces, where they spent most of their time.

◆ Literary Works

The Poetry Much of Emily Brontë's poetry relates to the Gondal saga she worked on from childhood until her death. Many address the reader directly, making use of characters to explore experiences of nature, religion, death, and the power of imagination. Her ideas were considered unusual, her poetry considered uneven, yet readers should remember that she did not write for an audience. Her poems, as a result, contain an unself-conscious intensity.

Poems by Currer, Ellis, and Acton Bell (1846), which include poems by Charlotte, Emily, and Anne Brontë

The Novel Brontë's only work of fiction, a tale from the brooding Yorkshire moors of a love that reaches beyond death, is one of the most widely read novels in the English language. Her hero, Heathcliff, is a living protest against the civility and propriety demanded by Victorian customs.

Wuthering Heights (1847)

TIMELINE

Brontë's Life		World Events	
1818	Born on July 30 at Thornton, Yorkshire	1813	Robert Southey becomes Poet Laureate
1821	Children's mother, Maria Branwell Brontë, dies of cancer; Aunt Elizabeth Branwell moves in to help raise the children	1818	First steamship crosses Atlantic
		1819	Peterloo Massacre in Manchester; Shelley's "Ode to the West Wind"
1824	Four eldest Brontë sisters—Maria, Elizabeth, Charlotte, and Emily—enter Cowan Bridge School	1821	Death of Keats
		1822	Death of Shelley; Heinrich Heine's *Poems* published in Germany
1825	Maria and Elizabeth leave school ill; within months, both die of tuberculosis; Charlotte and Emily return home	1824	Death of Byron
		1825	Horse-drawn buses in London
		1827	Death of William Blake
1826	Charlotte, Branwell, Emily, and Anne write "great plays" about Branwell's toy soldiers	1829	Robert Peel establishes Metropolitan Police in London
		1831	Victor Hugo's *The Hunchback of Notre Dame* published in France
1835	Charlotte teaches at Roe Head School; Emily begins as a pupil, but is sent home ill in October	1832	First Reform Act expands voting rights
1836	First surviving poem by Emily: "Will the day be bright"	1833	Slavery abolished in British Empire
		1834	Death of Coleridge
1837	Emily teaches at Law Hill School, near Halifax	1837	Accession of Queen Victoria; Dickens' *Oliver Twist* published
1838–42	More than half of Emily's surviving poems written	1843	Death of Robert Southey
		1844	J.M.W. Turner paints *Rain, Steam, and Speed*
1842	Charlotte and Emily visit Brussels to study languages	1845	Irish Potato Famine begins
1843	Emily productive and content, alone at Haworth with her father	1850	Death of Wordsworth; Tennyson's "In Memoriam A.H.H." published
1845	Charlotte discovers Emily's poems; *Wuthering Heights* begun	1850	Nathaniel Hawthorne's *The Scarlet Letter* published
1846	Charlotte, Emily, and Anne publish joint volume of poems	1851	Herman Melville's *Moby-Dick* published
1847	Charlotte's *Jane Eyre*, Emily's *Wuthering Heights,* and Anne's *Agnes Grey* published under the pseudonyms Currer, Ellis, and Acton Bell	1854	Japan reopens trade with West; Britain enters Crimean War
1848	Death of Branwell in September; death of Emily in December		
1850	Charlotte publishes second edition of *Wuthering Heights* with corrections, "Editor's Preface," and "Biographical Notice" which makes clear Emily's identity as author		

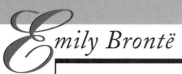

High waving heather

December 13, 1836

High waving heather 'neath stormy blasts bending
Midnight and moonlight and bright shining stars
Darkness and glory rejoicingly blending
Earth rising to heaven and heaven descending
5   Man's spirit away from its drear dungeon sending
Bursting the fetters and breaking the bars

All down the mountainsides wild forests lending
One mighty voice to the life giving wind
Rivers their banks in the jubilee rending
10   Fast through the valleys a reckless course wending
Wider and deeper their waters extending
Leaving a desolate desert behind

Shining and lowering and swelling and dicing
Changing forever from midnight to noon
15   Roaring like thunder like soft music sighing
Shadows on shadows advancing and flying
Lightning bright flashes the deep gloom defying
Coming as swiftly and fading as soon

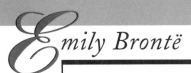
Emily Brontë

Love is like the wild rose-briar

Love is like the wild rose-briar,
Friendship, like the holly tree–
The holly is dark when the rose-briar blooms,
But which will bloom most constantly?

5   The wild rose-briar is sweet in spring,
Its summer blossoms scent the air;
Yet wait till winter comes again
And who will call the wild-briar fair?

Then scorn the silly rose-wreath now
10   And deck thee with the holly's sheen,
That when December blights thy brow
He still may leave thy garland green.

My heart is not enraptured now

My heart is not enraptured now
My eyes are full of tears
And constant sorrow on my brow
Has done the work of years

5   It was not hope that wrecked at once
The spirit's ocean storm
But a long life of solitude
Hopes quenched and rising thoughts subdued
A bleak November's calm

Emily Brontë

The day is done

February 2, 1844

The day is done—the winter sun
Is setting in its sullen sky
And drear the course that has been run
And dim the beams that slowly die

5   No star will light my coming night
No moon of hope for me will shine
I mourn not heaven would blast my sight
And I never longed for harp divine

Through life hard task I did not ask
10   Celestial aid celestial cheer
I saw my fate without its mask
And met it too without a tear

The grief that pressed my dreary breast
Was heavier far than earth can be
15   And who would dread eternal rest
When labour's hire was agony

Dark falls the fear of this despair
On hearts that drink of happiness
But I was bred the mate of care
20   The foster child of sore distress

No sighs for me no sympathy
No wish to keep my soul below
The heart is dead since infancy
Unwept for let the body go

Song

October 15, 1839

O between distress and pleasure
Fond affection cannot be
Wretched hearts in vain would treasure
Friendship's joys when others flee

5   Well I know thine eye would never
Smile while mine grieved willingly
Yet I know thine eye forever
Could not weep in sympathy

Let us part the time is over
10   When I thought and felt like thee
I will be an ocean rover
I will sail the desert sea

Isles there are beyond its billow
Lands where woe may wander free
15   And beloved thy midnight pillow
Will be soft unwatched by me

Not on each returning morrow
When thy heart bounds ardently
Needst thou then dissemble[1] sorrow
20   Marking my despondency[2]

Day by day some dreary token
Will forsake thy memory
Till at last all old links broken
I shall be a dream to thee

---

1. dissemble: Conceal.
2. despondency: Despair, hopelessness.

☑ Check Your Comprehension

1. What is the setting of "High waving heather"?
2. In "Love is like the wild rose-briar," to what (a) emotions and (b) seasons are the wild rose-briar and the holly tree linked?
3. In "My heart is not enraptured now," what is responsible, according to the speaker, for the aged appearance of her brow?
4. What does the speaker describe herself as the "mate" of and the "foster child" of in "The day is done"?
5. The last line of "Song" is "I shall be a dream to thee." What kind of dream is the speaker talking about?

◆ Critical Thinking

INTERPRET

1. When you consider lines in "High waving heather" such as "Bursting the fetters and breaking the bars" or "Rivers their banks in the jubilee rending," how would you characterize the mood of this poem? [Interpret]
2. Given that the rose-wreath is called "silly" in the third stanza of "Love is like the wild rose-briar," what do the speaker's feelings about love and friendship seem to be? [Infer]
3. Judging from the final stanzas of "My heart is not enraptured now," "The day is done," and "Song," how would you describe the speaker's personality? List three to five words from the stanzas that lead you to this conclusion. [Evaluate]
4. Victorian critics considered the ideas in Emily Brontë's poems unconventional and disturbing. Given that Victorian social codes valued conformity, cheerfully doing one's duty, and love as a sacred emotion, what might have been so disturbing about them? [Apply]

Emily Brontë

Hope

December 18, 1843

Hope was but a timid friend—
She sat without[1] the grated den
Watching how my fate would tend
Even as selfish-hearted men—

5   She was cruel in her fear—
Through the bars, one dreary day,
I looked out to see her there
And she turned her face away!

Like a false guard false watch keeping
10   Still in strife she whispered, peace
She would sing while I was weeping,
If I listened, she would cease—

False she was, and unrelenting,
When my last joys strewed the ground
15   Even Sorrow saw repenting
Those sad relics scattered round—

Hope—whose whisper would have given
Balm to all my frenzied pain—
Stretched her wings and soared to heaven—
20   Went—and ne'er returned again!

---

1. **without:** Outside.

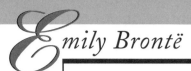

Emily Brontë

To Imagination

September 3, 1844

When weary with the long day's care
And earthly change from pain to pain
And lost and ready to despair
Thy kind voice calls me back again—
5   O my true friend, I am not lone
While thou canst speak with such a tone!

So hopeless is the world without
The world within I doubly prize
Thy world, where guile and hate and doubt
10   And cold suspicion never rise—
Where thou and I and Liberty
Have undisputed sovereignty

What matters it that all around
Danger and guilt and darkness lie
15   If but within our bosom's bound
We hold a bright untroubled sky
Warm with ten thousand mingled rays
Of suns that know no winter days—

Reason indeed may oft complain
20   For Nature's sad reality
And tell the suffering heart how vain
Its cherished dreams must always be
And Truth may rudely trample down
The flowers of fancy newly blown

25   But thou art ever there to bring
The hovering vision back and breathe
New glories o'er the blighted Spring
And call a lovelier life from death
And whisper with a voice divine
30   Of real worlds as bright as thine

I trust not to thy phantom bliss
Yet still, in evening's quiet hour
With never failing thankfulness
I welcome thee benignant power
35   Sure Solacer of human cares
And sweeter hope when hope despairs—

Stanzas

Often rebuked, yet always back returning
    To those first feelings that were born with me,
And leaving busy chase of wealth and learning
    For idle dreams of things which cannot be:

5   Today, I will seek not the shadowy region,
    Its unsustaining vastness waxes drear;
And visions rising, legion after legion,
    Bring the unreal world too strangely near.

I'll walk, but not in old heroic traces,
10   And not in paths of high morality,
And not among the half-distinguished faces,
    The clouded forms of long-past history.

I'll walk where my own nature would be leading:
    It vexes me to choose another guide:
15   Where the grey flocks in ferny glens are feeding;
    Where the wild wind blows on the mountain side.

What have those lonely mountains worth revealing?
    More glory and more grief than I can tell:
The earth that wakes one human heart to feeling
20   Can centre both the worlds of Heaven and Hell.

☑ Check Your Comprehension

1. Is the ending of "Hope" hopeful?

2. In stanza 3 of "To Imagination," why doesn't it matter that " . . . all around / Danger and guilt and darkness lie"?

3. In "Stanzas," where does the speaker decide to walk?

◆ Critical Thinking

INTERPRET

1. Would you call "Hope" a realistic or unrealistic poem? Why? **[Interpret]**

2. What values of the writer are demonstrated by "To Imagination" and "Stanzas"? **[Infer]**

3. Consider the last stanza of "To Imagination." In what way does this poem provide an answer to the poem "Hope"? **[Connect]**

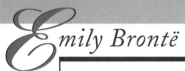

Emily Brontë

A Diary Note—No. 5

This is a note that Emily Brontë wrote on her birthday in 1845 and stored away, intending to read it again three years later on her thirtieth birthday.

Haworth, Thursday, July 30th, 1845

My birthday—showery, breezy, cool. I am twenty-seven years old to-day. This morning Anne and I opened the papers we wrote four years since, on my twenty-third birthday. This paper we intend, if all be well, to open on my thirtieth—three years hence, in 1848. Since the 1841 paper the following events have taken place. Our school scheme has been abandoned, and instead Charlotte and I went to Brussels on the 8th of February 1842.

Branwell left his place at Luddenden Foot. C. and I returned from Brussels, November 8th, 1842, in consequence of aunt's death.

Branwell went to Thorp Green as a tutor, where Anne still continued, January 1843.

Charlotte returned to Brussels the same month, and after staying a year, came back again on New Year's Day 1844.

Anne left her situation at Thorp Green of her own accord, June 1845.

Anne and I went our first long journey by ourselves together, leaving home on the 30th of June, Monday, sleeping at York, returning to Keighley Tuesday evening, sleeping there and walking home on Wednesday morning. Though the weather was broken we enjoyed ourselves very much, except during a few hours at Bradford. And during our excursion we were, Ronald Macalgin, Henry Angora, Juliet Angusteena, Rosabella Esmaldan, Ella and Julian Egremont, Catharine Navarre, and Cordelia Fitzaphnold, escaping from the palaces of instruction to join the Royalists who are hard driven at present by the victorious Republicans. The Gondals still flourish bright as ever. I am at present writing a work on the First Wars. Anne has been writing some articles on this, and a book by Henry Sophona. We intend sticking firm by the rascals as long as they delight us, which I am glad to say they do at present. I should have mentioned that last summer the school scheme was revived in full vigor. We had prospectuses printed, dispatched letters to all acquaintances imparting our plans, and did our little all; but it was found no go. Now I don't desire a school at all, and none of us have any great longing for it.

We have cash enough for our present wants, with a prospect of accumulation. We are all in decent health, only that papa has a complaint in his eyes, and with the exception of B., who, I hope, will be better and do better hereafter. I am quite contented for myself: not as idle as formerly, altogether as hearty, and having learnt to make the most of the present and long for the future with the fidgetiness that I cannot do all I wish; seldom or never troubled with nothing to do, and merely desiring that everybody could be as comfortable as myself and as undesponding, and then we should have a very tolerable world of it.

By mistake I find we have opened the paper on the 31st instead of the 30th. Yesterday was much such a day as this, but the morning was divine.

Tabby, who was gone in our last paper, is come back, and has lived with us two years and a half, and is in good health. Martha, who also departed, is here too.[1] We have got Flossy; got and lost Tiger; lost the hawk Hero, which, with the geese, was given away, and is doubtless dead, for when I came back from Brussels, I inquired on all hands and could hear nothing of him. Tiger died early last year. Keeper and Flossy are well, also the canary acquired four years since. We are now all at home, and likely to be there some time. Branwell went to Liverpool on Tuesday to stay a week. Tabby has just been teasing me to turn as formerly to "Pilloputate." Anne and I should have picked the black currants if it had been fine and sunshiny. I must hurry off now to my turning[2] and ironing. I have plenty of work on hands, and writing, and am altogether full of business. With best wishes for the whole house till 1848, July 30th, and as much longer as may be,—I conclude.

---

1. **"...is here too.":** Tabby and Martha are servants.
2. **turning:** A type of sewing.

☑ Check Your Comprehension

1. Who are the "rascals" that Emily and Anne intend "sticking firm by"?
2. Why did the Brontës abandon their plan for a school?
3. The diary note was supposed to be opened on Emily's birthday, July 30th, but was instead opened accidentally on the 31st. Why doesn't it seem to matter?

◆ Critical Thinking

1. How do the Gondal Chronicles seem to function in the everyday lives of the Brontës? [Analyze]
2. How would you describe, overall, the character of the Brontë children's lives in the years described by this birthday note? [Interpret]
3. How would you describe the tone of the birthday note, as compared to the tone of many of the poems? [Compare and Contrast]
4. How might you account for any difference in tone that you perceive between the poems and the note? [Draw Conclusions]

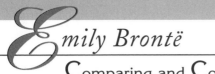

Emily Brontë

Comparing and Connecting the Author's Works

◆ Literary Focus: Imagery

Critics, over time, have defined **imagery** as a poetic device in many different ways. In our era, poetic imagery is generally understood to have two meanings. One is the use of language to produce mental pictures—images. The other meaning refers to the language itself; imagery is the use of figures of speech like **simile** (comparing two unlike things by using the words *like* or *as,* for example, "Love is like the wild rose-briar") and **personification** (giving human qualities to something that is not alive, for example, "Celestial aid celestial cheer"). A poet's imagery is the unique way that the poet uses figurative language to produce mental pictures.

Brontë uses metaphor, simile, and personification often in her poems. Look through Brontë's poems and find an example of each of them. Copy the lines from the poems and write which figure of speech they represent.

◆ Drawing Conclusions About Emily Brontë's Work

Charlotte Brontë, Emily's sister and author of the novel *Jane Eyre,* wrote about Emily's poems: *these were not common effusions [an outpouring of emotion]... I found them condensed and terse, vigorous and genuine.*

1. Emily Brontë's poems are very emotional. What makes them unlike "common effusions?" Find an example of terse and condensed writing in one of Brontë's poems and use it to support Charlotte Brontë's statement. Write a paragraph that explains why your selection could be considered terse and concise.
2. Charlotte Brontë also wrote that her sister's poems had "a peculiar music—wild, melancholy and elevating." Poems are not meant to be sung, but an important trait of a poem is that the language must possess emotion, rhythm, and meter, all of which can evoke music in the mind of the reader. Find a selection from Emily's poems that fits Charlotte's description. Write a paragraph that supports your selection and identify what is wild and melancholic (sad) in the selection.

◆ Idea Bank

Writing

1. **Diary Entry** As you saw in "A Diary Note," the Brontës wrote letters to themselves and then stored them away to be opened a few years later. This custom gave them the opportunity to record their lives and a chance to speculate about the future. Then, when they reread them, they had the opportunity to reminisce and recover memories that they had forgotten. Write a letter to yourself in which you describe what your life is currently like, any events that seem significant to you, and what your hopes and plans for the future may be.
2. **Writing Poetry** (a) One typical feature of Emily Brontë's poems is the personification of nature by attributing human emotions to natural elements, like "lonely mountains." Write a poem in which you describe a natural scene in emotional terms. (b) Brontë also writes poems that use imagery to describe an emotion, something that cannot be depicted objectively. Her poem "Hope" is an example. Write a poem that has an emotion as its title and that uses imagery to describe that emotion.

3. **Film Criticism** One definition of imagery is what your mind perceives as you read a poem. Watching a film based on an author's work is a way to see how a filmmaker has visually interpreted the author's imagery. Watch the movie *Wuthering Heights* and write an essay that shows how the film uses visual imagery to evoke Brontë's literary imagery.
   [Media Link]

4. **Compare and Contrast Poetry** Emily Dickinson (1830–1886) was an American poet with some interesting similarities to Emily Brontë. Both were reclusive and neither anticipated that her work would be widely read, and in fact, they both kept their poetry hidden from others. Following is Emily Dickinson's poem "'Hope' is the thing with feathers." Write an essay that compares and contrasts the two poems.

> "Hope" is the thing with feathers—
> That perches in the soul—
> And sings the tune without words—
> And never stops—at all—
>
> And sweetest—in the Gale—is heard—
> And sore must be the storm—
> That could abash the little Bird
> That kept so many warm—
>
> I've heard it in the chillest land—
> And on the strangest Sea—
> Yet, never, in Extremity,
> It asked a crumb—of Me.

To help you organize your thoughts, fill in the rest of the following diagram:

"Hope is the thing with feathers."	"Hope"
Similarities	Differences
The subject of both poems is the emotion, hope.	Hope is a friend Hope is a bird

5. **Interpretation of Music** Opera combines voice with music and tells a story often based on a heroic myth. In a way, the Gondal epics that the Brontë children composed resemble opera. One of the best known Romantic opera composers was the German, Richard Wagner (1813–1883). Listen to a section of one of his most famous operas, *Tristan und Isolde,* and make notes on your impressions of the music. **[Music Link]**

Researching and Representing

6. **Historical/Medical Research** Tuberculosis, which killed Emily Brontë and other members of her family, was a terrible plague in the Victorian era. Form a group and research the history of the disease. Develop your research into a report and present it to your class.
   [Social Studies Link; Group Activity]

◆ Further Reading, Listening, and Viewing

- C. W. Hatfield, editor: *The Complete Poems of Emily Brontë* (1941)
- Emily Brontë: *Wuthering Heights* (1847)
- Edward Chitham: *A Life of Emily Brontë* (1987) Biography
- Richard Wagner: *Lohengrin, Der Ring des Nibelungen, Tristan und Isolde, Parsifal* Operas. Recordings and videos of these operas are available.
- *Wuthering Heights:* Director Peter Kominsky (1992) Film starring Ralph Fiennes and Juliette Binoche

On the Web:

http://www.phschool.com/atschool/literature
Go to the student edition *Platinum*. Proceed to Unit 5. Then, click Hot Links to find Web sites featuring Emily Brontë.

Gwendolyn Brooks In Depth

> "My last defense/Is the present tense.
>
> —*Gwendolyn Brooks, from "Old Mary"*

GWENDOLYN **B**ROOKS is one of America's most distinguished contemporary poets. Her work draws on traditional, modern, and contemporary verse forms, all of which reflect the society and culture of African Americans. Her later poems are characterized by intense voices and lean forms that convey the urgency and outrage of what came to be known in the 1960's as the Black Arts Movement.

Family History David Brooks and Keziah Wims, Gwendolyn's father and mother, were married in 1916 and settled in Chicago, where they were the second African American family to move into their neighborhood. David completed high school, and attended Fisk University for one year. He hoped to become a doctor. Brooks's mother, Keziah, came from a family of ten children and studied to be a classical pianist.

Gwendolyn Brooks was born on June 7, 1917, and her brother Raymond was born sixteen months later. Their mother encouraged the children to play quietly and kept them sheltered from racial strife. This helped young Gwendolyn to develop the powerful imagination that allowed her to become an important poet. When she entered elementary school, however, she was shocked by the racism that surrounded her.

An Early Start Shy and dark-skinned, Brooks found it difficult to gain social acceptance among her peers, but her enthusiasm for writing grew. In 1930,

her first published poem, "Eventide," was printed in *American Childhood,* and by 1934, her poems were appearing regularly in a weekly column in the newspaper *Chicago Defender.*

Brooks graduated from Englewood High School, then went on to Wilson Junior College and graduated in 1936. Afterward she worked several miserable jobs, including selling religious objects door-to-door and being a maid. These experiences eventually became the inspiration for her books *Maud Martha* (1953), her only novel, and *In the Mecca* (1968). After college, Brooks married Henry Lowington Blakely II in 1939. Their son, Henry III, was born a year later.

First Book In 1945, Brooks won the Midwestern Writers Conference Prize with her poem "the progress." Her work was soon forwarded to Richard Wright, author of *Native Son* and *Black Boy*. Impressed with Brooks's poetry, Wright recommended her work for publication. The collection was published as *A Street in Bronzeville* in 1944.

The next few years were very successful for Brooks. She won two Guggenheim Fellowships, a National Institute of Arts and Letters award in 1946, and an award from the American Academy of Arts and Letters.

The Pulitzer Prize In 1949, she was the first African American to be awarded the Pulitzer Prize for Poetry. The publication of *Annie Allen*, and its favorable reviews, brought Brooks national attention.

Gwendolyn's daughter, Nora, was born in September 1951. Brooks continued to draw from her own experiences in her novel *Maud Martha*, published in 1953. *Maud Martha* tells the story of an African American woman coming to terms with prejudice and poverty. In 1956, she wrote *Bronzeville Boys and Girls*, followed by *Bronzeville Men and Women*, which was published in 1960, as *The Bean Eaters*.

Black Activist, Black Artist During the 1960's, Brooks became involved with the civil rights movement and later with the Black Power and Black Arts movement. During this time, Brooks began to support young black writers by subsidizing their publications, donating cash awards for writing contests, and giving financial aid directly to writers.

Throughout the 1970's, Brooks published a number of books of poetry as well as her autobiography, *Report From Part One*. A second autobiographical work, *Report From Part Two*, was published in 1996. In January 1980, Brooks read at the White House, and in 1985, she was made the Library of Congress's poetry consultant, one of the country's most prestigious literary appointments.

◆ African American History in The Twentieth Century

The Civil War led to the end of slavery in the United States, but not the end of discrimination, especially in the South. Consequently, many African Americans migrated north to urban areas in the early 1900's. World War I created professional and educational opportunities for African Americans and a black urban middle class was established.

This period was marred by racial violence, but also saw great artistic and cultural advances for African Americans. One example of this new pride and culture is the Harlem Renaissance, named for the cultural explosion in the 1920's in Harlem, an African American section of New York City.

The economic depression of the 1930's ended the cultural and economic prosperity of the Harlem Renaissance, and it took World War II to prompt reforms. In 1954, the U.S. Supreme Court ruled that segregation in public schools was illegal, beginning the civil rights era. Throughout the latter half of the 1950's and the 1960's, leaders like Martin Luther King, Jr., fought against discrimination.

In the wake of King's assassination, there were again riots in most large American cities. In the 1970's, gradual steps were made toward racial equality and, increasingly, African American popular culture influenced national tastes. Racial equality remains a goal in the United States but progress continues to be made.

◆ Literary Works

Poetry

A Street in Bronzeville (1945); *Annie Allen* (1949); *Bronzeville Boys and Girls* (1956); *The Bean Eaters* (1960); *Selected Poems* (1963); *In the Mecca* (1968); *Family Pictures* (1970); Beckonings (1975); Blacks (1987)

Fiction

Maud Martha (1953)

Prose

Primer for Blacks (1980); *Young Poet's Primer (1981)*; *Very Young Poets (1983)*

Autobiography

Report From Part One (1972); *Report From Part Two* (1996)

Edited by Gwendolyn Brooks

A Broadside Treasury (1971); *Jump Bad: A New Chicago Anthology* (1971)

TIMELINE

Brooks's Life		World Events	
1917	Born in Topeka, Kansas on June 7	1910	National Association for the Advancement of Colored People (NAACP) formed
1930	"Eventide," her first poem, is published in *American Childhood Magazine*	1911	Fire at Triangle Shirtwaist Company factory kills 146, leads to reforms in working conditions and fire safety
1934	Publishes in *Chicago Defender*; graduates from Englewood High School	1917	U.S. declares war on Germany; October Revolution in Russia
1936	Graduates from Wilson Junior College	1918	Germany and Allies sign armistice; 22 million die in influenza epidemic
1938	Joins NAACP Youth Council	1920	Women gain right to vote in U.S.A.
1939	Marries Henry Lowington Blakely II		
1944	*A Street in Bronzeville* published	1924	Robert Frost awarded Pulitzer Prize in Poetry
1946	Wins Guggenheim Fellowship	1925	James Weldon Johnson publishes *The Book of American Negro Spirituals*; John Scopes tried for violating Tennessee law against teaching evolution.
1950	*Annie Allen* wins the Pulitzer Prize for Poetry		
1953	Only novel, *Maud Martha*, published		
1956	*Bronzeville Boys and Girls* published	1927	First talkie, Al Jolson in "The Jazz Singer"
1960	*The Bean Eaters* published	1954	*Brown vs. Board of Education* ends segregation in public schools
1962	President Kennedy invites her to read at Library of Congress; meets Robert Frost	1955	Rosa Parks's defiance initiates the Montgomery, Alabama, bus strike
1963	*Selected Poems* published		
1967	Attends Second Fisk Writers Conference; meets LeRoi Jones (Amiri Baraka)	1957	Soviet launching of the first satellite, Sputnik; Little Rock, Arkansas, becomes symbol for struggle against segregation
1968	Appointed Poet Laureate of Illinois		
1971	*The World of Gwendolyn Brooks* published	1963	March on Washington, organized by A. Philip Randolph
1975	*Beckonings* published; edits *A Capsule Course in Black Poetry Writing*	1966	Black Panther Party founded
		1972	U.S. Congress passes Equal Opportunity Act
1981	*Black Love* and *To Disembark* published	1991–92	Persian Gulf War
1986–87	*The Near–Johannesburg Boy and Other Poems*; and *Blacks* published	1994	Nelson Mandela inaugurated as first black president of South Africa
1996	*Report From Part Two* published		

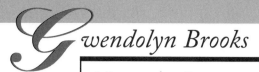
Gwendolyn Brooks

Horses Graze

Cows graze.
Horses graze.
They
eat
5   eat
eat.
Their graceful heads
are bowed
bowed
10   bowed
in majestic oblivion.
They are nobly oblivious
to your follies,
your inflation,
15   the knocks and nettles of administration.
They
eat
eat
eat.
20   And at the crest of their brute satisfaction,
with wonderful gentleness, in affirmation,
they lift their clean calm eyes and they lie down
and love the world.
They speak with their companions.
25   They do not wish that they were otherwise.
Perhaps they know that creature feet may press
only a few earth inches at a time,
that earth is anywhere earth,
that an eye may see,
30   wherever it may be,
the Immediate arc, alone, of life, of love.

In Sweden,
China,
Afrika,
35   in India or Maine
the animals are sane;
they know and know and know
there's ground below
and sky
40   up high.

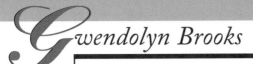

The Last Quatrain of the Ballad of Emmett Till

after the murder,
after the burial

Emmett's mother is a pretty-faced thing;
    the tint of pulled taffy.

5   She sits in a red room,
        drinking black coffee.

She kisses her killed boy.
    And she is sorry.

Chaos in windy grays
10   through a red prairie.

Speech to the Young.
Speech to the Progress—Toward.

For Nora Brooks Blakely.
For Henry Blakely Ill.

Say to them,
say to the down-keepers,
the sun-slappers,
the self-soilers,
5   the harmony-hushers,
"Even if you are not ready for day
it cannot always be night."
You will be right.
For that is the hard home-run.

10   And remember:
live not for Battles Won.
Live not for The-End of-the-song.
Live in the along.

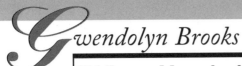

Gwendolyn Brooks

"When Handed a Lemon, Make Lemonade"

(title by Anonymous)

I've lived through lemons,
sugaring them.
"When handed a lemon,
make lemonade."
5   That is what
some sage[1] has said.
"When handed a lemon,
make lemonade."

10   There is always a use
for lemon juice.

Do you know what to do with
trouble, children?
Make lemonade. Make lemonade.
15   "Handed a lemon, make lemonade."

---

1. sage (saj) *n.*: A wise, experienced person.

☑ Check Your Comprehension

1. Does the speaker in "Horses Graze" perceive animals as wild and aggressive or as peaceful creatures?
2. In "Horse Graze," what kind of figure of speech is the phrase "the knocks and nettles of administration"?
3. What similar advice is given in the poems "Speech to the Young. Speech to the Progress—Toward." and "When Handed a Lemon, Make Lemonade"?
4. Which stanza is the rhyming couplet in "When Handed a Lemon, Make Lemonade"?

◆ Critical Thinking

INTERPRET

1. In "Horses Graze," Brooks uses the poetic device of repetition; the lines "eat/eat/eat." are repetitive. How does this repetition evoke an animal's life and concerns? **[Analyze]**

2. "The Last Quatrain of the Ballad of Emmett Till" is presented as a fragment of a longer (unwritten) poem. What do you think the whole poem could be about? **[Extend]**

3. "Speech to the Young. Speech to the Progress—Toward." is dedicated to Brooks's children. What message is she trying to give them? **[Interpret]**

4. How can trouble be like a lemon in the poem "When Handed a Lemon, Make Lemonade"? **[Extend]**

IX: truth

And if sun comes
How shall we greet him?
Shall we not dread him,
Shall we not fear him
5   After so lengthy a
Session with shade?

Though we have wept for him,
Though we have prayed
All through the night-years—
10   What if we wake one shimmering morning to
Hear the fierce hammering
Of his firm knuckles
Hard on the door?

Shall we not shudder?—
15   Shall we not flee
Into the shelter,
the dear thick shelter
Of the familiar
Propitious[1] haze?

20   Sweet is it, sweet is it
To sleep in the coolness
Of snug unawareness.

The dark hangs heavily
Over the eyes.

---

1. propitious (prə pi′ shəs) *adj.*: Favorable or kindly.

X

Exhaust the little moment. Soon it dies.
And be it gash or gold it will not come
Again in this identical disguise.

Gwendolyn Brooks

The Crazy Woman

I shall not sing a May song.
A May song should be gay.
I'll wait until November
And sing a song of gray.

5   I'll wait until November.
That is the time for me.
I'll go out in the frosty dark
And sing most terribly.

And all the little people
10   Will stare at me and say,
"That is the Crazy Woman
Who would not sing in May."

☑ Check Your Comprehension

1. In "IX: truth," why is it "sweet. . . To sleep in the coolness/Of snug unawareness"?
2. What do the words "gash and gold" mean in "X"?
3. Why is a "May song" gay and a "November song" gray in "The Crazy Woman"?
4. What do these poems have in common?

◆ Critical Thinking

INTERPRET

1. Personification is a figure of speech in which something is given human qualities. What kind of "person" is the sun in "IX: truth"? **[Analyze]**
2. The poem "X" is an epigram, a short, witty poem that makes a statement or observation. Using the poems in this section, give examples of other sayings that warn us to make the most of time? **[Apply]**
3. In "Crazy Woman," why would the speaker choose to wait to sing a May song until November? **[Draw Conclusions]**

In Honor of David Anderson Brooks, My Father

July 30, 1883–November 21, 1959

A dryness is upon the house
My father loved and tended.
Beyond his firm and sculptured door
His light and lease have ended.

5   He walks the valleys, now—replies
To sun and wind forever.
No more the cramping chamber's chill,
No more the hindering fever.

Now out upon the wide clean air
10   My father's soul revives,
All innocent of self-interest
And the fear that strikes and strives.

He who was Goodness, Gentleness,
And Dignity is free,
15   Translates to public Love
Old private charity.

Gwendolyn Brooks

Of Robert Frost

There is a little lightning in his eyes.
Iron at the mouth.
His brows ride neither too far up nor down.

He is splendid. With a place to stand.

5   Some glowing in the common blood.
Some specialness within.

Langston Hughes

is merry glory.

Is saltatory[1]
Yet grips his right of twisting free.

Has a long reach,
Strong speech,
5   Remedial fears.
Muscular tears.

Holds horticulture
In the eye of the vulture
Infirm profession.
10   In the Compression—
In mud and blood and sudden death—
In the breath
Of the holocaust he
Is helmsman, hatchet, headlight.
15   See
One restless in the exotic time! and ever,
Till the air is cured of its fever.

---

1. saltatory (səl′ tə′ tōrē) *adj.*: Leaping or dancing.

Gwendolyn Brooks

Excerpt *from* Report From Part One

Langston Hughes! The words and deeds of Langston Hughes were rooted in kindness, and in pride. His point of departure was always a clear pride in his race. Race pride may be craft, art, or a music that combines the best of jazz and hymn. Langston frolicked and chanted to the measure of his own race-reverence.

It is now almost a cliche to squeal "Such one was out and fighting before you were *born*!" But at least all may admit that Langston held high and kept warm the weapons until the youngsters could cut the caul, could wipe away the webs of birth and get to work. Indeed, he preceded them with a couple of chores, a couple of bleedings. Langston Hughes admired the word "black" when that word was less than a darling flag. He believed in the beauty of blackness when belief in the beauty of blackness was not the fashion, not "the thing," not the sweet berry of the community tooth.

He was an easy man. You could rest in his company. No one possessed a more serious understanding of life's immensities. No one was firmer in recognition of the horrors man imposes upon man, in hardy insistence on reckonings. But when those who knew him remember him the memory inevitably will include laughter of an unusually warm and tender kind. The wise man, he knew, will take some juice out of this one life that is his gift.

We squeezed perhaps a hundred people into our Langston Hughes two-room kitchenette party. Langston was the merriest and the most colloquial of them all. "*Best* party I've ever been given!" He enjoyed everyone: he enjoyed all the talk, all the phonograph blues, all the festivity in the crowded air. And— I remember him dropping in unexpectedly some years later. His dignified presence decorated our droll[1] little quarters. We asked him to share our dinner of mustard greens, ham hocks and candied sweet potatoes, and he accepted. "Just what I want!" exclaimed the noble poet, the efficient essayist, the adventurous dramatist.

---

1. droll: Funny; quaint.

He loved the young. He helped and advised hundreds. On more than one occasion he devoted his column to work of mine, before and after my books were published. Others he knew and aided and encouraged . . . One of my prides is that he dedicated to me his book of short stories *Something In Common*.

One of the indelibles.

Langston Hughes loved literature. He loved it not fearfully, not with awe. His respect for it was never stiff nor cold. His respect for it was gaily deferential. He considered literature not his private inch, but great acreage. The plantings of others he not only welcomed but busily enriched. He had an affectionate interest in those young writers. He was intent, he was careful. The young manuscript-bearing applicant never felt himself an intruder, never went away with Oak turned ashes in the hand.

Mightily did he use the street. He found its multiple heart, its tastes, smells, alarms, formulas, flowers, garbage and convulsions. He brought them all to his table-top. He crushed them to a writing-paste. He himself became the pen. . . .

☑ Check Your Comprehension

1. How are the three selections similar?
2. Can "Langston Hughes" and "Of Robert Frost" be considered memorial poems?
3. How do you know that Gwendolyn Brooks respects Langston Hughes?
4. In the excerpt from *Report From Part One*, Brooks writes: "The wise man, he [Langston Hughes] knew, will take some juice out of this one life that is his gift." Which of Brooks's poems uses a similar metaphor?

◆ Critical Thinking

1. Brooks wrote "In Honor of David Anderson Brooks, My Father" after her father died. What images in this poem describe how Brooks felt about her father? **[Interpret]**

2. Langston Hughes (1902–1967) was a writer from the Harlem Renaissance cultural movement. Brooks uses figurative language to describe the man in verse. What personal qualities of Hughes is Brooks describing when she writes that "he's helmsman, hatchet, headlight."? **[Interpret]**

3. Robert Frost (1874–1963) was an American poet whom Brooks respected. What do you think Brooks meant by the phrase "common blood"? **[Interpret]**

4. In *Report From Part One*, Brooks describes Langston Hughes in prose. She also describes him in verse in "Langston Hughes." What poetic techniques does she use in the poem to express the same feelings she writes about in this prose selection? **[Analyze]**

Gwendolyn Brooks
Comparing and Connecting the Author's Works

◆ Literary Focus: Social Protest Poetry

Gwendolyn Brooks employs a combination of classical and modern poetic techniques and forms in her work. However, the subject of her poems is almost always a protest against racism. Though her subject matter is contemporary, she is participating in the ancient literary tradition of **social protest poetry**. Although Brooks draws from many different literary traditions in her work, many of her poems can be considered works of social protest because they are directed at racism in American society. Brooks's poetry aims to attack the source of the racism or support those who fight against it. Social protest poetry may take the form of

- **Directives** (advice on how to behave)
- **Portraits** of victims, heroes, and enemies
- **Encomiums** (public compliments)
- **Elegies** (poems that mourn the loss of someone or something)
- **Satires** (witty attacks on human folly)

Turn back to Brooks's poems. Write down the titles of the poems that are elegies.

1. Who or what is being mourned in these poems? How might society be improved by mourning this loss?
2. Now try the same for Brooks's directive poems. Write down the titles of the poems that give advice on behavior. Who do you think Brooks intended to read these poems? Is the advice in these poems applicable to more than her intended audience?

◆ Drawing Conclusions About Brooks's Work

Gwendolyn Brooks has always encouraged the literary development of young people. She has even written books of poetry for children. In a 1990 interview in *Ebony* magazine, Brooks said *Looking at poetry and saluting it, they [children] realize that in the world there is beauty. That there is horror they know and have always known . . . Their nature is not frugal, it is expansive and lifting. It reacts. It reacts to clouds, sunshine. It reacts to dryness, waste, oppression. Some of these young people . . . have found that poetry is a friend to whom you can say too much.*

In this interview excerpt, Brooks was speaking about children's writing. She also reveals, however, some of what she values in poetry. In the diagram below, examples of her poetic values taken from her interview are linked to examples of how these values are expressed in her poems.

◆ Idea Bank

Writing

1. **Advice** Some of Brooks's poems, "Speech to the Young," for example, offer advice to children. If you had children, what kind of advice would you like to give them? Make a list of what you would like to tell them.

2. **Portrait Poem** In the poem "Langston Hughes," Brooks paints a portrait of a man she admires. Write your own portrait of somebody you respect.

3. **Compare and Contrast** Write a brief essay that compares and contrasts "The Last Quatrain of the Ballad of Emmett Till" and "In Honor of David Anderson Brooks."

Brooks's poetic values	Examples of value in a poem
"In the world there is beauty	"Their graceful heads are bowed/bowed/ bowed in majestic oblivion." From "Horses Graze"
"there is horror"	"In the breath/Of the holocaust he/Is helmsman, hatchet, headlight." From "Langston Hughes"
"to reconcile onions and roses"	And be it gash or gold it will"

Speaking and Listening

4. **Poetry Reading** In an *Ebony* magazine interview, Brooks said, "I like the youthful zest of Right Rap, which features an intoxicating beat, varieties of tone. In rock, rap, and reggae you will find pieces of poetry—powerful, pitiful, perpendicular...You will find love light loss liberty lunacy and laceration." Pick one of her poems and perform it as rap. **[Performing Arts Link]**

Researching and Representing

5. **Compare and Contrast** In books such as *A Street in Bronzeville* and *Annie Allen,* Gwendolyn Brooks depicted the harsh realities and simple pleasures of black people living in a Chicago neighborhood during the 1940's. Duke Ellington, the jazz composer, did the same thing with his composition, *Black, Brown, and Beige.* Find and listen to a recording of *Black, Brown, and Beige.* Write your impressions of the composition and then reread Brooks's poems. Write an essay comparing your impressions of both of the works.

◆ Further Reading, Listening, and Viewing

- Gwendolyn Brooks: *Report From Part One* (1972) Autobiography.

- Gwendolyn Brooks: *Report From Part Two* (1996) Autobiography.

- Gwendolyn Brooks: *Blacks* (1987) Selected works.

- George E. Kent: *A Life of Gwendolyn Brooks* (1990) Biography.

- *Gwendolyn Brooks Reading Her Poetry* (1973) Sound recording.

- *A Conversation With Gwendolyn Brooks* (1986) Video recording.

On the Web:

http://www.phschool.com/atschool/literature
Go to the student edition *Platinum*. Proceed to Unit 3. Then, click Hot Links to find Web sites featuring Gwendolyn Brooks

Anton Chekhov In Depth

> "Our typical response to some signal moment of moral discovery in a Chekhov story . . . is almost always, consolingly enough, recognition rather than shock, as though we really knew in our hearts that people were like that. . . . "
>
> —*Richard Ford*

ANTON CHEKHOV (än ´tôn chek´ ôf) is an acknowledged master of two genres, the short story and the play—but critics argue over where he made the greater literary contribution. A doctor and a writer, Chekhov examined the precise workings of everyday life—at times with clinical detachment, at times with deep compassion. Chekhov's characters tell us, not what to believe, but how people actually behave. "The artist is not meant to be a judge of his characters and what they say," he once wrote. "His only job is to be an impartial witness."

A Difficult Childhood Chekhov was born on January 17, 1860, in Taganrog, a small seaport in southern Russia. He was the third son in a family of five boys and one girl. His mother was the daughter of a textile merchant; his father owned a general store that stayed open from 5 A.M. to midnight. The Chekhov's children all worked in the shop from an early age.

When Chekhov was sixteen, his father went bankrupt. The family fled to Moscow, leaving Anton behind to finish school and tutor the son of his father's creditor. He lived on his own for three years, sending money to his mother.

A Double Life In 1879, Chekhov rejoined his family and entered medical school at Moscow University. To support his impoverished family, he began writing short comic sketches and "little stories" for humor magazines, using silly pen names.

Chekhov graduated from medical school in 1884 and entered into general practice in Moscow. He continued to write his "frivolous tales." That year he also began experiencing the early symptoms of tuberculosis. In 1885, Chekhov achieved his first serious literary success with his story "The Huntsman." He also met Alexei Suvorin, the rich owner of Russia's leading newspaper, who became Chekhov's patron and close friend. Suvorin encouraged him to write longer, more sophisticated fiction and to publish his work under his own name.

By 1888, Chekhov was a literary celebrity. He had published two collections of stories, won the prestigious Pushkin Prize, and had his first play, *Ivanov*, performed. Though he never completely abandoned humor, his stories were growing more complex and psychologically probing.

Sakhalin In 1890, Chekhov journeyed across Siberia to the island of Sakhalin, a Russian penal colony. Appalled by the misery he saw, he wrote *The Island of Sakhalin*, an enormous book that brought about some reforms.

Chekhov returned home a changed man and wrote two of his greatest stories, "Gusev" and "The Duel." Struggling over his Sakhalin book, he threw himself into a new cause: disaster relief during the famine of 1891–1892.

Country Life In 1892, Chekhov bought a country estate in Melikhovo, where he lived for the next six years with his parents and sister. He resumed his work as a doctor, treating the local peasants and serving as district cholera superintendent during an epidemic. He also wrote some of his finest stories, including "Neighbors"; "Ward 6"; "My Life"; and "Peasants", whose savage portrayal of peasant life caused a sensation. Chekhov also turned to drama, but a disastrous production of *The Seagull* (1896) made him vow never to write another play.

Dramatic Masterpieces In 1897, Chekhov was hospitalized after a lung hemorrhage caused by tuberculosis. Following his father's sudden death, he moved with his mother and sister to Yalta, a resort on the Black Sea. Despite failing health, Chekhov continued to write, producing the stories "Lady with Lapdog" and "The Darling." Increasingly, Chekhov turned his attention to drama, writing three masterpieces that forever changed the direction of modern theater: *Uncle Vanya*, *Three Sisters*, and *The Cherry Orchard*. Chekhov insisted these plays were comedies, yet all deal with a tragic theme: the destruction of beauty in the world.

Love and Death In 1901, Chekhov married Olga Knipper, a star of the Moscow Art Theater. Three years later, at the age of forty-four, and six months after the triumphant opening of *The Cherry Orchard*, Chekhov died in Badenweiler, Germany.

◆ Political Reform and Unrest

Chekhov's lifetime was a period of great political upheaval in Russian history. In 1861, the year after Chekhov was born, Tsar Alexander II realized his nation needed to be modernized, and her institutions liberalized. His first step was the Emancipation Act, which abolished serfdom for Russia's 52 million peasants. An overhaul of the legal system, and the creation of elected local assemblies, called *zemstvos,* followed.

Conservatives were outraged by the tsar's reforms. But liberals and radicals, were also upset. They felt more drastic changes were needed, including a national parliament. In 1866, terrorists made the first of several attempts to assassinate the tsar. In 1881, a group called the People's Will finally succeeded by throwing a bomb into his carriage. Alexander II was killed on the very day he had signed a decree promising to set up two nationally elected "advisory" commissions—a tentative step toward democracy.

When Alexander III became tsar, he cancelled his father's decrees. Throughout his reign (1881–1894), government repression led to widespread political unrest. During his son Nicholas II's rule, that unrest culminated in a bloody uprising called the Revolution of 1905. The Russian Revolution in 1917 finally toppled the tsarist regime.

◆ Literary Works

Major Short Stories "The Kiss" (1887), "The Steppe" (1888), "A Dreary Story" (1889) "Gusev" (1890), "The Duel" (1891), "Neighbors" (1892), "Ward 6" (1894), "My Life" (1896), "Peasants" (1897), "Lady with Lapdog" (1899), "The Darling" (1899), "The Bishop" (1902)

Major Plays *Ivanov* (1887), *The Seagull* (1896), *Uncle Vanya* (1897), *Three Sisters* (1901), *The Cherry Orchard* (1904)

T I M E L I N E

Chekhov's Life		World Events	
1860	Anton Chekhov is born on January 17 in Taganrog, Russia	1861	Serfs emancipated in Russia; Ivan Turgenev publishes *Fathers and Sons;* Charles Dickens publishes *Great Expectations*
1868	Enters Taganrog School for Boys		
1876	Stays in Taganrog to finish school after father goes bankrupt and family flees to Moscow	1861–65	U.S. Civil War
		1864	Tsar Alexander II institutes judicial and other reforms
1879	Joins family in Moscow; enters medical school	1865–69	Leo Tolstoy publishes *War and Peace*
1880	Begins writing comic sketches for newspapers and magazines	1866	Fyodor Dostoevsky publishes *Crime and Punishment;* attempted assassination of Alexander II
1882	Begins writing weekly column		
1884	Graduates from medical school; begins working as doctor; *The Shooting Party* published as serial; begins experiencing signs of tuberculosis	1867	Russia sells Alaska to U.S.; Karl Marx begins publishing *Kapital*
		1870	Franco-Prussian War
			George Eliot publishes *Middlemarch*
1885	Publishes "The Huntsman" to critical acclaim; befriends Alexei Suvorin, rich newspaper owner		First Impressionist art exhibition, included Monet's picture "Impression: Sunrise" at Marmottan Museum in Paris
1886	Publishes first book of stories		
1887	Publishes second book of stories; *Ivanov* performed in Moscow	1874–77	Tolstoy publishes *Anna Karenina*
		1877–78	Russo-Turkish War
1888	"The Steppe" published; wins Pushkin Prize	1879	Henrik Ibsen publishes *A Doll's House*
1890	Makes expedition to Sakhalin		
1891	Publishes "The Duel"; travels to western Europe with Suvorin; helps with famine relief	1880	Dostoevsky publishes *The Brothers Karamazov*
		1881	Alexander II assassinated; Alexander III becomes tsar; anti-Jewish pogroms; Henry James publishes *The Portrait of a Lady*
1892	Buys country estate at Melikhovo; cholera superintendent during epidemic; publishes "Ward 6"		
1895	Publishes *Sakhalin Island*	1882	Robert Koch identifies the bacterium that causes tuberculosis
1896	*The Seagull* flops in Petersburg		
1897	Enters clinic after severe hemorrhage; *Uncle Vanya* published	1885	Friedrich Nietzsche publishes *Beyond Good and Evil*
			Terrible famine in Russia
1898	Begins association with Moscow Arts Theatre; *Seagull* is big hit	1892–93	Cholera epidemic in Russia
1899	Publishes "The Darling" and "Lady with Lapdog"; settles in Yalta with mother and sister after father's death	1894	Nicolas II becomes tsar after the death of Alexander III
			Sigmund Freud publishes *The Interpretation of Dreams*
1901	*Three Sisters* performed; marries actress Olga Knipper	1900	Widespread political unrest in Russia
	The Cherry Orchard performed; dies July 2 in Badenweiler, Germany	1904–05	Russo-Japanese War
		1905	Revolution of 1905

nton Chekhov

The Bet

Translated by Constance Garnett

It was a dark autumn night. The old banker was walking up and down his study and remembering how, fifteen years before, he had given a party one autumn evening. There had been many clever men, there, and there had been interesting conversations. Among other things, they had talked of capital punishment. The majority of the guests, among whom were many journalists and intellectual men, disapproved of the death penalty. They considered that form of punishment out of date, immoral, and unsuitable for Christian States. In the opinion of some of them the death penalty ought to be replaced everywhere by imprisonment for life.

"I don't agree with you," said their host the banker. "I have not tried either the death penalty or imprisonment for life, but if one may judge *a priori*[1] the death penalty is more moral and more humane than imprisonment for life. Capital punishment kills a man at once, but lifelong imprisonment kills him slowly. Which executioner is the more humane, he who kills you in a few minutes or he who drags the life out of you in the course of many years?"

"Both are equally immoral," observed one of the guests, "for they both have the same object—to take away life. The State is not God. It has not the right to take away what it cannot restore when it wants to."

Among the guests was a young lawyer, a young man of five-and-twenty. When he was asked his opinion, he said:

"The death sentence and the life sentence are equally immoral, but if I had to choose between the death penalty and imprisonment for life, I would certainly choose the second. To live anyhow is better than not at all."

A lively discussion arose. The banker, who was younger and more nervous in those days, was suddenly carried away by excitement; he struck the table with his fist and shouted at the young man:

"It's not true! I'll bet you two millions you wouldn't stay in solitary confinement for five years."

"If you mean that in earnest," said the young man, "I'll take a bet, but I would stay not five but fifteen years."

"Fifteen? Done!" cried the banker. "Gentlemen, I stake two millions!"

---

1. *a priori* (ä prē ôrē): Based on theory instead of experience or experiment.

"Agreed! You stake your millions and I stake my freedom!" said the young man.

And this wild, senseless bet was carried out! The banker, spoilt and frivolous, with millions beyond his reckoning, was delighted at the bet. At supper he made fun of the young man, and said:

"Think better of it, young man, while there is still time. To me two millions are a trifle, but you are losing three or four of the best years of your life. I say three or four, because you won't stay longer. Don't forget either, you unhappy man, that voluntary confinement is a great deal harder to bear than compulsory. The thought that you have the right to step out in liberty at any moment will poison your whole existence in prison. I am sorry for you."

And now the banker, walking to and fro, remembered all this, and asked himself. "What was the object of that bet? What is the good of that man's losing fifteen years of his life and my throwing away two millions? Can it prove that the death penalty is better or worse than imprisonment for life? No, no. It was all nonsensical and meaningless. On my part it was the caprice of a pampered man, and on his part simple greed for money. . . ."

Then he remembered what followed that evening. It was decided that the young man should spend the years of his captivity under the strictest supervision in one of the lodges in the banker's garden. It was agreed that for fifteen years he should not be free to cross the threshold of the lodge, to see human beings, to hear the human voice, or to receive letters and newspapers. He was allowed to have a musical instrument and books, and was allowed to write letters, to drink wine, and to smoke. By the terms of the agreement, the only relations he could have with the outer world were by a little window made purposely for that object. He might have anything he wanted—books, music, wine, and so on—in any quantity he desired by writing an order, but could only receive them through the window. The agreement provided for every detail and every trifle that would make his imprisonment strictly solitary, and bound the young man to stay there exactly fifteen years, beginning from twelve o'clock of November 14, 1870, and ending at twelve o'clock of November 14, 1885. The slightest attempt on his part to break the conditions, if only two minutes before the end, released the banker from the obligation to pay him two millions.

For the first year of his confinement, as far as one could judge from his brief notes, the prisoner suffered severely from loneliness and depression. The sounds of the piano could be heard continually day and night from his lodge. He refused wine and tobacco. Wine, he wrote, excites the desires, and desires are the worst foes of the prisoner; and besides, nothing could be more dreary than drinking good wine and seeing no one. And tobacco spoilt the air of his room. In the first year the books he sent for were principally of a light character; novels with a complicated love plot, sensational and fantastic stories, and so on.

In the second year the piano was silent in the lodge, and the prisoner asked only for the classics. In the fifth year music was audible again, and the prisoner asked for wine. Those who watched him through the window said that all that year he spent doing nothing but eating and drinking and lying on his bed, frequently yawning and angrily talking to himself. He did not read books. Sometimes at night he would sit down to write; he would spend hours writing, and in the morning tear up all that he had written. More than once he could be heard crying.

In the second half of the sixth year the prisoner began zealously studying languages, philosophy, and history. He threw himself eagerly into these studies—so much so that the banker had enough to do to get him the books he ordered. In the course of four years some six hundred volumes were procured at his request. It was during this period that the banker received the following letter from his prisoner:

"My dear Jailer, I write you these lines in six languages. Show them to people who know the languages. Let them read them. If they find not one mistake I implore you to fire a shot in the garden. That shot will show me that my efforts have not been thrown away. The geniuses of all ages and of all lands speak different languages, but the same flame burns in them all. Oh, if you only knew what unearthly happiness my soul feels now from being able to understand them!" The prisoner's desire was fulfilled. The banker ordered two shots to be fired in the garden.

Then after the tenth year, the prisoner sat immovably at the table and read nothing but the Gospel. It seemed strange to the banker that a man who in four years had mastered six hundred learned volumes should waste nearly a year over one thin book easy of comprehension. Theology and histories of religion followed the Gospels.

In the last two years of his confinement the prisoner read an immense quantity of books quite indiscriminately. At one time he was busy with the natural sciences, then he would ask for Byron or Shakespeare. There were notes in which he demanded at the same time books on chemistry, and a manual of medicine, and a novel, and some treatise on philosophy or theology. His reading suggested a man swimming in the sea among the wreckage of his ship, and trying to save his life by greedily clutching first at one spar and then at another.

The old banker remembered all this, and thought:

"Tomorrow at twelve o'clock he will regain his freedom. By our agreement I ought to pay him two millions. If I do pay him, it is all over with me: I shall be utterly ruined."

Fifteen years before, his millions had been beyond his reckoning; now he was afraid to ask himself which were greater, his debts or his assets. Desperate gambling on the Stock Exchange, wild speculation, and the excitability which he could not get over even in advancing years, had by degrees led to the decline of his fortune, and the proud, fearless, self-confident millionaire had become a banker of middling rank, trembling at every rise and fall in his investments. "Cursed bet!" muttered the old man, clutching his head in despair. "Why didn't the man die? He is only forty now. He will take my last penny from me, he will marry, will enjoy life, will gamble on the Exchange; while I shall look at him with envy like a beggar, and hear from him every day the same sentence: 'I am indebted to you for the happiness of my life, let me help you!' No, it is too much! The one means of being saved from bankruptcy and disgrace is the death of that man!"

It struck three o'clock, the banker listened; everyone was asleep in the house, and nothing could be heard outside but the rustling of the chilled trees. Trying to make no noise, he took from a fireproof safe the key of the door which had not been opened for fifteen years, put on his overcoat and went out of the house.

It was dark and cold in the garden. Rain was falling. A damp cutting wind was racing about the garden, howling and giving the trees no rest. The banker strained his eyes, but could see neither the earth nor the white statues, nor the lodge, nor the trees. Going to the spot where the lodge stood, he twice called the watchman. No answer followed. Evidently the watchman had sought shelter from the weather, and was now asleep somewhere either in the kitchen or in the greenhouse.

"If I had the pluck to carry out my intention," thought the old man, "suspicion would fall first upon the watchman."

He felt in the darkness for the steps and the door, and went into the entry of the lodge. Then he groped his way into a little passage and lighted a match. There was not a soul there. There was a bedstead with no bedding on it, and in the corner there was a dark cast-iron stove. The seals on the door leading to the prisoner's rooms were intact.

When the match went out the old man, trembling with emotion, peeped through the little window. A candle was burning dimly in the prisoner's room. He was sitting at the table. Nothing could be seen but his back, the hair on his head, and his hands. Open books were lying on the table, on the two easy-chairs, and on the carpet near the table.

Five minutes passed and the prisoner did not once stir. Fifteen years' imprisonment had taught him to sit still. The banker tapped at the window with his finger, and the prisoner made no movement whatever in response. Then the banker cautiously broke the seals off the door and put the key in the keyhole. The rusty lock gave a grating sound and the door creaked. The banker expected to hear at once footsteps and a cry of astonishment, but three minutes passed and it was as quiet as ever in the room. He made up his mind to go in.

At the table a man unlike ordinary people was sitting motionless. He was a skeleton with the skin drawn tight over his bones, with long curls like a woman's and a shaggy beard. His face was yellow with an earthy tint in it, his checks were hollow, his back long and narrow, and the hand on which his shaggy head was propped was so thin and delicate that it was dreadful to look at it. His hair was already streaked with silver, and seeing his emaciated, aged-looking face, no one would have believed that he was only forty. He was asleep. . . . In front of his bowed head there lay on the table a sheet of paper on which there was something written in fine handwriting.

"Poor creature!" thought the banker, "he is asleep and most likely dreaming of the millions. And I have only to take this half-dead man, throw him on the bed, stifle him a little with the pillow, and the most conscientious expert would find no sign of a violent death. But let us first read what he has written here. . . ."

The banker took the page from the table and read as follows:

"Tomorrow at twelve o'clock I regain my freedom and the right to associate with other men, but before I leave this room and see the sunshine, I think it necessary to say a few words to you. With a clear conscience I tell you, as before God, who beholds me, that I despise freedom and life and health, and all that in your books is called the good things of the world.

"For fifteen years I have been intently studying earthly life. It is true I have not seen the earth nor men, but in your books I have drunk fragrant wine, I have sung songs, I have hunted stags and wild boars in the forests, have loved women. . . . Beauties as ethereal as clouds, created by the magic of your poets and geniuses, have visited me at night, and have whispered in my ears wonderful tales that have set my brain in a whirl. In your books I have climbed to the peaks of Elburz and Mont Blanc, and from there I have seen the sun rise and have watched it at evening flood the sky, the ocean, and the mountaintops with gold and crimson. I have watched from there the lightning flashing over my head and cleaving the storm clouds. I have seen green forests, fields, rivers, lakes, towns. I have heard the singing of the sirens[2], and the strains of the shepherds' pipes; I have touched the wings of comely devils who flew down to converse with me of God. . . .In your books I have flung myself into the bottomless pit, performed miracles, slain, burned towns, preached new religions, conquered whole kingdoms. . . .

"Your books have given me wisdom. All that the unresting thought of man has created in the ages is compressed into a small compass in my brain. I know that I am wiser than all of you.

"And I despise your books, I despise wisdom and the blessings of this world. It is all worthless, fleeting, illusory, and deceptive, like a mirage. You may be proud, wise, and fine, but death will wipe you off the face of the earth as though you were no more than mice burrowing under the floor, and your posterity, your history, your immortal geniuses will burn or freeze together with the earthly globe.

"You have lost your reason and taken the wrong path. You have taken lies for truth, and hideousness for beauty. You would marvel if, owing to strange events of some sorts, frogs and lizards suddenly grew on apple and orange trees instead of fruit, or if roses began to smell like a sweating horse; so I marvel at you who exchange heaven for earth. I don't want to understand you.

"To prove to you in action how I despise all that you live by, I renounce the two millions of which I once dreamed as of paradise and which now I despise. To deprive myself of the right to the money I shall go out from here five hours before the time fixed, and so break the compact. . . ."

When the banker had read this he laid the page on the table, kissed the strange man on the head, and went out of the lodge, weeping. At no other time, even when he had lost heavily on the Stock Exchange, had he felt so great a contempt for himself. When he got home he lay on his bed, but his tears and emotion kept him for hours from sleeping.

Next morning the watchmen ran in with pale faces, and told him they had seen the man who lived in the lodge climb out of the window into the garden, go to the gate, and disappear. The banker went at once with the servants to the lodge and made sure of the flight of his prisoner. To avoid arousing unnecessary talk, he took from the table the writing in which the millions were renounced, and when he got home locked it up in the fireproof safe.

---

2. sirens (sī ′ rənz)**:** In Greek mythology, sea nymphs whose beautiful singing lured passing sailors to their death by causing them to steer too close to the rocky coast of the sirens' island.

☑ Check Your Comprehension

1. Describe the terms of the bet.
2. (a) Fifteen years later, what does the banker believe was his own motivation for making this bet? (b) Why does he think the lawyer made the bet?
3. (a) How does the banker feel about the bet now? (b) What does he assume the lawyer is feeling?
4. (a) Why does the banker go to the lodge the night before the lawyer is to be set free? (b) What does he discover there?

◆ Critical Thinking

1. (a) How has the banker changed during the fifteen years the lawyer has been imprisoned? (b) In what key way is he still the same? **[Interpret]**
2. The lawyer has also changed during his imprisonment, what kinds of transformation does Chekhov show us? **[Analyze]**
3. How do you think the banker's own attitudes and values shape his assumptions about the lawyer? **[Infer]**
4. How do you think the lawyer's transformation relates to the story's **theme**, or central insight about life? **[Apply]**
5. Do you find the lawyer's transformation believable? Why or why not? **[Evaluate]**
6. Do you believe that it's really possible to have the kinds of experiences the lawyer claims to have had while imprisoned— simply through reading? Why or why not? **[Relate]**

nton Chekhov

Difficult People

Translated by Constance Garnett

Yevgraf Ivanovitch Shiryaev, a small farmer, whose father, a parish priest, now deceased, had received a gift of three hundred acres of land from Madame Kuvshinnikov, a general's widow, was standing in a corner before a copper washing-stand, washing his hands. As usual, his face looked anxious and ill-humored, and his beard was uncombed.

"What weather!" he said. "It's not weather, but a curse laid upon us. It's raining again!"

He grumbled on, while his family sat waiting at table for him to have finished washing his hands before beginning dinner. Fedosya Semyonovna, his wife, his son Pyotr, a student, his eldest daughter Varvara, and three small boys, had been sitting waiting a long time. The boys—Kolka, Vanka, and Arhipka—grubby, snub-nosed little fellows with chubby faces and tousled hair that wanted cutting, moved their chairs impatiently, while their elders sat without stirring, and apparently did not care whether they ate their dinner or waited. . . .

As though trying their patience, Shiryaev deliberately dried his hands, deliberately said his prayer, and sat down to the table without hurrying himself. Cabbage soup was served immediately. The sound of carpenter's axes (Shiryaev was having a new barn built) and the laughter of Fomka, their laborer, teasing the turkey, floated in from the courtyard.

Big, sparse drops of rain pattered on the window.

Pyotr, a round-shouldered student in spectacles, kept exchanging glances with his mother as he ate his dinner. Several times he laid down his spoon and cleared his throat, meaning to begin to speak, but after an intent look at his father he fell to eating again. At last, when the porridge had been served, he cleared his throat resolutely and said:

"I ought to go tonight by the evening train. I ought to have gone before; I have missed a fortnight as it is. The lectures begin on the first of September."

"Well, go," Shiryaev assented; "why are you lingering here? Pack up and go, and good luck to you."

A minute passed in silence.

"He must have money for the journey, Yevgraf Ivanovitch," the mother observed in a low voice.

"Money? To be sure, you can't go without money. Take it at once, since you need it. You could have had it long ago!"

The student heaved a faint sigh and looked with relief at his mother. Deliberately Shiryaev took a pocketbook out of his coat pocket and put on his spectacles.

"How much do you want?" he asked.

"The fare to Moscow is eleven roubles forty-two kopecks. . . ."

"Ah, money, money!" sighed the father. (He always sighed when he saw money, even when he was receiving it.) "Here are twelve roubles for you. You will have change out of that which will be of use to you on the journey."

"Thank you."

After waiting a little, the student said:

"I did not get lessons quite at first last year. I don't know how it will be this year; most likely it will take me a little time to find work. I ought to ask you for fifteen roubles for my lodging and dinner."

Shiryaev thought a little and heaved a sigh.

"You will have to make ten do," he said. "Here, take it."

The student thanked him. He ought to have asked him for something more, for clothes, for lecture fees, for books, but after an intent look at his father he decided not to pester him further.

The mother, lacking in diplomacy and prudence, like all mothers, could not restrain herself, and said:

"You ought to give him another six roubles, Yevgraf Ivanovitch, for a pair of boots. Why, just see, how can he go to Moscow in such wrecks?"

"Let him take my old ones; they are still quite good."

"He must have trousers, anyway; he is a disgrace to look at."

And immediately after that a storm-signal showed itself, at the sight of which all the family trembled.

Shiryaev's short, fat neck turned suddenly red as a beetroot. The color mounted slowly to his ears, from his ears to his temples, and by degrees suffused his whole face. Yegraf Ivanovitch shifted in his chair and unbuttoned his shirt collar to save himself from choking. He was evidently struggling with the feeling that was mastering him. A deathlike silence followed. The children held their breath. Fedosya Semyonova, as though she did not grasp what was happening to her husband, went on:

"He is not a little boy now, you know; he is ashamed to go about without clothes."

Shiryaev suddenly jumped up, and with all his might flung down his fat pocketbook in the middle of the table, so that a hunk of bread flew off a plate. A revolting expression of anger, resentment, avarice—all mixed together—flamed on his face.

"Take everything!" he shouted in an unnatural voice; "plunder me! Take it all! Strangle me!"

He jumped up from the table, clutched at his head, and ran staggering about the room.

"Strip me to the last thread!" he shouted in a shrill voice. "Squeeze out the last drop! Rob me! Wring my neck!"

The student flushed and dropped his eyes. He could not go on eating. Fedosya Semyonovna, who had not after twenty-five years grown used to her husband's difficult character, shrank into herself and muttered something in self-defense. An expression of amazement and dull terror came into her wasted and birdlike face, which at all times looked dull and scared. The little boys and the elder daughter Varvara, a girl in her teens, with a pale ugly face, laid down their spoons and sat mute.

Shiryaev, growing more and more ferocious, uttering words each more terrible than the one before, dashed up to the table and began shaking the notes out of his pocketbook.

"Take them!" he muttered, shaking all over. "You've eaten and drunk your fill, so here's money for you too! I need nothing! Order yourself new boots and uniforms!"

The student turned pale and got up.

"Listen, papa," he began, gasping for breath. "I . . . I beg you to end this, for. . . ."

"Hold your tongue!" the father shouted at him, and so loudly that the spectacles fell off his nose; "hold your tongue!"

"I used . . . I used to be able to put up with such scenes, but . . . but now I have got out of the way of it. Do you understand? I have got out of the way of it!"

"Hold your tongue!" cried the father, and he stamped with his feet. "You must listen to what I say! I shall say what I like, and you hold your tongue. At your age I was earning my living, while you . . . Do you know what you cost me, you scoundrel? I'll turn you out! Wastrel!"[1]

"Yevgraf Ivanovitch," muttered Fedosya Semyonovna, moving her fingers nervously; "you know he . . . you know Petya . . .!"

"Hold your tongue!" Shiryaev shouted out to her, and tears actually came into his eyes from anger. "It is you who have spoilt them—you! It's all your fault! He has no respect for us, does not say his prayers, and earns nothing! I am only one against the ten of you! I'll turn you out of the house!"

The daughter Varvara gazed fixedly at her mother with her mouth open, moved her vacant-looking eyes to the window, turned pale, and, uttering a loud shriek, fell back in her chair. The father, with a curse and a wave of the hand, ran out into the yard.

This was how domestic scenes usually ended at the Shiryaevs'. But on this occasion, unfortunately, Pyotr the student was carried

---

1. wastrel (wā′ strəl) *n.:* Spendthrift; good-for-nothing.

away by overmastering anger. He was just as hasty and ill-tempered as his father and his grandfather the priest, who used to beat his parishioners about the head with a stick. Pale and clenching his fists, he went up to his mother and shouted in the very highest tenor note his voice could reach:

"These reproaches are loathsome! sickening to me! I want nothing from you! Nothing! I would rather die of hunger than eat another mouthful at your expense! Take your nasty money back! take it!"

The mother huddled against the wall and waved her hands, as though it were not her son, but some phantom before her.

"What have I done?" she wailed. "What?"

Like his father, the boy waved his hands and ran into the yard. Shiryaev's house stood alone on a ravine which ran like a furrow for four miles along the steppe.[2] Its sides were overgrown with oak saplings and alders, and a stream ran at the bottom. On one side the house looked toward the ravine, on the other toward the open country, there were no fences nor hurdles. Instead there were farm buildings of all sorts close to one another, shutting in a small space in front of the house which was regarded as the yard, and in which hens, ducks, and pigs ran about.

Going out of the house, the student walked along the muddy road toward the open country. The air was full of a penetrating autumn dampness. The road was muddy, puddles gleamed here and there, and in the yellow fields autumn itself seemed looking out from the grass, dismal, decaying, dark. On the right-hand side of the road was a vegetable garden cleared of its crops and gloomy-looking, with here and there sunflowers standing up in it with hanging heads already black.

Pyotr thought it would not be a bad thing to walk to Moscow on foot; to walk just as he was, with holes in his boots, without a cap, and without a farthing of money. When he had gone eighty miles his father, frightened and aghast, would overtake him, would begin begging him to turn back or take the money, but he would not even look at him, but would go on and on. . . . Bare forests would be followed by desolate fields, fields by forests again; soon the earth would be white with the first snow, and the streams would be coated with ice. . . .Somewhere near Kursk or near Serpuhovo, exhausted and dying of hunger, he would sink down and die. His corpse would be found, and there would be a paragraph in all the papers saying that a student called Shiryaev had died of hunger. . . .

---

2. steppe (step) *n.:* Vast, grassy plain stretching across southeastern Europe and Siberia; similar to the U.S. prairie.

A white dog with a muddy tail who was wandering about the vegetable garden looking for something gazed at him and sauntered after him. . . .

He walked along the road and thought of death, of the grief of his family, of the moral sufferings of his father, and then pictured all sorts of adventures on the road, each more marvelous than the one before—picturesque places, terrible nights, chance encounters. He imagined a string of pilgrims, a hut in the forest with one little window shining in the darkness; he stands before the window, begs for a night's lodging. . . .They let him in, and suddenly he sees that they are robbers. Or, better still, he is taken into a big manor house, where, learning who he is, they give him food and drink, play to him on the piano, listen to his complaints, and the daughter of the house, a beauty, falls in love with him.

Absorbed in his bitterness and such thoughts, young Shiryaev walked on and on. Far, far ahead he saw the inn, a dark patch against the gray background of cloud. Beyond the inn, on the very horizon, he could see a little hillock;[3] this was the railway station. That hillock reminded him of the connection existing between the place where he was now standing and Moscow, where street lamps were burning and carriages were rattling in the streets, where lectures were being given. And he almost wept with depression and impatience. The solemn landscape, with its order and beauty, the deathlike stillness all around, revolted him and moved him to despair and hatred!

"Look out!" He heard behind him a loud voice.

An old lady of his acquaintance, a landowner of the neighborhood, drove past him in a light, elegant landau.[4] He bowed to her, and smiled all over his face. And at once he caught himself in that smile, which was so out of keeping with his gloomy mood. Where did it come from if his whole heart was full of vexation and misery? And he thought nature itself had given man this capacity for lying, that even in difficult moments of spiritual strain he might be able to hide the secrets of his nest as the fox and the wild duck do. Every family has its joys and its horrors, but however great they may be, it's hard for an outsider's eye to see them; they are a secret. The father of the old lady who had just driven by, for instance, had for some offense lain for half his lifetime under the ban of the wrath of Tsar Nicholas I[5]; her husband had been a gambler; of her four sons, not one had turned out well. One could imagine how many terrible scenes there must have been in her life, how many tears must have been shed. And

---

3. hillock (hĭ´ lək) *n.:* Small hill.
4. landau (lan´ dou) *n.:* Four-wheeled carriage with front and back passenger seats and a two-part roof. The top is opened by folding back the rear section and removing the front section.
5. Tsar Nicholas I (zär): Ruler of Russia from 1825 to 1855.

yet the old lady seemed happy and satisfied, and she had answered his smile by smiling too. The student thought of his comrades, who did not like talking about their families; he thought of his mother, who almost always lied when she had to speak of her husband and children. . . .

Pyotr walked about the roads far from home till dusk, abandoning himself to dreary thoughts. When it began to drizzle with rain he turned homeward. As he walked back he made up his mind at all costs to talk to his father, to explain to him, once and for all, that it was dreadful and oppressive to live with him.

He found perfect stillness in the house. His sister Varvara was lying behind a screen with a headache, moaning faintly. His mother, with a look of amazement and guilt upon her face, was sitting beside her on a box, mending Arhipka's trousers. Yevgraf Ivanovitch was pacing from one window to another, scowling at the weather. From his walk, from the way he cleared his throat, and even from the back of his head, it was evident he felt himself to blame.

"I suppose you have changed your mind about going today?" he asked.

The student felt sorry for him, but immediately suppressing that feeling, he said:

"Listen . . . I must speak to you seriously . . . yes, seriously. I have always respected you, and . . . and have never brought myself to speak to you in such a tone, but your behavior . . . your last action . . ."

The father looked out of the window and did not speak. The student, as though considering his words, rubbed his forehead and went on in great excitement:

"Not a dinner or tea passes without your making an uproar. Your bread sticks in our throat . . . nothing is more bitter, more humiliating, than bread that sticks in one's throat. . . . Though you are my father, no one, neither God nor nature, has given you the right to insult and humiliate us so horribly, to vent your ill-humor on the weak.

"You have worn my mother out and made a slave of her, my sister is hopelessly crushed, while I. . . ."

"It's not your business to teach me," said his father.

"Yes, it is my business! You can quarrel with me as much as you like, but leave my mother in peace! I will not allow you to torment my mother!" the student went on, with flashing eyes. "You are spoilt because no one has yet dared to oppose you. They tremble and are mute toward you, but now that is over! Coarse, ill-bred man! You are coarse . . . do you understand? You are coarse, ill-humored, unfeeling. And the peasants can't endure you!"

The student had by now lost his thread, and was not so much speaking as firing off detached words. Yevgraf Ivanovitch listened in silence, as though stunned; but suddenly his neck turned crimson, the color crept up his face, and he made a movement.

"Hold your tongue!" he shouted.

"That's right!" the son persisted; "you don't like to hear the truth! Excellent! Very good! begin shouting! Excellent!"

"Hold your tongue, I tell you!" roared Yevgraf Ivanovitch.

Fedosya Semyonovna appeared in the doorway, very pale, with an astonished face; she tried to say something, but she could not, and could only move her fingers.

"It's all your fault!" Shiryaev shouted at her. "You have brought him up like this!"

"I don't want to go on living in this house!" shouted the student, crying, and looking angrily at his mother. "I don't want to live with you!"

Varvara uttered a shriek behind the screen and broke into loud sobs. With a wave of his hand, Shiryaev ran out of the house.

The student went to his own room and quietly lay down. He lay till midnight without moving or opening his eyes. He felt neither anger nor shame, but a vague ache in his soul. He neither blamed his father nor pitied his mother, nor was he tormented by stings of conscience; he realized that every one in the house was feeling the same ache, and God only knew which was most to blame, which was suffering most. . . .

At midnight he woke the laborer, and told him to have the horse ready at five o'clock in the morning for him to drive to the station; he undressed and got into bed, but could not get to sleep. He heard how his father, still awake, paced slowly from window to window, sighing, till early morning. No one was asleep; they spoke rarely, and only in whispers. Twice his mother came to him behind the screen. Always with the same look of vacant wonder, she slowly made the cross over him, shaking nervously.

At five o'clock in the morning he said good-bye to them all affectionately, and even shed tears. As he passed his father's room, he glanced in at the door. Yevgraf Ivanovitch, who had not taken off his clothes or gone to bed, was standing by the window, drumming on the panes.

"Good-bye; I am going," said his son.

"Good-bye . . . the money is on the round table," his father answered, without turning around.

A cold, hateful rain was falling as the laborer drove him to the station.

The sunflowers were drooping their heads still lower, and the grass seemed darker than ever.

☑ Check Your Comprehension

1. At the beginning of the story, what does Pyotr want from his father?
2. (a) At first, how does his father respond to his request? (b) Why does his father then explode in rage?
3. As Pyotr walks down the road after storming out of the house, what does he imagine might happen—both bad and good—if he were to leave home?
4. Why is Pyotr so shocked to find himself smiling at the old lady in the landau?
5. Describe the confrontation that occurs when he returns home that night.
6. How does Pyotr feel afterward?

◆ Critical Thinking

1. (a) Where in the story does the narrator show that Pyotr is like his father—that he too is a difficult person? (b) In what ways do you think Pyotr is different from his father? **[Analyze]**
2. What important insight does Pyotr gain from his encounter with the old woman? In other words, what does he learn, and why does it have such an effect on him? **[Interpret]**
3. How does this insight relate to the story's **theme**, or central idea about life? **[Infer]**
4. How do you feel about the story's resolution? Would you have preferred a more clear-cut conclusion to the conflict within this family? Explain your response. **[Evaluate]**
5. This story was written more than one hundred years ago. Do you think families still treat each other the way the Shiryaevs do? Take a position and support your opinion. **[Relate]**

Anton Chekhov

Comparing and Connecting the Author's Works

◆ Literary Focus: Static and Dynamic Characters

Usually the main character in a story is a **dynamic character**—someone whose behavior, attitudes, or beliefs change in some crucial way as a result of the story's action. A **static character,** on the other hand, stays essentially the same throughout the story, without developing or learning anything meaningful along the way. A dynamic character changes by making a key decision, gaining an important insight, or learning something about human nature. What a dynamic character comes to recognize is often essential to interpreting the story's **theme**—its central insight about life.

1. In "The Bet," both the banker and the lawyer change dramatically over the course of fifteen years. Compare and contrast the changes they experience.
2. (a) Explain why Pyotr in "Difficult People" is a dynamic character. (b) Do you think his father is also a dynamic character? Support your interpretation with details from the story.
3. Compare and contrast the lawyer's gradual transformation with Pyotr's sudden moment of insight.
4. According to one commentator, "Chekhov shows you that it is not important to be happy but to understand." Explain how this statement applies to the lawyer and Pyotr.

◆ Drawing Conclusions About Chekhov's Work

Here's how one literary critic has generalized about Chekhov's work:

Almost all of Chekhov's characters are trapped—in their families, in their villages, in their marriages, in themselves—and long for escape. In his stories, Chekhov administers the jolt that forces them to see ... that they are living false lives and must grasp the truth.
— James Wood

Below is a cluster diagram that explores how the lawyer in "The Bet" exemplifies Wood's generalization about Chekhov's characters. Create a similar cluster diagram exploring the idea that Pyotr in "Difficult People" also represents a trapped character. Then write a brief essay either summarizing the ideas in your diagram or comparing and contrasting ideas in both diagrams. (You may, of course, incorporate your own ideas about the lawyer.)

◆ Idea Bank

Writing

1. **News Report** Write a news report investigating the strange events of "The Bet." Will you manage to get to the bottom of the story, or will you be thrown off by the banker's attempts at a cover-up? Use a chart like this one to gather your facts. (The first box has been partially filled in for you.) If you like, you may invent details that are not in the story, such as names, dates, or addresses. **[Media Link]**

Who?	forty-year-old man voluntarily imprisoned for fifteen years because of a bet . . .
What?	
When?	
Where?	
Why?	
How?	

2. **Letter** In his letter the lawyer in "The Bet" explains what he has learned during his imprisonment and why he is renouncing the money. Write a letter explaining something important you've learned or decided.

3. **Compare and Contrast Stories** Chekhov's characters are frequently worried, if not obsessed, about money. Write an essay comparing and contrasting these characters attitude toward money and materialism.

Speaking and Listening

4. **Debate** Chekhov believed that it wasn't the writer's responsibility to solve problems, but simply to state problems correctly. Form two groups and debate the problem presented in "The Bet", using evidence from current events, and the story itself to support your argument. **[Social Studies Link; Group Activity]**

5. **Performance** Working with a partner or small group, perform a scene from "Difficult People." You'll need to create a script that includes both dialogue and stage directions.
[Performing Arts Link]

Researching and Representing

6. **Set Design** Imagine that you are the set designer for a dramatic adaptation of either "The Bet" or "Difficult People." Draw or build a model of a stage set for one scene, or do a series of sketches showing your conception of the set design for a whole production. **[Art Link]**

◆ Further Reading, Listening, and Viewing

• *The Essential Tales of Chekhov*, translated by Constance Garnett, edited by Richard Ford (1998) A well-rounded collection selected by a contemporary short story master

• *The Plays of Anton Chekhov*, translated by Paul Schmidt (1997) New translations by a Russian-language scholar and Chekhovian actor

• *The Selected Letters of Anton Chekhov*, translated by Sidonie Lederer and edited by Lillian Hellman (1994) The best edition of Chekhov's letters for the general reader

• Serge Schmemann: *Echoes of a Native Land: Two Centuries of a Russian Village* (1997) A *New York Times* reporter's memoir about returning to his ancestral village

• Anton Chekhov: *The Black Monk and Other Stories* (1994). Three audio-casettes of Chekhov stories

• *Great Russian Writers: Anton Chekhov* (1999) A film biography

• *Vanya on 42nd Street* (1995). Movie (PG) about rehearsals for a production of Chekhov's *Uncle Vanya*. Directed by Louis Malle, starring Wallace Shawn and André Gregory

On the Web:

http://www.phschool.com/atschool/literature
Go to the student edition *Platinum*. Proceed to Unit 6. Then, click Hot Links to find Web sites featuring Anton Chekhov.

Annie Dillard In Depth

> "The goal of Dillard's work is to make the reader see, to hold his eyes open 'with toothpicks, with trees.' She insists that each person has his own creative capacity to awaken from blindness to a state of perception that discovers the world with new meaning."
>
> —*Eudora Welty*

ANNIE DILLARD has carved a unique place for herself in American literature. She has written essays, a memoir, poetry, and a novel. In every genre, she distinguishes herself with carefully crafted language and keen observations.

An American Childhood Annie (Meta Ann Doak) Dillard was born April 30, 1945, in Pittsburgh, Pennsylvania. Her memoir, *An American Childhood,* chronicles her early years of collecting insects, playing baseball, and reading—especially her favorite book, *The Field Book of Ponds and Streams.* She used her fertile imagination to "see" what is not observable—a notion that has become a common theme in her writing.

She left home at seventeen to attend Hollins College. She fell in love with her professor of creative writing, Richard H. W. Dillard, marrying him at the end of her sophomore year. She continued her education, graduating with a bachelor's degree in 1967 and receiving her master's degree in English in 1968. She was involved in an anti-poverty program, spent time painting, and developed an insatiable appetite for reading.

Literary Beginnings Dillard wrote a column for the Wilderness Society in *The Living Wilderness* from 1973–75 and was a contributing editor to *Harper's Magazine* from 1973–85. She wrote a book of poetry, *Tickets for a Prayer Wheel,* published in 1974.

In 1971, Annie Dillard almost died of pneumonia. After this experience, Dillard decided she needed to do more than read about life—she needed to experience it first hand. She began taking extended camping trips, spending most of the day observing nature and most of the evenings reading or writing. One result was *Pilgrim at Tinker Creek,* a personal narrative focusing on the paradox of beauty and violence existing side by side in the natural world.

The book was an instant success. When it won the Pulitzer Prize in 1975, Annie Dillard, with only one other book to her name, was suddenly a well-known writer at the age of twenty-nine.

Teaching Career Uncomfortable with the acclaim and in the middle of a divorce, Dillard moved to Washington State to become scholar-in-residence at Western Washington University in Bellingham. There, Dillard met an anthropologist, Gary Clevidence, whom she married in 1980. The couple moved to Middletown, Connecticut, where Dillard began teaching at Wesleyan University. After the birth of their daughter Rosie (Cody Rose), Dillard began writing about her own childhood in *An American Childhood.*

During the years between *Pilgrim at Tinker Creek* and *An American Childhood,* Dillard wrote three nonfiction works: *Holy the Firm, Living by Fiction,* and *Teaching a Stone to Talk. The Writing Life* was published in 1989, and her first novel, *The Living,* came out in 1992. Dillard continues to spend a great deal of time reading, writing, and teaching literature and writing.

◆ Writing About Nature

"I am no scientist," writes Annie Dillard, "but a poet and a walker with a background in theology and a penchant for quirky facts." In fact, many poets and other writers like Dillard have been people who "see a world in a grain of sand / and a heaven in a wild flower" (William Blake) and help others to see this world through their writing. Such writers are often able to see lessons about life, religion, beauty, goodness, and love through nature.

Many critics have compared Dillard to Henry David Thoreau, who also left the comfort of home to live close to nature. In the woods near Walden Pond, Thoreau wrote his thoughts about nature and mankind. Like his friend and contemporary, Ralph Waldo Emerson, he believed that the natural world relflects the human spirit and can help mankind understand himself, his place in the universe, and universal truths.

Laura Ingalls Wilder, Willa Cather, Sarah Orne Jewett, and Gene Stratton Porter were popular writers of the late eighteenth and early nineteenth centuries who wrote about nature on the American frontier. A host of poets— from Emily Dickinson, Edna St. Vincent Millay, and Ina Coolbrith to modern poets like Elizabeth Bishop, Mary Oliver, and Elizabeth Coatsworth—have expressed their poetic insights on nature.

Recently, many nature writers have also voiced their concerns about mankind's abuse of the earth. Rachel Carson in *Silent Spring* was one of the first to raise the environmental consciousness of her readers. Others include Wallace Stegner, Loren Eiseley, and Mary Austin.

◆ Literary Works

Early Works Most of Dillard's writing is nonfiction narrative. Her poetry has also been published in many popular magazines.

Tickets for a Prayer Wheel (poems), 1974

Pilgrim at Tinker Creek, 1974

Holy the Firm, 1978

Teaching a Stone to Talk: Expeditions and Encounters, 1982

An American Childhood, 1987

Recent Works

The Writing Life, 1989

The Living, 1992

Mornings Like This: Found Poems, 1995

T I M E L I N E

Dillard's Life		World Events	
1945	Annie Doak born on April 30 in Pittsburgh, Pennsylvania	1945	World War II ends
1958	Receives microscope for Christmas	1947	*Diary of Anne Frank* published
		1949	Arthur Miller wins Pulitzer Prize for drama for *Death of a Salesman*
1965	Marries Richard Henry Wilde Dillard	1950	Korean War begins
1967	Graduates with BA from Hollins College	1951	Color television first introduced in the U.S.
1968	Receives MA from Hollins College	1954	Televised hearings of Senator Joe McCarthy seeking to prove Communist infiltration in the United States
1973–75	Columnist for *Living Wilderness*		
1973–85	Contributing editor for *Harper's Magazine*	1957	Sputnik launched by U.S.S.R.
1974	Book of poems, *Tickets for a Prayer Wheel,* published	1961	Alan Shepard makes first U.S. space flight
1975	Wins Pulitzer Prize for general nonfiction for *Pilgrim at Tinker Creek*	1963	President John F. Kennedy assassinated
1974–79	Scholar in residence at Western Washington University	1965	Freedom march from Selma to Montgomery, Alabama, led by Martin Luther King
1979–87	Professor at Wesleyan University		
1987– present	Writer in residence, Wesleyan University	1967	50,000 people demonstrate against the Vietnam War at the Lincoln Memorial
1980	Marries Gary Clevidence	1968	Robert Kennedy assassinated
1982	*Teaching a Stone to Talk* published; member of U.S. cultural delegation to China	1968	Martin Luther King assassinated
		1969	Neil Armstrong walks on the moon
1984	Daughter Cody Rose born	1974	President Nixon resigns over Watergate cover-up
1987	*An American Childhood* published		
1988	Marries Robert D. Richardson, Jr.	1977	George Lucas's movie *Star Wars* premiers
1990	Converts to Catholicism		
1992	Novel *The Living* published	1981	IBM produces first personal computer
1995	*Mornings Like This: Found Poems* published	1986	Space shuttle *Challenger* explodes
		1989	Berlin Wall demolished by ecstatic Berliners
		1994	Nelson Mandela becomes president of South Africa

Annie Dillard

from The Writing Life

I write this in the most recent of my many studies—a pine shed on Cape Cod. The pine lumber is unfinished inside the study; the pines outside are finished trees. I see the pines from my two windows. Nuthatches[1] spiral around their long, coarse trunks. Sometimes in June a feeding colony of mixed warblers flies through the pines; the warblers make a racket that draws me out the door. The warblers drift loosely through the stiff pine branches, and I follow through the thin long grass between the trunks.

The study—sold as a prefabricated toolshed—is eight feet by ten feet. Like a plane's cockpit, it is crammed bulkhead to bulkhead with high-tech equipment. All it needs is an altimeter; I never quite know where I am. There is a computer, a printer, and a photocopying machine. My backless chair, a prie-dieu[2] on which I kneel, slides under the desk; I give it a little kick when I leave. There is an air conditioner, a heater, and an electric kettle. There is a low-tech bookshelf, a shelf of gull and whale bones, and a bed. Under the bed I stow paints—a one-pint can of yellow to touch up the windows' trim, and five or six tubes of artists' oils. The study affords ample room for one. One who is supposed to be writing books. You can read in the space of a coffin, and you can write in the space of a toolshed meant for mowers and spades.

I walk up here from the house every morning. The study and its pines, and the old summer cottages nearby, and the new farm just north of me, rise from an old sand dune high over a creeky salt marsh. From the bright lip of the dune I can see oyster farmers working their beds on the tide flats and sailboats under way in the saltwater bay. After I have warmed myself standing at the crest of the dune, I return under the pines, enter the study, slam the door so the latch catches—and then I cannot see. The green spot in front of my eyes outshines everything in the shade. I lie on the bed and play with a bird bone until I can see it.

Appealing workplaces are to be avoided. One wants a room with no view, so imagination can meet memory in the dark. When I furnished this study seven years ago, I pushed the long desk against a blank wall, so I could not see from either window. Once, fifteen years ago, I wrote in a cinder-block cell over a parking lot. It overlooked a tar-and-gravel roof. This pine shed under trees is not quite so good as the cinder-block study was, but it will do.

"The beginning of wisdom," according to a West African proverb, "is to get you a roof."

---

1. **Nuthatches:** Small tree-climbing birds common in wooded areas.
2. **prie-dieu** (prē dyē') *n.*: Low bench designed for kneeling.

Annie Dillard

from An American Childhood

After I read *The Field Book of Ponds and Streams* several times, I longed for a microscope. Everybody needed a microscope. Detectives used microscopes, both for the FBI and at Scotland Yard. Although usually I had to save my tiny allowance for things I wanted, that year for Christmas my parents gave me a microscope kit.

In a dark basement corner, on a white enamel table, I set up the microscope kit. I supplied a chair, a lamp, a batch of jars, a candle, and a pile of library books. The microscope kit supplied a blunt black three-speed microscope, a booklet, a scalpel, a dropper, an ingenious device for cutting thin segments of fragile tissue, a pile of clean slides and cover slips, and a dandy array of corked test tubes.

One of the test tubes contained "hay infusion." Hay infusion was a wee brown chip of grass blade. You added water to it, and after a week it became a jungle in a drop, full of one-celled animals. This did not work for me. All I saw in the microscope after a week was a wet chip of dried grass, much enlarged.

Another test tube contained "diatomaceous earth." This was, I believed, an actual pinch of the white cliffs of Dover. On my palm it was an airy, friable chalk. The booklet said it was composed of the siliceous[1] bodies of diatoms—one-celled creatures that lived in, as it were, small glass jewelry boxes with fitted lids. Diatoms, I read, come in a variety of transparent geometrical shapes. Broken and dead and dug out of geological deposits, they made chalk, and a fine abrasive used in silver polish and toothpaste. What I saw in the microscope must have been the fine abrasive—grit enlarged. It was years before I saw a recognizable, whole diatom. The kit's diatomaceous earth was a bust.

All that winter I played with the microscope. I prepared slides from things at hand, as the books suggested. I looked at the transparent membrane inside an onion's skin and saw the cells. I looked at a section of cork and saw the cells, and at scrapings from the inside of my cheek, ditto. I looked at my blood and saw not much; I looked at my urine and saw long iridescent[2] crystals, for the drop had dried.

All this was very well, but I wanted to see the wildlife I had read about. I wanted especially to see the famous amoeba, who had eluded me. He was supposed to live in the hay infusion, but I hadn't found him there. He lived outside in warm ponds and streams, too, but I lived in Pittsburgh, and it had been a cold winter.

---

1. silicaceous (si lə kā′ shəs) *adj.*: Wholly or partly made of the mineral silicon dioxide.
2. iridescent (ir′ ə de′ sənt) *adj.*: Having a brilliant rainbow-like luster.

Finally late that spring I saw an amoeba. The week before, I had gathered puddle water from Frick Park; it had been festering in a jar in the basement. This June night after dinner I figured I had waited long enough. In the basement at my microscope table I spread a scummy drop of Frick Park puddle water on a slide, peeked in, and lo, there was the famous amoeba. He was as blobby and grainy as his picture; I would have known him anywhere.

Before I had watched him at all, I ran upstairs. My parents were still at table, drinking coffee. They, too, could see the famous amoeba. I told them, bursting, that he was all set up, that they should hurry before his water dried. It was the chance of a lifetime.

Father had stretched out his long legs and was tilting back in his chair. Mother sat with her knees crossed, in blue slacks, smoking a Chesterfield. The dessert dishes were still on the table. My sisters were nowhere in evidence. It was a warm evening; the big dining-room windows gave onto blooming rhododendrons.

Mother regarded me warmly. She gave me to understand that she was glad I had found what I had been looking for, but that she and Father were happy to sit with their coffee, and would not be coming down.

She did not say, but I understood at once, that they had their pursuits (coffee?) and I had mine. She did not say, but I began to understand then, that you do what you do out of your private passion for the thing itself.

I had essentially been handed my own life. In subsequent years my parents would praise my drawings and poems, and supply me with books, art supplies, and sports equipment, and listen to my troubles and enthusiasms, and supervise my hours, and discuss and inform, but they would not get involved with my detective work, nor hear about my reading, nor inquire about my homework or term papers or exams, nor visit the salamanders I caught, nor listen to me play the piano, nor attend my field hockey games, nor fuss over my insect collection with me, or my poetry collection or stamp collection or rock collection. My days and nights were my own to plan and fill.

When I left the dining room that evening and started down the dark basement stairs, I had a life. I sat to my wonderful amoeba, and there he was, rolling his grains more slowly now, extending an arc of his edge for a foot and drawing himself along by that foot, and absorbing it again and rolling on. I gave him some more pond water.

I had hit pay dirt. For all I knew, there were paramecia, too, in that pond water, or daphniae, or stentors, or any of the many other creatures I had read about and never seen: volvox, the spherical algal colony; euglena with its one red eye; the elusive, glassy diatom; hydra, rotifers, water bears, worms. Anything was possible. The sky was the limit.

☑ Check Your Comprehension

1. What serves as Annie Dillard's study in the selection from *The Writing Life*?
2. How big is the study?
3. What is in her study? Why do you think she lists everything in it?
4. In Dillard's opinion, why are "appealing workplaces . . . to be avoided"?
5. What book does the selection from *An American Childhood* tell us that Annie read over and over?
6. How did Annie feel when she finally saw an amoeba?

◆ Critical Thinking

INTERPRET

1. What is the effect on the reader of comparing Dillard's study in *The Writer's Life* to a plane's cockpit? **[Analyze; Apply]**

2. Why does Dillard use the word "stow" in the phrase "Under the bed I stow paints?" **[Speculate; Infer]**
3. What is funny or unusual about the use of the term "low-tech bookshelf" in *The Writer's Life?* Why do you think Dillard uses this term? **[Analyze]**
4. What might Dillard mean in the selection from *An American Childhood* when she says "I had essentially been handed my own life"? **[Analyze; Draw a Conclusion]**
5. Why do you think Dillard felt as she did when her mother did not come to the basement to see the amoeba? **[Relate]**

COMPARE LITERARY WORKS

6. How are the styles of the selections from *The Writing Life* and *An American Childhood* similar? Support your answer with quotations from the works. **[Compare; Support]**

Annie Dillard

from Intricacy

A rosy, complex light fills my kitchen at the end of these lengthening June days. From an explosion on a nearby star eight minutes ago, the light zips through space, particle-wave, strikes the planet, angles on the continent, and filters through a mesh of land dust: clay bits, sod bits, tiny wind-borne insects, bacteria, shreds of wing and leg, gravel dust, grits of carbon, and dried cells of grass, bark, and leaves. Reddened, the light inclines into this valley over the green western mountains; it sifts between pine needles on northern slopes, and through all the mountain blackjack oak and haw, whose leaves are unclenching, one by one, and making an intricate, toothed and lobed haze. The light crosses the valley, threads through the screen on my open kitchen window, and gilds the painted wall. A plank of brightness bends from the wall and extends over the goldfish bowl on the table where I sit. The goldfish's side catches the light and bats it my way; I've an eyeful of fish-scale and star.

This Ellery cost me twenty-five cents. He is a deep red-orange, darker than most goldfish. He steers short distances mainly with his slender red lateral fins; they seem to provide impetus for going backward, up or down. It took me a few days to discover his ventral fins; they are completely transparent and all but invisible—dream fins. He also has a short anal fin, and a tail that is deeply notched and perfectly transparent at the two tapered tips. He can extend his mouth, so that it looks like a length of pipe; he can shift the angle of his eyes in his head so he can look before and behind himself, instead of simply out to his side. His belly, what there is of it, is white ventrally, and a patch of this white extends up his sides—the variegated Ellery. When he opens his gill slits he shows a thin crescent of silver where the flap overlapped—as though all his brightness were sunburn.

For this creature, as I said, I paid twenty-five cents. I had never bought an animal before. It was very simple; I went to a store in Roanoke called "Wet Pets"; I handed the man a quarter, and he handed me a knotted plastic bag bouncing with water in which a green plant floated and the goldfish swam. This fish, two bits' worth, has a coiled gut, a spine radiating fine bones, and a brain. Just before I sprinkle his food flakes into his bowl, I rap three times on the bowl's edge; now he is conditioned, and swims to the surface when I rap. And, he has a heart.

Once, years ago, I saw red blood cells whip, one by one,

through the capillaries in a goldfish's transparent tail. The goldfish was etherized.[1] Its head lay in a wad of wet cotton wool; its
tail lay on a tray under a dissecting microscope, one of those
wonderful light-gathering microscopes with two eyepieces like a
stereoscope in which the world's fragments—even the skin on
my finger—look brilliant with myriads of colored lights, and as
deep as any alpine landscape. The red blood cells in the goldfish's tail streamed and coursed through narrow channels invisible save for glistening threads of thickness in the general
translucency. They never wavered or slowed or ceased flowing,
like the creek itself; they streamed redly around, up, and on,
one by one, more, and more, without end. (The energy of that
pulse reminds me of something about the human body: if you
sit absolutely perfectly balanced on the end of your spine, with
your legs either crossed tailor-fashion or drawn up together, and
your arms forward on your legs, then even if you hold your
breath, your body will rock with the energy of your heartbeat,
forward and back, effortlessly, for as long as you want to remain
balanced.) Those red blood cells are coursing in Ellery's tail
now, too, in just that way, and through his mouth and eyes as
well, and through mine. I've never forgotten the sight of those
cells; I think of it when I see the fish in his bowl; I think of it
lying in bed at night, imagining that if I concentrate enough I
might be able to feel in my fingers' capillaries the small knock-
ings and flow of those circular dots, like a string of beads drawn
through my hand.

Something else is happening in the goldfish bowl. There on
the kitchen table, nourished by the simple plank of complex
light, the plankton[2] is blooming. The water yellows and clouds;
a transparent slime coats the leaves of the water plant, elodea; a
blue-green film of single-celled algae clings to the glass. And I
have to clean the doggone bowl. I'll spare you the details: it's the
plant I'm interested in. While Ellery swims in the stoppered
sink, I rinse the algae down the drain of another sink, wash the
gravel, and rub the elodea's many ferny leaves under running
water until they feel clean.

The elodea is not considered much of a plant. Aquarists use
it because it's available and it gives off oxygen completely submersed; laboratories use it because its leaves are only two cells
thick. It's plentiful, easy to grow, and cheap—like the goldfish.
And, like the goldfish, its cells have unwittingly performed for
me on a microscope's stage.

I was in a laboratory, using a very expensive microscope. I
peered through the deep twin eyepieces and saw again that

---

1. **etherized** (ē´ thə rīzd) v.: Made numb, as if by the chemical ether.
2. **plankton** n.: Minute water-borne plants and animals.

color-charged glistening world. A thin, oblong leaf of elodea, a quarter of an inch long, lay on a glass slide sopping wet and floodlighted brilliantly from below. In the circle of light formed by the two eyepieces trained at the translucent leaf, I saw a clean mosaic of almost colorless cells. The cells were large—eight or nine of them, magnified four hundred and fifty times, packed the circle—so that I could easily see what I had come to see: the streaming of chloroplasts.

Chloroplasts bear chlorophyll; they give the green world its color, and they carry out the business of photosynthesis.[3] Around the inside perimeter of each gigantic cell trailed a continuous loop of these bright green dots. They spun like paramecia; they pulsed, pressed, and thronged. A change of focus suddenly revealed the eddying currents of the river of transparent cytoplasm, a sort of "ether" to the chloroplasts or "space-time," in which they have their tiny being. Back to the green dots: they shone, they swarmed in ever-shifting files around and around the edge of the cell; they wandered, they charged, they milled, raced, and ran at the edge of apparent nothingness, the empty-looking inner cell; they flowed and trooped greenly, up against the vegetative wall.

All the green in the planted world consists of these whole, rounded chloroplasts wending their ways in water. If you analyze a molecule of chlorophyll itself, what you get is one hundred thirty-six atoms of hydrogen, carbon, oxygen, and nitrogen arranged in an exact and complex relationship around a central ring. At the ring's center is a single atom of magnesium. Now: If you remove the atom of magnesium and in its exact place put an atom of iron, you get a molecule of hemoglobin. The iron atom combines with all the other atoms to make red blood, the streaming red dots in the goldfish's tail.

---

3. photosynthesis *n.*: Production of complex sugars by plants with the aid of sunlight.

Annie Dillard

from Untying the Knot

Yesterday I set out to catch the new season, and instead I found an old snakeskin. I was in the sunny February woods by the quarry; the snakeskin was lying in a heap of leaves right next to an aquarium someone had thrown away. I don't know why that someone hauled the aquarium deep into the woods to get rid of it; it had only one broken glass side. The snake found it handy, I imagine; snakes like to rub against something rigid to help them out of their skins, and the broken aquarium looked like the nearest likely object. Together the snakeskin and the aquarium made an interesting scene on the forest floor. It looked like an exhibit at a trial—circumstantial evidence—of a wild scene, as though a snake had burst through the broken side of the aquarium, burst through his ugly old skin, and disappeared, perhaps straight up in the air, in a rush of freedom and beauty.

The snakeskin had unkeeled scales, so it belonged to a non-poisonous snake. It was roughly five feet long by the yardstick, but I'm not sure because it was very wrinkled and dry, and every time I tried to stretch it flat it broke. I ended up with seven or eight pieces of it all over the kitchen table in a fine film of forest dust.

The point I want to make about the snakeskin is that, when I found it, it was whole and tied in a knot. Now there have been stories told, even by reputable scientists, of snakes that have deliberately tied themselves in a knot to prevent larger snakes from trying to swallow them—but I couldn't imagine any way that throwing itself into a half hitch would help a snake trying to escape its skin. Still, ever cautious, I figured that one of the neighborhood boys could possibly have tied it in a knot in the fall, for some whimsical boyish reason, and left it there, where it dried and gathered dust. So I carried the skin along thoughtlessly as I walked, snagging it sure enough on a low branch and ripping it in two for the first of many times. I saw that thick ice still lay on the quarry pond and that the skunk cabbage was already out in the clearings, and then I came home and looked at the skin and its knot.

The knot had no beginning. Idly I turned it around in my hand, searching for a place to untie; I came to with a start when I realized I must have turned the thing around fully ten times. Intently, then, I traced the knot's lump around with a finger: it was continuous. I couldn't untie it any more than I could untie a doughnut; it was a loop without beginning or end. These snakes *are* magic, I thought for a second, and then of course I reasoned what must have happened. The skin had been pulled inside-out like a peeled sock for several inches; then an inch or so of the inside-out part—a piece whose length was coincidentally equal to the diameter of the skin—had somehow been turned right-side out again, making a thick lump whose edges were lost in wrinkles, looking exactly like a knot.

So. I have been thinking about the change of seasons. I don't want to miss spring this year. I want to distinguish the last winter frost from the out-of-season one, the frost of spring. I want to be there on the spot the moment the grass turns green. I always miss this radical revolution; I see it the next day from a window, the yard so suddenly green and lush I could envy Nebuchadnezzar[1] down on all fours eating grass. This year I want to stick a net into time and say "now," as men plant flags on the ice and snow and say, "here." But it occurred to me that I could no more catch spring by the tip of the tail than I could untie the apparent knot in the snakeskin; there are no edges to grasp. Both are continuous loops.

---

1. Nebuchadnezzar (ne´ byə kəd ne´ zər): King of Babylon from 605–562 B.C.

Annie Dillard

from Living Like Weasels

A weasel is wild. Who knows what he thinks? He sleeps in his underground den, his tail draped over his nose. Sometimes he lives in his den for two days without leaving. Outside, he stalks rabbits, mice, muskrats, and birds, killing more bodies than he can eat warm, and often dragging the carcasses home. Obedient to instinct, he bites his prey at the neck, either splitting the jugular vein at the throat or crunching the brain at the base of the skull, and he does not let go. One naturalist refused to kill a weasel who was socketed into his hand deeply as a rattlesnake. The man could in no way pry the tiny weasel off, and he had to walk half a mile to water, the weasel dangling from his palm, and soak him off like a stubborn label.

And once, says Ernest Thompson Seton[1]—once, a man shot an eagle out of the sky. He examined the eagle and found the dry skull of a weasel fixed by the jaws to his throat. The supposition is that the eagle had pounced on the weasel and the weasel swiveled and bit as instinct taught him, tooth to neck, and nearly won. I would like to have seen that eagle from the air a few weeks or months before he was shot: was the whole weasel still attached to his feathered throat, a fur pendant? Or did the eagle eat what he could reach, gutting the living weasel with his talons before his breast, bending his beak, cleaning the beautiful airborne bones?

I have been reading about weasels because I saw one last week. I startled a weasel who startled me, and we exchanged a long glance.

Twenty minutes from my house, through the woods by the quarry and across the highway, is Hollins Pond, a remarkable piece of shallowness, where I like to go at sunset and sit on a tree trunk. Hollins Pond is also called Murray's Pond; it covers two acres of bottomland near Tinker Creek with six inches of water and six thousand lily pads. In winter, brown-and-white steers stand in the middle of it, merely dampening their hooves; from the distant shore they look like miracle itself, complete with miracle's nonchalance. Now, in summer, the steers are

---

1. **Ernest Thompson Seton:** (1860–1946) American naturalist and writer.

gone. The water lilies have blossomed and spread to a green horizontal plane that is terra firma[2] to plodding blackbirds, and tremulous ceiling to black leeches, crayfish, and carp.

This is, mind you, suburbia. It is a five-minute walk in three directions to rows of houses, though none is visible here. There's a 55 mph highway at one end of the pond, and a nesting pair of wood ducks at the other. Under every bush is a muskrat hole or a beer can. The far end is an alternating series of fields and woods, fields and woods, threaded everywhere with motor-cycle tracks—in whose bare clay wild turtles lay eggs.

So. I had crossed the highway, stepped over two low barbed-wire fences, and traced the motorcycle path in all grati-tude through the wild rose and poison ivy of the pond's shore-line up into high grassy fields. Then I cut down through the woods to the mossy fallen tree where I sit. This tree is excellent. It makes a dry, upholstered bench at the upper, marshy end of the pond, a plush jetty raised from the thorny shore between a shallow blue body of water and a deep blue body of sky.

The sun had just set. I was relaxed on the tree trunk, ensconced in the lap of lichen, watching the lily pads at my feet tremble and part dreamily over the thrusting path of a carp. A yellow bird appeared to my right and flew behind me. It caught my eye; I swiveled around—and the next instant, inexplicably, I was looking down at a weasel, who was looking up at me.

Weasel! I'd never seen one wild before. He was ten inches long, thin as a curve, a muscled ribbon, brown as fruitwood, soft-furred, alert. His face was fierce, small and pointed as a lizard's; he would have made a good arrowhead. There was just a dot of chin, maybe two brown hairs' worth, and then the pure white fur began that spread down his underside. He had two black eyes I didn't see, any more than you see a window.

The weasel was stunned into stillness as he was emerging from beneath an enormous shaggy wild rose bush four feet away. I was stunned into stillness twisted backward on the tree trunk. Our eyes locked, and someone threw away the key.

Our look was as if two lovers, or deadly enemies, met unex-pectedly on an overgrown path when each had been thinking of something else: a clearing blow to the gut. It was also a bright blow to the brain, or a sudden beating of brains, with all the charge and intimate grate of rubbed balloons. It emptied our lungs. It felled the forest, moved the fields, and drained the pond; the world dismantled and tumbled into that black hole of

---

2. **terra firma** (ter′ ə fer′ mə) *n.*: Solid ground.

eyes. If you and I looked at each other that way, our skulls would split and drop to our shoulders. But we don't. We keep our skulls. So.

He disappeared. This was only last week, and already I don't remember what shattered the enchantment. I think I blinked, I think I retrieved my brain from the weasel's brain, and tried to memorize what I was seeing, and the weasel felt the yank of separation, the careening splashdown into real life and the urgent current of instinct. He vanished under the wild rose. I waited motionless, my mind suddenly full of data and my spirit with pleadings, but he didn't return.

Please do not tell me about "approach-avoidance conflicts." I tell you I've been in that weasel's brain for sixty seconds, and he was in mine. Brains are private places, muttering through unique and secret tapes—but the weasel and I both plugged into another tape simultaneously, for a sweet and shocking time. Can I help it if it was a blank?

What goes on in his brain the rest of the time? What does a weasel think about? He won't say. His journal is tracks in clay, a spray of feathers, mouse blood and bone: uncollected, unconnected, loose-leaf, and blown.

I would like to learn, or remember, how to live. I come to Hollins Pond not so much to learn how to live as, frankly, to forget about it. That is, I don't think I can learn from a wild animal how to live in particular—shall I suck warm blood, hold my tail high, walk with my footprints precisely over the prints of my hands?—but I might learn something of mindlessness, something of the purity of living in the physical senses and the dignity of living without bias or motive. The weasel lives in necessity and we live in choice, hating necessity and dying at the last ignobly in its talons. I would like to live as I should, as the weasel lives as he should. And I suspect that for me the way is like the weasel's: open to time and death painlessly, noticing everything, remembering nothing, choosing the given with a fierce and pointed will.

nnie Dillard

from Sojourner

If survival is an art, then mangroves[1] are artists of the beautiful: not only that they exist at all—smooth-barked, glossy-leaved, thickets of lapped mystery—but that they can and do exist as floating islands, as trees upright and loose, alive and homeless on the water.

I have seen mangroves, always on tropical ocean shores, in Florida and in the Galápagos.[2] There is the red mangrove, the yellow, the button, and the black. They are all short, messy trees, waxy-leaved, laced all over with aerial roots, woody arching buttresses, and weird leathery berry pods. All this tangles from a black muck soil, a black muck matted like a mud-sopped rag, a muck without any other plants, shaded, cold to the touch, tracked at the water's edge by herons and nosed by sharks.

It is these shoreline trees which, by a fairly common accident, can become floating islands. A hurricane flood or a riptide can wrest a tree from the shore, or from the mouth of a tidal river, and hurl it into the ocean. It floats. It is a mangrove island, blown.

There are floating islands on the planet; it amazes me. Credulous Pliny[3] described some islands thought to be mangrove islands floating on a river. The people called these river islands *the dancers*, "because in any consort of musicians singing, they stir and move at the stroke of the feet, keeping time and measure."

Trees floating on rivers are less amazing than trees floating on the poisonous sea. A tree cannot live in salt. Mangrove trees exude salt from their leaves; you can see it, even on shoreline black mangroves, as a thin white crust. Lick a leaf and your tongue curls and coils; your mouth's a heap of salt.

Nor can a tree live without soil. A hurricane-born mangrove island may bring its own soil to the sea. But other mangrove trees make their own soil—and their own islands—from scratch. These are the ones which interest me. The seeds germinate in the fruit on the tree. The germinated embryo can drop anywhere—say, onto

---

1. **mangroves** (man' grōvz) *n.:* Trees of a kind that grows at water's edge.
2. **Galapagos** (gə lä' pə gəs): Island group off the coast of Ecuador.
3. **Pliny** (pli' nē): (A.D. 23–79) Roman scholar.

a dab of floating muck. The heavy root end sinks; a leafy plumule[4] unfurls. The tiny seedling, afloat, is on its way. Soon aerial roots shooting out in all directions trap debris. The sapling's networks twine, the interstices narrow, and water calms in the lee. Bacteria thrive on organic broth; amphipods[5] swarm. These creatures grow and die at the trees' wet feet. The soil thickens, accumulating rainwater, leaf rot, seashells, and guano; the island spreads.

More seeds and more muck yield more trees on the new island. A society grows, interlocked in a tangle of dependencies. The island rocks less in the swells. Fish throng to the backwaters stilled in snarled roots. Soon, Asian mudskippers—little four-inch fish—clamber up the mangrove roots into the air and peer about from periscope eyes on stalks, like snails. Oysters clamp to submersed roots, as do starfish, dog whelk, and the creatures that live among tangled kelp. Shrimp seek shelter there, limpets a holdfast, pelagic birds[6] a rest.

And the mangrove island wanders on, afloat and adrift. It walks teetering and wanton before the wind. Its fate and direction are random. It may bob across an ocean and catch on another mainland's shores. It may starve or dry while it is still a sapling. It may topple in a storm, or pitchpole. By the rarest of chances, it may stave into another mangrove island in a crash of clacking roots, and mesh. What it is most likely to do is drift anywhere in the alien ocean, feeding on death and growing, netting a makeshift soil as it goes, shrimp in its toes and terns[7] in its hair.

---

4. **plumule** (plü′ myül) *n.*: Primary leaf bud of a newly-germinated plant.
5. **amphipods** (am′ fi pädz) *n.*: Small crustaceans with flattened bodies.
6. **pelagic birds** (pē la′ jik) *n.*: Birds of the open sea.
7. **terns** (tərnz) *n.*: Gull-like marine birds.

☑ Check Your Comprehension

1. In "Intricacy," who (or what) is Ellery? How much did he cost?
2. What makes plants green?
3. What was unusual about the knot in "Untying the Knot"?
4. In "Living Like Weasels," what was unusual about the eagle that someone shot from the sky?
5. In "Living Like Weasels," what does Dillard say she wants to learn from wild animals? What does she say she cannot learn from them?
6. In "Sojourner," what are mangroves? What is unusual about them?

◆ Critical Thinking

INTERPRET

1. In "Intricacy," why do you suppose Dillard thinks so often about the red blood cells in Ellery's tail after she sees them in a microscope? **[Speculate; Analyze]**
2. In "Untying the Knot," the snakeskin serves as a metaphor for something else. This metaphor helps Dillard to gain an insight about that thing. What does the metaphor stand for and what insight does it give her? **[Interpret]**
3. Dillard says "Our eyes locked, and someone threw away the key" when she met the weasel. What might she mean by this? How does the metaphor she uses help you understand the passage? **[Interpret; Analyze]**
4. Humans and animals have very different ways of telling their histories. What does Dillard say these different ways are? What metaphor does she use to describe this difference? **[Compare; Support]**
5. In "Sojourner," what metaphors does Dillard use to describe mangroves? How do these metaphors help describe the wonder she feels about mangroves? **[Infer; Support]**

COMPARE LITERARY WORKS

6. What are some of the things Dillard learns about nature in these selections? What are some of the conclusions she draws from observing nature? **[Support; Analyze]**

Annie Dillard

Comparing and Connecting the Author's Works

◆ Literary Focus: Descriptive Writing

Descriptive Writing is writing in which the author endeavors to recreate for the reader what he or she has experienced through the five senses: sight, touch, taste, smell, and hearing. To paint this picture, the author selects details using specific, concrete nouns, vivid verbs, and often unusual adjectives to evoke the senses. Look at the vivid verbs Dillard uses in the following passage from "Intricacy". "The red blood cells in the goldfish's tail <u>streamed</u> and <u>coursed</u> . . . never <u>wavered</u> or <u>slowed</u> or <u>ceased flowing</u>." Then note the specific nouns and adjectives she uses in the same sentence. "[It]. . . coursed through <u>narrow channels</u> <u>invisible</u> save for <u>glistening threads</u> of <u>thickness</u> in the <u>general translucency</u>." To which sense does each of these underlined words appeal?

1. In the first paragraph of "Intricacy," Dillard uses many vivid verbs to describe what happens to the light in her kitchen. List these verbs.

2. In the first paragraph of the excerpt from *The Writing Life,* to what sense does each of the following words appeal: spiral, coarse, warblers, racket, drift?

◆ Drawing Conclusions About Dillard's Work

Annie Dillard wrote the following to a creative writing class she had taught at the University of North Carolina.

The way to a reader's emotions is, oddly enough, through the senses. . . . Capturing the typical isn't a virtue. Only making something new and interesting is.

Check Dillard's work for words that appeal, in unusual ways, to the five senses. The following chart includes words from "Living Like Weasels." On a separate piece of paper, create a similar chart for the first two paragraphs of the excerpt from "Sojourner." Choose at least six words that seem to appeal to the senses. For each word, write the part of speech, the sense(s) it appeals to, and whether it is a metaphor or a simile. Then, in a brief paragraph, write how well you think Dillard follows her own advice about using the five senses and making "something new and interesting" in her writing.

Word	Part of Speech	Sense(s)
thin	adjective	sight
ribbon	noun	sight
soft-furred	adjective	touch

◆ Idea Bank

Writing

1. **Journal** Go to your favorite place in nature, or, if possible, a natural place you've never been before. Observe as much as you can and then write about what you have seen in a journal.

2. **Essay** Dillard wrote, "I walk out; I see something, some event that would otherwise have been utterly missed and lost . . . .I am an explorer, then, and I am also a stalker." Using examples from the selections, write an essay that explores what Dillard means by this and what you think of Dillard's assessment of herself.

3. **Descriptive Essay** Write a descriptive essay about a place in nature that you like, a favorite landscape painting, or an imaginary place. (The place may include animals or people.) Before you begin, use a chart like the one below to brainstorm words that evoke the five senses and could be used to describe the place you've chosen. Then use as many of those words as you can in your essay.

Smell	Taste	Touch	Sight	Sound

Speaking and Listening

4. **Oral Interpretation** Good descriptive writing almost begs to be read out loud. With a partner, select two different passages from "Intricacy," "Living Like Weasels," or "Sojourner." On your own, practice reading your passage out loud, paying attention to pronunciation, rhythm, emphasis, and volume. Then take turns presenting your oral interpretations to each other. **[Performing Arts Link]**

5. **Report** In small groups, do research on subjects having to do with protecting the environment. You may focus on famous environmentalists and their writing or activities, such as Rachel Carson, or you may research areas of the world where environments are threatened, such as the rain forests of South America. Brainstorm specifically what your group will research and assign each group member a subsection of the topic. Have each person write a summary of his or her topic and then present your report to the class. **[Group Activity; Science Link]**

6. **Television Documentary** Have small groups write a television documentary about mangroves, weasels, or snakes. Include information from the material in the selections, but assign members of your group to add more information from their own research. Ask for volunteers in your group to draw pictures or select photographs about your subject; assign others to select appropriate music and others to write and read the script. Then present the documentary to the class. **[Group Activity; Performing Arts Link]**

◆ Further Reading, Listening, and Viewing

- Lee Gutkind, editor: *The Essayist at Work: Profiles of Creative Nonfiction Writers*
- Ellen Hansen, editor: *The New England Transcendentalists: Life of the Mind and of the Spirit*
- *Pilgrim at Tinker Creek,* audiobook read by Grace Conlin (Blackstone Audiobooks)
- Rachel Carson, *Silent Spring,*
- Henry David Thoreau, *Walden*

On the Web:

http://www.phschool.com/languagearts/literature.
Go to the student edition *Platinum*. Proceed to Unit 4. Then click Hot Links to find Web sites featuring Annie Dillard.

Sophocles In Depth

> Count no mortal happy until he has passed the final limit of his death secure from pain.
>
> *-Sophocles*

SOPHOCLES' life spanned the fifth century B.C.E. During that time he enjoyed a long and successful career as one of the foremost Greek tragic poets. He saw the rise of Athens to imperial greatness and lived through the period of cultural and intellectual enlightenment in which Athens was "an education to Greece." He witnessed the deterioration of Athens brought about by plague and warfare. In 404, two years after the death of Sophocles, Sparta defeated Athens at the end of a long and bitter struggle. Tyranny replaced democracy.

496-480 Childhood Sophocles was born in Colonus, a suburb of Athens. His father, Sophillus, was a wealthy manufacturer. Sophocles received a traditional training in literature as well as lyre playing, singing and dancing. There are references to Sophocles' striking good looks and to his skill as a dancer and a musician. In 480, the Greeks defeated the Persians in naval battle at Salamis. At age sixteen, Sophocles played his lyre and led a chorus of boys at the public victory celebration.

480-468 Young Man Sophocles had a brief career as an actor and was remembered for his virtuoso lyre playing in the role of Thamyris. Sophocles' voice, however, was not strong enough to continue as an actor. He then devoted himself to writing.

468-440 Adult Years After the Persian Wars, Athens controlled a vast empire and became the cosmopolitan center of the world. Artistic and intellectual life in Athens was in full bloom. It was a time and place in which philosophers and poets challenged time-honored beliefs. At age 26, Sophocles flashed into prominence as a tragic poet by defeating Aeschylus at the height of his powers. The next twenty-five years are a blank page. In 443, Sophocles was elected as an administrator of the Athenian Treasury, an office that he performed competently. In 440, Sophocles was elected as one of ten generals, on the strength of his achievements as a poet! The play that supposedly earned him this distinction was *Antigone*.

440-406 Final Years During the final period of Sophocles' career, war and disease spread through Athens. A campaign against Sparta, led by Pericles in 431 and begun with high hopes, ended in catastrophe. Two years into the war, a great plague broke out in Athens and took the life of Pericles. His death marks a turning point in the fortunes of Athens. During this period, Sophocles belonged to a religious group that worshipped the doctor-hero Amynus, and in 421 was instrumental in establishing the Athenian sanctuary of Asclepius, the god of healing. Of the five Sophoclean plays from this final period, four involve characters whose physical or psychological suffering shows decidedly plague-like symptoms. The world of these tragedies is one in which good men are unexpectedly and undeservedly brought low, and in which faith in divine justice is put to an extreme test. It is a world very much like that of Athens in the final years of the Peloponnesian War. After the Sicilian expedition ended in disaster in 411, there was a military coup in Athens. Sophocles served on a Council of 400, which replaced the democratic government. "I'm not for it," he said, "but there's no other way." When Euripides, his innovative rival, died in 406, Sophocles is said to have dressed his chorus in black as they marched into the theatre of Dionysus. This gesture is an eloquent symbol of the times: a funeral march that marks not only the loss of a fellow tragedian, but the passing of the golden age of tragedy and the expiration of a great civilization as well. In the same year, Sophocles himself died. So universal was respect for him, that the Spartan commander who presided over the siege of Athens, ordered his soldiers to step aside for the funeral cortege as it made its way from the outlying district of Colonus. There the citizens worshipped Sophocles as a hero under the name Dexios, "the Welcomer." Two years later, a defeated Athens extended bitter welcome to the armies of their Spartan conquerors.

◆ War, Plague, and the Death of Pericles

In 430 Athens went to war with Sparta. Athens was at the pinnacle of power and had, in Pericles, a general of intelligence and foresight. Victory seemed assured. Then two unexpected catastrophes occurred. First, a deadly plague swept through Athens. The city was crowded with the dead and the dying. The disease did not distinguish between the weak and the strong, the good and the evil, or the just and the unjust. The historian, Thucydides, survived the plague. He observed a breakdown of moral and religious values and gave the following explanation for it: "The great lawlessness that was everywhere in the city began with this disease, for people saw before their eyes such quick reversals of fortune, as the rich suddenly died and men previously worth nothing took over their estates." Pericles managed to restore order and revive popular morale. "What heaven sends," he declared, "we must bear with a sense of

necessity, what the enemy does to us we must bear with courage." Then the second calamity occurred: Pericles, the one leader able to hold things together, died from the plague. The city became divided between those who favored democracy and those who favored oligarchy, government by the few. Strategic errors, political discord, private quarrels, rebellions among the allies, and monumental lack of foresight brought about the eventual downfall of Athens. It is important to keep these events in mind when considering the impact that *Oedipus the King* had on the audience of Sophocles' time. It is curious that *Oedipus the King*, now considered to be one of the greatest dramatic masterpieces of all time, won second place, defeated by a play that time has forgotten. One wonders whether Sophocles touched on matters that were a little too close to home?

◆ The Plays

Sophocles wrote 124 plays and won first prize on nineteen occasions. The exact dates of Sophocles' plays are, for the most part, unknown, but the order below is fairly certain.

Ajax The hero goes mad when the arms of Achilles are awarded to Odysseus.

Antigone The daughter of Oedipus buries her outlawed brother in defiance of a royal edict.

Oedipus the King The King of Thebes discovers that he unwittingly killed his father, thereby fulfilling an old prophecy.

The Women of Trachis The wife of Herakles mistakenly gives her husband poison.

Electra The daughter of Agamemnon avenges the death of her father.

Philoctetes The Greeks seek out Philoctetes, when they learn they can't conquer Troy without his bow.

Oedipus at Colonus Sophocles' final play tells of the death and heroization of blind Oedipus.

TIMELINE

Sophocles' Life		World Events	
496	Sophocles is born in Colonus, a district of Athens.	**776**	First Olympic Games.
480	Aeschylus, the tragic poet, fights in the battle of Salamis as the Greeks defeat the Persians. Euripides is born on the same day. Sophocles leads the chorus at the victory celebration over Persians at Salamis.	**699-600**	Greeks adopt Phoenician alphabet. Homer's *Iliad* and *Odyssey* are set in writing.
		563	Birth of Gautama Buddha.
		551	Confucius is born.
		509	End of monarchy and beginning of the Republic in Rome.
468	Sophocles defeats Aeschylus for his first victory in tragic competition, launching a long and successful career as a popular dramatist.	**490**	Persian invasion of Greece repelled at Marathon and Salamis.
		481	Birth of Protagoras, greatest of the itinerant professors
460–450	Sophocles shocks the Athenian public with his *Ajax*.	**480**	Persian War
443–442	Sophocles elected to Treasury post.	**c.480**	Herodotus, the "father of history," is born.
442–441	*Antigone* wins first prize.	**480**	Birth of Euripides.
440	Sophocles serves as one of 10 generals, under the command of Pericles.	**470**	Birth of Socrates.
		460's	Pericles expands Athenian Empire
		460	Birth of Hippocrates, "father of medicine."
430?	Sophocles presents *Women of Trachis,* telling of the final agonies of Herakles.	**460**	Birth of Thucydides, author of *History of the Peloponnesian Wars.*
429?	*Oedipus the King* wins second place.	**450's**	Democritus develops his atomic theory.
424	Sophocles writes a poem honoring his friend Herodotus.	**458**	Aeschylus produces the *Oresteia,* the only surviving trilogy from Greek tragedy.
421	Sophocles helps to establish the Athenian cult of Asclepius.	**c.446**	Birth of Aristophanes, the comic playwright.
410	Sophocles thought to have staged his *Electra*.	**440**	The Theban lyric poet, Pindar, dies.
409	*Philoctetes* is performed.	**437**	The Parthenon is completed.
406	Sophocles dies and is buried at Colonus, where he receives honors of a hero.	**431**	Peloponnesian War, between Athens and Sparta, begins. Pericles rules Athens.
		430	Plague breaks out in Athens. Ezra the Scribe establishes the Torah.
401	*Oedipus at Colonus,* containing some of Sophocles' finest poetry, is produced posthumously by his grandson.	**429**	Plato is born: philosopher, and founder of the first university in the western world.
		411	Revolution takes place in Athens.
		406	Euripides dies.
		404	Athens falls and thirty tyrants run the government.
		403	Democracy is restored to Athens.
		399	Death of Socrates.

Sophocles

from Oedipus the King

Translated by David Greene

THE OEDIPUS MYTH

A Dire Prophecy Laius, king of Thebes, and his queen, Jocasta received a prophecy that their son was fated to kill his father. When a son was born, they pierced and chained his feet and instructed a shepherd to abandon him on Mt. Cithaeron to die. The shepherd gave him to a Corinthian shepherd, who returned home and gave the boy to a childless couple. They named the boy Oedipus, which means "swollen foot."

Prophecy Fulfilled When Oedipus grew up, he learned of the prophecy that he would kill his father and marry his mother. He fled from Corinth. On the road to Thebes, he killed a traveler who tried to drive him off the road. He did not know that the victim was his real father, Laius, King of Thebes. In attempting to run from the prophecy he had begun to fulfill it.

The Riddle of the Sphinx At Thebes he rid the city of the Sphinx, a monster that ate those men who failed to solve her riddle: "What walks on four legs at dawn, two legs at noon, and three legs in the evening?" Oedipus answered correctly, "Man, who crawls in infancy, walks upright in his prime and walks with a cane in old age." The Sphinx destroyed herself, and the Thebans made Oedipus their king. He married Jocasta, not knowing that she was his mother.

The Fall of Oedipus Oedipus the King opens with the outbreak of a plague in Thebes. Oedipus tries once again to save the city. The oracle at Delphi informs Oedipus that he can end the plague only if he finds the killer of King Laius. Oedipus determines to hunt down and punish the murderer, unaware that the trail will lead him back to himself. Even when he begins to suspect that he is the guilty one, Oedipus courageously goes on in his search for the truth. When the pieces of the puzzle finally fall into place, Jocasta takes her own life. Oedipus plucks the brooches from her gown and gouges his eyes out, a fitting punishment for having failed to see the truth of his identity. The chorus laments the fall of Oedipus and the instability of mortal happiness.

```
CHARACTERS:
Oedipus, King of Thebes
Jocasta, His Wife
Creon, His Brother-in-Law
Teiresias, an Old Blind Prophet
A Priest
First Messenger, from Corinth (received
        the infant, Oedipus, from the Herdsman)
Second Messenger
Herdsman (ordered by Jocasta to expose
        infant Oedipus on Mt. Cithaeron)
Chorus of Old Men of Thebes
```

SCENE: *In front of the palace of Oedipus at Thebes¹. To the right of the stage near the altar stands the Priest with a crowd of children. Oedipus emerges from the central door.*

OEDIPUS.

Children, young sons and daughters of old Cadmus²,
why do you sit here with your suppliant crowns?
The town is heavy with a mingled burden

5   of sounds and smells, of groans and hymns and incense;
I did not think it fit that I should hear
of this from messengers but came myself,—
I Oedipus whom all men call the Great.

                              (He turns to the Priest.)

You're old and they are young; come, speak for them.

10   What do you fear or want, that you sit here
suppliant? Indeed I'm willing to give all
that you may need; I would be very hard
should I not pity suppliants like these.

PRIEST.

O ruler of my country, Oedipus,

15   you see our company around the altar;
you see our ages; some of us, like these,
who cannot yet fly far, and some of us
heavy with age; these children are the chosen
among the young, and I the priest of Zeus.³

---

1. **Thebes** (thēbz): A city in central Greece, midway between Delphi and Athens.
2. **Cadmus** (kadˊməs): The founder and first king of Thebes. The people of Thebes are referred to as his children.
3. **Zeus** (zūs): The most powerful of the twelve Olympian gods. His attributes are the eagle, the oak, and the lightning bolt.

20	Within the market place sit others crowned
	with suppliant garlands, at the double shrine
	of Pallas[4] and the temple where Ismenus[5]
	gives oracles[6] by fire. King, you yourself
	have seen our city reeling like a wreck
	already; it can scarcely lift its prow
	out of the depths, out of the bloody surf.
25	A blight is on the fruitful plants of the earth,
	a blight is on the cattle in the fields,
	a blight is on our women that no children
	are born to them; a God that carries fire,
	a deadly pestilence, is on our town,
	strikes us and spares not, and the house of Cadmus[6]
	is emptied of its people while black Death
30	grows rich in groaning and in lamentation.
	We have not come as suppliants to this altar
	because we thought of you as of a God,
	but rather judging you the first of men
	in all the chances of this life and when
	we mortals have to do with more than man.
35	You came and by your coming saved our city,
	freed us from tribute which we paid of old
	to the Sphinx[7], cruel singer. This you did
	in virtue of no knowledge we could give you,
	in virtue of no teaching; it was God
	that aided you, men say, and you are held
	with God's assistance to have saved our lives.
40	Now Oedipus, Greatest in all men's eyes,
	here falling at your feet we all entreat you,
	find us some strength for rescue.
	Perhaps you'll hear a wise word from some God,
	perhaps you will learn something from a man
	(for I have seen that for the skilled of practice
45	the outcome of their counsels live the most).
	Noblest of men, go, and raise up our city,

---

4. double shrine of Pallas (pal` əs): Two temples of Athena, the goddess of wisdom.

5. temple where Ismenus (iz mē´ nəs) **gives oracles by fire:** The temple of Apollo, located by the river Ismenus, in Thebes. There the priests read the future by studying patterns in sacrificial ashes.

6: House of Cadmus: The priest refers to the citizens of Thebes as descendants of Cadmus, who founded the city.

7. Sphinx (sfinks) *n.*: A winged female monster, half-lioness and half-human, who ate those men who could not solve her riddle: "What is it that walks on four legs at dawn, two legs at noon, and three legs in the evening; when it walks on the most feet it is slowest?" Oedipus saved Thebes by answering correctly, "Man, who crawls in infancy, walks upright in the prime of life, and walks with a cane in old age." Enraged, the Sphinx destroyed herself. Oedipus won the hand of Jocasta and became king of Thebes.

go,—and give heed. For now this land of ours
calls you its savior since you saved it once.
So, let us never speak about your reign
as of a time when first our feet were set
50 secure on high, but later fell to ruin.
Raise up our city, save it and raise it up.
Once you have brought us luck with happy omen;
be no less now in fortune.
If you will rule this land, as now you rule it,
better to rule it full of men than empty.
55 For neither tower nor ship is anything
when empty, and none live in it together.

OEDIPUS.

I pity you, children. You have come full of longing,
but I have known the story before you told it
only too well. I know you are all sick,
60 yet there is not one of you, sick though you are,
that is as sick as I myself.
Your several sorrows each have single scope
and touch but one of you. My spirit groans
for city and myself and you at once.
65 You have not roused me like a man from sleep;
know that I have given many tears to this,
gone many ways wandering in thought,
but as I thought I found only one remedy
and that I took. I sent Menoeceus' son
70 Creon, Jocasta's brother, to Apollo,[8]
to his Pythian[9] temple,
that he might learn there by what act or word
I could save this city. As I count the days,
it vexes me what ails him; he is gone
75 far longer than he needed for the journey.
But when he comes, then, may I prove a villain,
if I shall not do all the God commands.

PRIEST.

Thanks for your gracious words. Your servants here
signal that Creon is this moment coming.

OEDIPUS.

80 His face is bright. O holy Lord Apollo,

---

8. Apollo (ə päl′ ō): The god of prophecy, knowledge, music, sunlight and healing. He is the son of Zeus and Leto, and the brother of Artemis. His emblems are
the bow and the lyre.
9. Pythean (pith′ e ən) **temple:** The oracular shrine of Apollo at Delphi, below Mt.
Parnassus in central Greece.

grant that his news too may be bright for us
and bring us safety.

PRIEST.

It is happy news,
I think, for else his head would not be crowned
with sprigs of fruitful laurel.

OEDIPUS.

We will know soon,
85   he's within hail. Lord Creon, my good brother,
what is the word you bring us from the God?

(Creon enters.)

CREON.

A good word,—for things hard to bear themselves
if in the final issue all is well
I count complete good fortune.

OEDIPUS.

What do you mean?
What you have said so far
90   leaves me uncertain whether to trust or fear.

CREON.

If you will hear my news before these others
I am ready to speak, or else to go within.

OEDIPUS.

Speak it to all;
the grief I bear, I bear it more for these
than for my own heart.

CREON.

95   I will tell you, then,
what I heard from the God.
King Phoebus[10] in plain words commanded us
to drive out a pollution from our land,
pollution grown ingrained within the land;
drive it out, said the God, not cherish it,
till it's past cure.

---

10. **Phoebus:** Apollo.

OEDIPUS.

What is the rite
of purification? How shall it be done?

CREON.

100   By banishing a man, or expiation
of blood by blood, since it is murder guilt
which holds our city in this destroying storm.

OEDIPUS.

Who is this man whose fate the God pronounces?

CREON.

My Lord, before you piloted the state
we had a king called Laius.[11]

OEDIPUS.

105   I know of him by hearsay. I have not seen him.

CREON.

The God commanded clearly: let some one
punish with force this dead man's murderers.

OEDIPUS.

Where are they in the world? Where would a trace
of this old crime be found? It would be hard
to guess where.

CREON.

110   The clue is in this land;
that which is sought is found;
the unheeded thing escapes:
so said the God.

OEDIPUS.

Was it at home,
or in the country that death came upon him,
or in another country travelling?

---

11. Laius: (lai′ us): The king of Thebes and husband of Jocasta. Prophecy foretold that the son of Laius and Jocasta would kill his father and marry his mother. To avoid this fate, Laius drove a nail through the ankles of Oedipus and commanded a servant to leave the child on Mt. Cithaeron to die. The servant pitied the child and, without revealing its identity, gave it to a shepherd from Corinth. This shepherd handed the crippled child over to King Polybus and Queen Merope who adopted him and gave him the name Oedipus, which means "swollen foot."

CREON.

He went, he said himself, upon an embassy,[12]
115   but never returned when he set out from home.

OEDIPUS.

Was there no messenger, no fellow traveller
who knew what happened? Such a one might tell
something of use.

CREON.

They were all killed save one. He fled in terror
and he could tell us nothing in clear terms
of what he knew, nothing, but one thing only.

OEDIPUS.

120   What was it?
If we could even find a slim beginning
in which to hope, we might discover much.

CREON.

This man said that the robbers they encountered
were many and the hands that did the murder
were many; it was no man's single power.

OEDIPUS.

How could a robber dare a deed like this
were he not helped with money from the city,
125   money and treachery?

CREON.

                      That indeed was thought.
But Laius was dead and in our trouble
there was none to help.

OEDIPUS.

What trouble was so great to hinder you
inquiring out the murder of your king?

CREON.

130   The riddling Sphinx induced us to neglect
mysterious crimes and rather seek solution
of troubles at our feet.

---

12. embassy: An important mission or errand.

OEDIPUS.

I will bring this to light again. King Phoebus
fittingly took this care about the dead,
and you too fittingly.

135 And justly you will see in me an ally,
a champion of my country and the God.
For when I drive pollution from the land
I will not serve a distant friend's advantage,
but act in my own interest. Whoever
he was that killed the king may readily

140 wish to dispatch me with his murderous hand;
so helping the dead king I help myself.
Come, children, take your suppliant boughs and go;
up from the altars now. Call the assembly
and let it meet upon the understanding

145 that I'll do everything. God will decide
whether we prosper or remain in sorrow.

PRIEST.

Rise, children—it was this we came to seek,
which of himself the king now offers us.
May Phoebus who gave us the oracle

150 come to our rescue and stay the plague.

(Exeunt all but the Chorus.)

CHORUS.

   STROPHE.[13]

What is the sweet spoken word of God from the shrine of Pytho
   rich in gold
that has come to glorious Thebes?
I am stretched on the rack of doubt, and terror and trembling
   hold
my heart, O Delian Healer, and I worship full of fears

155 for what doom you will bring to pass, new or renewed in the
   revolving years.
Speak to me, immortal voice,
child of golden Hope.

---

13. Strophe: Choral passages, or odes, were accompanied by music. Members of the
chorus sang the lyrics and danced to the music. The sections of an ode were divided into
two parts, a strophe, which was sung by one half of the chorus, and an antistrophe which
was sung by the other half, in response.

ANTISTROPHE.[14]

First I call on you, Athene,[15] deathless daughter of Zeus,
160   and Artemis, Earth Upholder,[16]
who sits in the midst of the market place in the throne
       which men call Fame,
and Phoebus, the Far Shooter, three averters of Fate,
165   come to us now, if ever before, when ruin rushed upon the state,
you drove destruction's flame away
out of our land.

   STROPHE.

Our sorrows defy number;
all the ship's timbers are rotten;
170   taking of thought is no spear for the driving away of the
          plague.
There are no growing children in this famous land;
there are no women bearing the pangs of childbirth.
You may see them one with another, like birds swift on
175   the wing,
quicker than fire unmastered,
speeding away to the coast of the Western God.

   ANTISTROPHE.

In the unnumbered deaths
of its people the city dies;
those children that are born lie dead on the naked earth
unpitied, spreading contagion of death; and grey haired mothers
       and wives
182-185 everywhere stand at the altar's edge, suppliant, moaning;
the hymn to the healing God rings out but with it
the wailing voices are blended.
From these our sufferings grant us, O golden Daughter of Zeus[17],
glad-faced deliverance.

   STROPHE.

There is no clash of brazen shields but our fight is with the War
       God,
191   a War God ringed with the cries of men, a savage God who burns
       us;
grant that he turn in racing course backwards out of our
       country's bounds

---

14. Antistrophe: Section of a choral ode that responds to a strophe. A choral ode may contain as many as three pairs of odes and antistrophe.
15. Athene: The goddess of wisdom. Athene had no mother but was born from the head of Zeus.
16. Artemis the Upholder: The daughter of Zeus and Leto, chaste goddess of the hunt, protector or "upholder" of earth's creatures.
17. Golden Daughter of Zeus: Athena.

195   to the great palace of Amphitrite[18] or where the waves of the
          Thracian sea[19]
      deny the stranger safe anchorage.
      Whatsoever escapes the night
      at last the light of day revisits;
      so smite the War God, Father Zeus,
200   beneath your thunderbolt,
      for you are the Lord of the lightning, the lightning
          that carries fire.

ANTISTROPHE.

      And your unconquered arrow shafts, winged by the golden
          corded bow,
205   Lycean King, I beg to be at our side for help;
      and the gleaming torches of Artemis with which she scours the
          Lycean hills,
      and I call on the God with the turban of gold, who gave his name
          to this country of ours,
210   the Bacchic God[20] with the wind flushed face,
      Evian One, who travel
      with the Maenad[21] company,
      combat the God that burns us
      with your torch of pine;
      for the God that is our enemy is a God unhonoured among the
          Gods.

(Oedipus returns.)

OEDIPUS.

215   For what you ask me—if you will hear my words,
      and hearing welcome them and fight the plague,
      you will find strength and lightening of your load.
      Hark to me; what I say to you, I say
      as one that is a stranger to the story
      as stranger to the deed. For I would not
220   be far upon the track if I alone
      were tracing it without a clue. But now,
      since after all was finished, I became
      a citizen among you, citizens—
      now I proclaim to all the men of Thebes:
225   who so among you knows the murderer

---

18. Amphitrite (am fi trit e): Sea goddess who was wife of Poseidon, god of the sea.
19. Thracian Sea: The Black sea, whose shores were inhabited by Thracians, a warlike people.
20. the Bacchic God: Bacchus means the frantic god and refers to Dionysus, the god of wine, who was born of Zeus and a woman of Thebes, the first city to honor him.
21. Maenads: Female followers of Dionysus.

by whose hand Laius, son of Labdacus,
died—I command him to tell everything
to me,—yes, though he fears himself to take the blame
on his own head; for bitter punishment
230   he shall have none, but leave this land unharmed.
Or if he knows the murderer, another,
a foreigner, still let him speak the truth.
For I will pay him and be grateful, too.
But if you shall keep silence, if perhaps
some one of you, to shield a guilty friend,
or for his own sake shall reject my words—
235   hear what I shall do then:
I forbid that man, whoever he be, my land,
my land where I hold sovereignty and throne;
and I forbid any to welcome him
240   or cry him greeting or make him a sharer
in sacrifice or offering to the Gods,
or give him water for his hands to wash.
I command all to drive him from their homes,
since he is our pollution, as the oracle
of Pytho's God proclaimed him now to me.
So I stand forth a champion of the God
245   and of the man who died.
Upon the murderer I invoke this curse—
whether he is one man and all unknown,
or one of many—may he wear out his life
in misery to miserable doom!
250   If with my knowledge he lives at my hearth
I pray that I myself may feel my curse.
On you I lay my charge to fulfill all this
for me, for the God, and for this land of ours
destroyed and blighted, by the God forsaken.

255   Even were this no matter of God's ordinance
it would not fit you so to leave it lie,
unpurified, since a good man is dead
and one that was a king. Search it out.
Since I am now the holder of his office,
260   and have his bed and wife that once was his,
and had his line not been unfortunate
we would have common children—(fortune leaped
upon his head)—because of all these things,
I fight in his defense as for my father,
265   and I shall try all means to take the murderer
of Laius the son of Labdacus
the son of Polydorus and before him

of Cadmus and before him of Agenor.
Those who do not obey me, may the Gods
270 grant no crops springing from the ground they plough
nor children to their women! May a fate
like this, or one still worse than this consume them!
For you whom these words please, the other Thebans,
may Justice as your ally and all the Gods
275 live with you, blessing you now and for ever!

CHORUS.
As you have held me to my oath, I speak:
I neither killed the king nor can declare
the killer; but since Phoebus set the quest
it is his part to tell who the man is.

OEDIPUS.
280 Right; but to put compulsion on the Gods
against their will—no man can do that.

CHORUS.
May I then say what I think second best?

OEDIPUS.
If there's a third best, too, spare not to tell it.

CHORUS.
I know that what the Lord Teiresias
285 sees, is most often what the Lord Apollo
sees. If you should inquire of this from him
you might find out most clearly.

OEDIPUS.
Even in this my actions have not been sluggard.
On Creon's word I have sent two messengers
and why the prophet is not here already
I have been wondering.

CHORUS.
290   His skill apart
there is besides only an old faint story.

OEDIPUS.
What is it?
I look at every story.

CHORUS.

It was said
that he was killed by certain wayfarers.

OEDIPUS.

I heard that, too, but no one saw the killer.

CHORUS.

Yet if he has a share of fear at all,
295   his courage will not stand firm, hearing your curse.

OEDIPUS.

The man who in the doing did not shrink
will fear no word.

CHORUS.

Here comes his prosecutor:
led by your men the godly prophet comes
in whom alone of mankind truth is native.

(Enter Teiresias, led by a little boy.)

OEDIPUS.

300   Teiresias, you are versed in everything,
things teachable and things not to be spoken,
things of the heaven and earth-creeping things.
You have no eyes but in your mind you know
with what a plague our city is afflicted.
My lord, in you alone we find a champion,
in you alone one that can rescue us.
305   Perhaps you have not heard the messengers,
but Phoebus sent in answer to our sending
an oracle declaring that our freedom
from this disease would only come when we
should learn the names of those who killed King Laius,
and kill them or expel from our country.
310   Do not begrudge us oracles from birds,
or any other way of prophecy
within your skill; save yourself and the city,
save me; redeem the debt of our pollution
that lies on us because of this dead man.
We are in your hands; pains are most nobly taken
315   to help another when you have means and power.

TEIRESIAS.

Alas, how terrible is wisdom when
it brings no profit to the man that's wise!

This I knew well, but had forgotten it,
else I would not have come here.

OEDIPUS.

What is this?
How sad you are now you have come!

TEIRESIAS.

320 Let me
go home. It will be easiest for us both
to bear our several destinies to the end
if you will follow my advice.

OEDIPUS.

You'd rob us
of this your gift of prophecy? You talk
as one who had no care for law
nor love for Thebes who reared you.

TEIRESIAS.

Yes, but I see that even your own words
325 miss the mark; therefore I must fear for mine.

OEDIPUS.

For God's sake if you know of anything,
do not turn from us; all of us kneel to you,
all of us here, your suppliants.

TEIRESIAS.

All of you here know nothing. I will not
bring to the light of day my troubles, mine—
rather than call them yours.

OEDIPUS.

What do you mean?
330 You know of something but refuse to speak.
Would you betray us and destroy the city?

TEIRESIAS.

I will not bring this pain upon us both,
neither on you nor on myself. Why is it
you question me and waste your labor? I
will tell you nothing.

OEDIPUS.

335 You would provoke a stone! Tell us, you villain,
tell us, and do not stand there quietly
unmoved and balking at the issue.

TEIRESIAS.

You blame my temper but you do not see
your own that lives within you; it is me
you chide.

OEDIPUS.

Who would not feel his temper rise
340   at words like these with which you shame our city?

TEIRESIAS.

Of themselves things will come, although I hide them
and breathe no word of them.

OEDIPUS.

               Since they will come
tell them to me.

TEIRESIAS.

               I will say nothing further.
Against this answer let your temper rage
as wildly as you will.

OEDIPUS.

345   Indeed I am
so angry I shall not hold back a jot
of what I think. For I would have you know
I think you were complotter[22] of the deed
and doer of the deed save in so far
as for the actual killing. Had you had eyes
I would have said alone you murdered him.

TEIRESIAS.

350   Yes? Then I warn you faithfully to keep
the letter of your proclamation and
from this day forth to speak no word of greeting
to these nor me; you are the land's pollution.

OEDIPUS.

How shamelessly you started up this taunt!
355   How do you think you will escape?

TEIRESIAS.

                    I have.
I have escaped; the truth is what I cherish
and that's my strength.

---

22. **complotter** (kəm plät′ ər): Someone who plots against another person.

OEDIPUS.

               And who has taught you truth?
Not your profession surely!

TEIRESIAS.

                  You have taught me,
for you have made me speak against my will.

OEDIPUS.

Speak what? Tell me again that I may learn it better.

TEIRESIAS.

Did you not understand before or would you
360   provoke me into speaking?

OEDIPUS.

                   I did not grasp it,
not so to call it known. Say it again.

TEIRESIAS.

I say you are the murderer of the king
whose murderer you seek.

OEDIPUS.

                 Not twice you shall
say calumnies like this and stay unpunished.

TEIRESIAS.

Shall I say more to tempt your anger more?

OEDIPUS.

365   As much as you desire; it will be said
in vain.

TEIRESIAS.

             I say that with those you love best
you live in foulest shame unconsciously
and do not see where you are in calamity.

OEDIPUS.

Do you imagine you can always talk
like this, and live to laugh at it hereafter?

TEIRESIAS.

Yes, if the truth has anything of strength.

OEDIPUS.

370 It has, but not for you; it has no strength
for you because you are blind in mind and ears
as well as in your eyes.

TEIRESIAS.

You are a poor wretch
to taunt me with the very insults which
every one soon will heap upon yourself.

OEDIPUS.

Your life is one long night so that you cannot
375 hurt me or any other who sees the light.

TEIRESIAS.

It is not fate that I should be your ruin,
Apollo is enough; it is his care
to work this out.

OEDIPUS.

Was this your own design
or Creon's?

TEIRESIAS.

Creon is no hurt to you,
but you are to yourself.

OEDIPUS.

380 Wealth, sovereignty and skill outmatching skill
for the contrivance of an envied life!
Great store of jealousy fill your treasury chests,
385 if my friend Creon, friend from the first and loyal,
thus secretly attacks me, secretly
desires to drive me out and secretly
suborns this juggling, trick devising quack,
this wily beggar who has only eyes
for his own gains, but blindness in his skill.
390 For, tell me, where have you seen clear, Teiresias,
with your prophetic eyes? When the dark singer,
the sphinx, was in your country, did you speak
word of deliverance to its citizens?
And yet the riddle's answer was not the province
of a chance comer. It was a prophet's task
395 and plainly you had no such gift of prophecy
from birds[23] nor otherwise from any God

---

23. Birds: Seers sometimes interpreted the will of the gods by observing the flight of the birds.

to glean a word of knowledge. But I came,
Oedipus, who knew nothing, and I stopped her.
I solved the riddle by my wit alone.
Mine was no knowledge got from birds. And now
you would expel me,
400   because you think that you will find a place
by Creon's throne. I think you will be sorry,
both you and your accomplice, for your plot
to drive me out. And did I not regard you
as an old man, some suffering would have taught you
that what was in your heart was treason.

CHORUS.

We look at this man's words and yours, my king,
405   and we find both have spoken them in anger.
We need no angry words but only thought
how we may best hit the God's meaning for us.

TEIRESIAS.

If you are king, at least I have the right
no less to speak in my defense against you.
410   Of that much I am master. I am no slave
of yours, but Loxias',[24] and so I shall not
enroll myself with Creon for my patron.
Since you have taunted me with being blind,
here is my word for you.
You have your eyes but see not where you are
in sin, nor where you live, nor whom you live with.
415   Do you know who your parents are? Unknowing
you are an enemy to kith and kin
in death, beneath the earth, and in this life.
A deadly footed, double striking curse,
from father and mother both, shall drive you forth
out of this land, with darkness on your eyes,
that now have such straight vision. Shall there be

---

24. Loxias': Apollo is the god of prophecy.

420   a place will not be harbor to your cries,
        a corner of Cithaeron[25] will not ring
        in echo to your cries, soon, soon,—
        when you shall learn the secret of your marriage,
        which steered you to a haven in this house,—
        haven no haven, after lucky voyage?
        And of the multitude of other evils
        establishing a grim equality
425   between you and your children, you know nothing.
        So, muddy with contempt my words and Creon's!
        Misery shall grind no man as it will you.

---

25. Cithaeron: Mountain near Thebes where Oedipus was abandoned as an infant.

☑ Check Your Comprehension

1. What are three places, mentioned in the Priest's opening speech, where suppliants are stationed?

2. What are three instances, mentioned in the Priest's opening speech, in which a God is mentioned in connection with Oedipus?

3. How does Oedipus show his concern for the welfare of his people in his response to the priest (lines 58–77)?

4. What does the chorus pray for in its entrance ode?

5. What specific words of the chorus provide a key to the emotional tone of the scene between Teiresias and Oedipus (lines 404–406)?

6. (a) According to the words of the Priest in lines 35–40, how did Oedipus earn his reputation as the savior of Thebes? (b) Why does he twice give credit to the gods?

7. When Oedipus says to Teiresias "I solved the riddle by my wit alone" (line 399), in what important respect does he contradict what the priest said earlier about Oedipus and the Sphinx?

◆ Critical Thinking

1. Where in the play does Sophocles equate blindness with ignorance, and seeing with knowledge? **[Analyze]**

2. How has Oedipus' failure to "see" affected him in the past? How does "blindness" affect him in the early scenes of the play? **[Interpret]**

3. How does this failure to see relate to the play's theme or central insight about life? **[Infer]**

EVALUATE

4. Do you think that Oedipus deserves blame when he angrily refuses to believe that what Teiresias tells him is the truth and, instead accuses Teiresias of conspiracy? **[Make a Judgment]**

APPLY

5. Relate the blindness of Oedipus to an event in your own experience. (Suggestion: Think of a time when you angrily accused someone else of being "blind" only to discover that you were the "blind" one, after all.) **[Relate]**

$\mathscr{S}$ophocles
Drawing Conclusions About Sophocles Work

◆ Changes of Fortune and the Limitations of Human Knowledge

Popular tradition blamed ruin on excessive good Fortune, which often breeds **hubris**, insolence, and blindness to the possibility of ruin. Tragedy repeatedly reminds us that no mortal is immune from disaster and that to believe otherwise is to risk the displeasure of the gods.

Some critics believe that Sophocles influenced the work of his friend Herodotus, who was famous for applying dramatic conventions to history writing. Herodotus told the story of Croesus, the ancient king of Lydia. He was a fabulously wealthy man and boasted that he was the happiest man in the world. He did not heed the wisdom of Solon the Athenian, who told him "in every enterprise it profits us to consider well the end; for often the gods give men a glimpse of happiness and then plunges them into ruin." Soon after, he learned in a prophecy that his son was doomed to die by the blow of an iron weapon. He removed all weapons from his palace and kept his son out of battle. Despite these precautions, his son was fatally wounded by a spear in a hunting expedition. The man responsible for his death was the very man to whom Croesus had entrusted his son's welfare. Croesus next received an oracle telling him that if he crossed the river Halys he would destroy a great empire. He crossed the river and suffered defeat. It had not occurred to him that, by crossing the river, he would destroy his own empire! Croesus learned too late that happiness is a fragile condition and that his pride had been excessive.

What features do the tales of Croesus and Oedipus have in common?

Make a table with three columns to list general features that the stories have in common. Follow the example below:

Both are kings at height of fortune	Oedipus is King of Thebes	Croesus is King of Lydia

◆ Literary focus: Dramatic Irony

Dramatic Irony is what happens when the audience knows something that one or more of the characters on stage do not. The audience understands a meaning in actions or words that differs from what a character intends or understands. The audience at a Greek tragedy knew how the story was going to turn out. The dramatic interest does not turn on how the story ends but on the suspense created by the discrepancy between what the audience knows and what the characters know. A character unknowingly makes an assumption, in word or deed, that the audience knows to be false. Irony intensifies the sense that a catastrophe is unavoidable.

Main features of dramatic irony

- Significance of words or actions known by the audience
- Significance of words or situation not understood by the characters.
- Actions, words or situations have a meaning that differs from what a character intends or understands.

I. Turn back to the speech of Oedipus to the chorus (lines 58–77). How does Oedipus' claim to be more affected than his subjects by the sickness mean something different to us, who know that he is the cause of the plague? Why is this irony?

2. Explain the dramatic irony of Oedipus' claim in line 105, that he has never seen Laius.

3. Review the speech in which Oedipus condemns the murderer of Laius in lines 226–275. Find two specific examples of irony.

4. Consider the heated exchanges between Oedipus and Teiresias. In what sense is Oedipus blind and Teiresias seeing? In what ways do the insults about blindness establish an irony and reinforce a significant theme in the play?

◆ **Idea Bank**

Writing

1. **News Article** Imagine that there were newspapers in ancient Greece and write a lead a story for *Theban Daily Oracle*. Retell the events of the meeting between Teiresias and Oedipus. Create a headline. If you like, you may invent details that are not in the play. You may also quote from interviews with "eyewitnesses" that you have created. **[Career Link]**

Speaking and Listening

2. **Dramatic Dialogue** Write a behind-the-scenes conversation that you think might take place between two servants, one loyal to Creon and the other loyal to Oedipus.

3. **Tragedy Today** Write about someone in modern times that has experienced a reversal of fortune. Consider the factors that contributed to that reversal. Was the reversal deserved? Is the reversal tragic? Make a table like the one below, which lists the features of a tragic reversal, to help you decide whether the reversal is tragic.

Features of Tragic reversal	My example of a reversal
Person is prominent, successful, or envied.	John Q. Citizen, the mayor of Anytown, U.S.A., is admired by all because…
Everything is going well, person is at height of good fortune.	_____ _____

4. **Debate** Divide into two teams and debate this question: "Does Oedipus show signs of hubris." **[Group activity]**

Researching and Representing

5. **Choreograph an Ode** Choreograph the Choral ode in lines 151–215 and direct a performance. **[Performance; Physical education]**

◆ **Further Reading, Listening, and Viewing**

- Aeschylus: *The Seven Against Thebes*

- Peter D. Arnott: *Public and Performance in the Greek Theatre* (1989)

- R.J. Cootes and L.E. Snellgrove: *The Ancient World* (1991).

- Edith Hamilton: *The Greek Way* (1993)

- Lilian B. Lawler: *The Dance In Ancient Greece* (1964) with 62 illustrations.

- Sophocles, *Antigone, Oedipus At Colonus*

- Sophocles, *Oedipus Rex* (Corinth Films, 1980) performance of the play with masks, directed by Sir Tyrone Guthrie.

On the Web:

http://www.phschool.com/atschool/literature
Go to the student edition *Platinum*. Proceed to Unit 8. Then, click Hot Links to find Web sites on Sophocles.

Alfred, Lord Tennyson In Depth

> "No writer has ever dominated his age so completely as Tennyson dominated Victorian England; no poet has ever been so completely a national poet. His writing entered the consciousness of the age." —*Brian Southam*

ALFRED LORD TENNYSON, while still in college, was viewed as destined to become the greatest poet of the century. During his lifetime he was as famous as any film or rock star is today. Poet laureate of England for nearly half the nineteenth century, Tennyson "was the voice and sometimes…the conscience" of his age. Today he is considered one of the greatest English poets, admired for both his control of language and his ability to evoke a sense of longing and loss.

Born to Be a Poet Tennyson was born on August 6, 1809, in Somersby, Lincolnshire. His father, George, was a bitter, unstable man who took out his unhappiness on his wife and eleven children. Since George had been disinherited by his father, he was forced to become a minister, which added to his discontent.

Yet George was devoted to his children, particularly their education. Alfred was tutored at home by his father, who instilled a love of classical literature in his son, as well as encouraged Alfred's talents as a poet. By the age of fifteen, Tennyson had composed verse in the style of Alexander Pope, John Milton, and Sir Walter Scott. At seventeen, he and his older brothers published *Poems by Two Brothers* (1827), actually written by three Tennyson brothers.

College and Friendship That year, Tennyson entered Cambridge University and soon attracted a circle of admirers. His poem "Timbuctoo" won the Chancellor's Medal in the spring of 1829. That spring he also made the most important friend of his life: Arthur Hallam, who later became engaged to Tennyson's sister Emily. In the fall of 1829, the two friends were invited to join an elite intellectual student club, the Apostles. Hallam, in particular, encouraged him as a poet, and in June 1830, Tennyson's *Poems, Chiefly Lyrical,* which included "The Kraken" and "Mariana" was published.

In early 1831, Tennyson was forced to leave Cambridge after his father died. He returned home and, in 1832, *Poems,* which included "The Lady of Shalott," "The Lotos-Eaters," and "The Palace of Art" was published. The reviews were harsh.

A Devastating Blow In the fall of 1833, while Hallam was traveling in Europe, he died suddenly of a brain hemorrhage. Tennyson was devastated. For the next nine years, he refused to publish—although he poured his grief into such poems as "Ulysses," "Tithonus," "Break, Break, Break," and "Morte d'Arthur."

In 1836, Tennyson became romantically involved with Emily Sellwood. They were engaged the following year but broke it off in 1840, possibly because Tennyson feared he had inherited his father's mental instability and epilepsy.

In 1842, Tennyson finally ended his so-called "Years of Silence" with *Poems,* a two-volume collection that catapulted him to fame. After several years of depression, Tennyson published his first long work, *The Princess,* in 1847. This narrative poem examines a serious social issue: the proper role of women. Today the poem is appreciated mainly for the beautiful lyric songs embedded within the story, such as "Tears, Idle Tears," "Come Down, O Maid," and "The Splendor Falls."

Marriage and Acclaim In 1849, Tennyson resumed contact with Emily Sellwood, and they married in 1850, two weeks after the publication of *In Memorium*. In this vast poem, Tennyson collected the elegies for Hallam that he had written over the years and arranged them into "a spiritual biography," moving from abject grief to a "happy sense of God's purpose." The poem established Tennyson as the greatest living poet. That year Queen Victoria invited him to become the nation's poet laureate.

Soon Tennyson had two sons, a big house on the Isle of Wight, and a new sense of stability. Yet his next work, *Maud* (1855), was a strange poem whose themes of violence and insanity shocked many readers. In 1859, Tennyson regained his popularity with *Idylls of the King*, the first four of a series of twelve poems about King Arthur that he completed in 1888. Tennyson considered the story of Arthur "the greatest of all poetic subjects," symbolizing his own society's moral decay. His next major work, *Enoch Arden* (1864), made Tennyson rich, and so famous that his once-secluded house had become a tourist attraction.

The Highest Honor In 1883, Tennyson reluctantly accepted a peerage, making him the first poet ever to be made a noble. Tennyson continued to write and publish poems, including his famous "Crossing the Bar" (1889), until he died in 1892, at the age of eighty-three.

◆ Scientific Inquiry in the Victorian Age

The Victorian age in England (1837–1901) was a period of tremen-dous technological, economic, political, and social change, from the development of the railroad to the expansion of democracy. It was also a period of intense scientific inquiry and upheaval. Works like Charles Lyell's *Principles of Geology* (1830–1833), Robert Chambers's *Vestiges of Creation* (1844), John Herschel's *Outlines of Astronomy* (1849), and above all Charles Darwin's *Origin of Species* (1859) challenged established religious ideas.

Tennyson was keenly interested in science—particularly the question of science versus religion, one of the dominant themes of *In Memorium*. He read widely in the scientific literature, befriended many prominent scientists, and in 1869, helped form the Metaphysical Society, a group of intellectuals.

◆ Literary Works

Early Poetry *Poems by Two Brothers* (1827, with Charles and Frederick), *Timbuctoo* (1829), *Poems, Chiefly Lyrical* (1830), *Poems* (1832, dated 1833)

Middle Poetry *Poems*, 2 vols. (1842), *The Princess: A Medley* (1847), *In Memorium* (1850), *Ode on the Death of the Duke of Wellington* (1852), *Maud, and Other Poems* (1855)

Later Poetry *Idylls of the King* (1859), *Enoch Arden, etc.* (1864), *The Holy Grail and Other Poems* (1870), *Gareth and Lynette Etc.* (1872), *Ballads and Other Poems* (1880), *Tiresias and Other Poems* (1885), *Locksley Hall Sixty Years After, Etc.* (1886), *Demeter and Other Poems* (1889), *The Death of Oenone, Akbar's Dream, and Other Poems* (1892)

Plays *Queen Mary* (1875), *Harold* (1876, dated 1877), *Becket* (1884), *The Cup and The Falcon* (1884), *The Foresters, Robin Hood and Maid Marian* (1892)

TIMELINE

Tennyson's Life	
1809	Alfred Tennyson born August 6 in Somersby, Lincolnshire, England
1820–27	Educated at home by father
1827	*Poems by Two Brothers* published; enters Cambridge
1829	Wins Chancellor's Medal for poem "Timbuctoo"; befriends Arthur Hallam; joins Apostles
1830	*Poems, Chiefly Lyrical* published; Hallam falls in love with Tennyson's sister Emily; he, Hallam, and other friends help Spanish rebels
1831	Father dies; leaves Cambridge
1832	*Poems* published; brother Edward enters insane asylum
1833	Hallam dies
1847	*The Princess* published
1850	Marries Emily Sellwood; *In Memorium* published; becomes poet laureate
1852	Son Hallam born
1854	Son Lionel born
1855	*Maud* published
1859	*Idylls of the King* published
1864	*Enoch Arden* published
1865	Mother dies
1874–82	Writes several unsuccessful plays
1883–84	Accepts peerage; becomes a noble
1886	Son Lionel dies of "jungle fever"
1888	Completes King Arthur idylls
1889	Writes "Crossing the Bar"
1892	Dies October 6 at Aldworth

World Events	
1808	Beethoven completes Fifth Symphony
1814	Steam locomotive introduced
1815	Napoleon defeated at Waterloo
1819	John Keats's odes and Percy Bysshe Shelley's "Ode to the West Wind" published
1821–24	Keats, Shelley, and Byron die
1832	Reform Bill expands voting rights
1833	Telegraph invented; slavery abolished in British Empire
1837	Victoria becomes Queen
1839–42	Opium War
1843	Wordsworth named poet laureate
1845–47	Irish Potato Famine
1847	Charlotte Brontë's *Jane Eyre* and Emily Brontë's *Wuthering Heights* published
1848	Karl Marx and Friedrich Engels's *The Communist Manifesto* published
1850	Elizabeth Barrett Browning's *Sonnets from the Portuguese* published
1853–56	Crimean War between Britain and Ottoman Empire
1855	Walt Whitman's *Leaves of Grass* published
1859	Charles Darwin's *The Origin of Species* published
1861–65	U.S. Civil War
1867	Second Reform Act
1871–72	George Eliot's *Middlemarch* published
1874	First Impressionist art exhibition
1876	Alexander Graham Bell invents the telephone
1886	Anton Chekhov's first book of short stories published
1899	Sigmund Freud's *The Interpretation of Dreams* published
1901	Queen Victoria dies

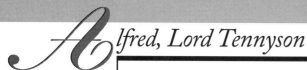

Alfred, Lord Tennyson

Tithonus[1]

The woods decay, the woods decay and fall,
The vapors weep their burthen[2] to the ground,
Man comes and tills the field and lies beneath,
And after many a summer dies the swan.[3]
5   Me only cruel immortality
Consumes; I wither slowly in thine arms,
Here at the quiet limit of the world,
A white-haired shadow roaming like a dream
The ever-silent spaces of the East,
10   Far-folded mists, and gleaming halls of morn.
     Alas! for this gray shadow, once a man—
So glorious in his beauty and thy choice,
Who madest him thy chosen, that he seemed
To his great heart none other than a God!
15   I asked thee, "Give me immortality."
Then didst thou grant mine asking with a smile,
Like wealthy men who care not how they give.
But thy strong hours indignant worked their wills,
And beat me down and marred and wasted me,
20   And though they could not end me, left me maimed
To dwell in presence of immortal youth,
Immortal age beside immortal youth,
And all I was in ashes. Can thy love,
Thy beauty, make amends, though even now,
25   Close over us, the silver star,[4] thy guide,
Shines in those tremulous eyes that fill with tears
To hear me? Let me go; take back thy gift.
Why should a man desire in any way
To vary from the kindly race of men,
30   Or pass beyond the goal of ordinance[5]
Where all should pause, as is most meet for all?
     A soft air fans the cloud apart; there comes
A glimpse of that dark world where I was born.

---

1. Tithonus (ti thō′ nəs): In Greek mythology, a handsome Trojan prince whom Aurora (Eos), the goddess of the dawn, fell in love with and brought to her palace. She asked Zeus to make Tithonus live forever, but she forgot to ask that he also remain young forever. He was eventually turned into a grasshopper. In Tennyson's poem, Tithonus is an old man, and he is addressing Eos.
2. burthen (bu′ th ən) *n.*: Burden (archaic form).
3. after many a summer dies the swan: Swans have a long life span.
4. the silver star: The morning star, which comes before the dawn.
5. ordinance (ôr d'n əns) *n.*: What is ordained as customary (in other words, mortality).

Once more the old mysterious glimmer steals

35 From thy pure brows, and from thy shoulders pure,
And bosom beating with a heart renewed.
Thy cheek begins to redden through the gloom,
Thy sweet eyes brighten slowly close to mine,
Ere yet they blind the stars, and the wild team[6]

40 Which love thee, yearning for thy yoke, arise,
And shake the darkness from their lossened manes,
And beat the twilight into flakes of fire.
       Lo! ever thus thou growest beautiful
In silence, then before thine answer given

45 Departest, and thy tears are on my cheek.
       Why wilt thou ever scare me with thy tears,
And make me tremble lest a saying learnt,
In days far-off, on that dark earth, be true?
"The Gods themselves cannot recall their gifts."

50   Ay me! Ay me! with what another heart
In days far-off, and with what other eyes
I used to watch—if I be he that watched—
The lucid outline forming round thee; saw
The dim curls kindle into sunny rings;

55 Changed with thy mystic change, and felt my blood
Glow with the glow that slowly crimsoned all
Thy presence and thy portals, while I lay,
Mouth, forehead, eyelids, growing dewy-warm
With kisses balmier than half-opening buds

60 Of April, and could hear the lips that kissed
Whispering I knew not what of wild and sweet,
Like that strange song I heard Apollo sing,
While Ilion[7] like a mist rose into towers.
       Yet hold me not forever in thine East;

65 How can my nature longer mix with thine?
Coldly thy rosy shadows bathe me, cold
Are all thy lights, and cold my wrinkled feet
Upon thy glimmering thresholds, when the steam
Floats up from those dim fields about the homes

70 Of happy men that have the power to die,
And grassy barrows of the happier dead.
Release me, and restore me to the ground.
Thou seest all things, thou wilt see my grave;
Thou wilt renew thy beauty morn by morn,

75 I earth in earth forget these empty courts,
And thee returning on thy silver wheels.

---

6. wild team: Team of horses that draws Eos' chariot across the sky at dawn.

7. Apollo . . . Ilion (ə päl′ ō; il′ ē ən): Apollo is the Greek god of music, poetry, and healing. The walls of Troy (Ilion) were supposedly built to the music of Apollo's lyre.

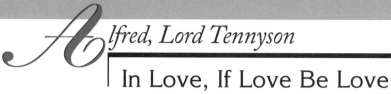

Alfred, Lord Tennyson

In Love, If Love Be Love

In love, if love be Love, if love be ours,
Faith and unfaith can ne'er be equal powers:
Unfaith in aught is want of faith in all.

It is the little rift within the lute,
5   That by and by will make the music mute,
And ever widening slowly silence all.

The little rift within the lover's lute
Or little pitted speck in garnered fruit,
That rotting inward slowly molders all.

10   It is not worth the keeping: let it go:
But shall it? Answer, darling, answer, no.
And trust me not at all or all in all.

☑ Check Your Comprehension

1. In "Tithonus," what does the speaker want? (Point out two lines in the poem where he directly makes this request.)

2. (a) Look at the images in the poem. What color does Tithonus associate with Eos (Aurora)? (b) What color does he associate with himself?

3. What two comparisons does the speaker make in "In Love, If Love Be Love"?

4. (a) What does the speaker of "In Love, If Love Be Love" want? (b) How would you paraphrase the speaker's argument? (To paraphrase something is to restate it in your own words.)

◆ Critical Thinking

INTERPRET

1. A paradox is a something that seems contradictory but actually presents a truth.

Why is the image in lines 65–66 of "Tithonus" a paradox? **[Analyze]**

2. (a) In "In Love, If Love Be Love," what does "it" refer to in lines 4 and 10? (b) How do you interpret the meaning of "shall it" in line 11? **[Interpret]**

3. Notice how many times the speaker of "In Love, If Love Be Love" uses the word "all." How does this repetition reinforce the poem's meaning? **[Analyze]**

APPLY

4. How would you react if someone made an argument (in everyday language) like the one the speaker is making in "In Love, If Love Be Love"? Why? **[Relate]**

5. In both of these poems, a speaker who is facing a problem is trying to persuade a lover to do or not to do something. Compare and contrast your responses to these two speakers. **[Compare; Contrast]**

Alfred, Lord Tennyson

The Splendor Falls

The splendor falls on castle walls
   And snowy summits old in story;
The long light shakes across the lakes,
   And the wild cataract[1] leaps in glory.
5   Blow, bugle, blow, set the wild echoes flying,
Blow, bugle; answer, echoes, dying, dying, dying.

0, hark, 0, hear! How thin and clear,
   And thinner, clearer, farther going!
0, sweet and far from cliff and scar[2]
10   The horns of Elfland faintly blowing!
Blow, let us hear the purple glens replying,
Blow, bugle; answer, echoes, dying, dying, dying.

0 love, they die in yon rich sky,
   They faint on hill or field or river;
15   Our echoes roll from soul to soul,
   And grow forever and forever.
Blow, bugle, blow, set the wild echoes flying,
And answer, echoes, answer, dying, dying, dying.

---

1. **cataract** (kat′ ə rakt) *n.*: Waterfall.
2. **scar** (skär) *n.*: Steep, rocky place or cliff.

Crossing the Bar[1]

Sunset and evening star,
    And one clear call for me!
And may there be no moaning of the bar,[2]
    When I put out to sea,

5   But such a tide as moving seems asleep,
    Too full for sound and foam,
When that which drew from out the boundless deep
    Turns again home.

Twilight and evening bell,
10   And after that the dark!
And may there be no sadness of farewell,
    When I embark;
For though from out our bourne[3] of Time and Place
    The flood may bear me far,
15   I hope to see my Pilot[4] face to face
    When 1 have crossed the bar.

---

1. Crossing the Bar: Written in 1889 while Tennyson was crossing the channel from the mainland to his home on the Isle of Wight. Before he died, he requested that the poem be placed "at the end of all editions" of his poetry. A bar is a sandbar, often found at the mouth of a harbor separating the shallower water from the open sea.

2. moaning of the bar: Literally, the sound of the ocean beating against the sandbar, or possibly the sound of a boat bottom scraping against the sandbar.

3. bourne (bôrn) *n.:* Boundary (archaic).

4. Pilot: A person who guides ships in or out of a harbor or through dangerous waters.

Alfred, Lord Tennyson

Break, Break, Break

Break, break, break,
    On thy cold gray stones, 0 Sea!
And I would that my tongue could utter
    The thoughts that arise in me.

5   O, well for the fisherman's boy,
    That he shouts with his sister at play!
0, well for the sailor lad,
    That he sings in his boat on the bay!

And the stately ships go on
10   To their haven under the hill;
But O for the touch of a vanished hand,
    And the sound of a voice that is still!

Break, break, break,
    At the foot of thy crags, 0 Sea!
15   But the tender grace of a day that is dead
    Will never come back to me.

Lines

Here often, when a child I lay reclined,
   I took delight in this locality.
Here stood the infant Ilion[1] of the mind,
   And here the Grecian ships did seem to be.
5   And here again I come, and only find
   The drain-cut levels of the marshy lea[2]—
Gray sea banks and pale sunsets—dreary wind,
Dim shores, dense rains, and heavy-clouded sea!

---

1. **Ilion** (il´ ē ən): Troy.
2. **lea** (lē) n.: Meadow, grassland.

☑ Check Your Comprehension

1. (a) Describe the setting in "The Splendor Falls." (b) What sounds does the speaker hear?
2. (a) In "Crossing the Bar," what does the speaker want in the first three stanzas? (b) What does the speaker hope for in the last stanza?
3. (a) In "Break, Break, Break," what is literally breaking on the stones? (b) In the last line, what "[w]ill never come back" to the speaker?
4. (a) In "Lines," what is the speaker doing? (b) How has his response to this setting changed since he was a child?

◆ Critical Thinking

INTERPRET

1. (a) In "The Splendor Falls," how do the **internal rhymes** (rhymes within, rather than at the end of, lines) reinforce the sounds and sights the speaker is describing? (b) In line 15, what do you think the speaker means by "our echoes"? **[Analyze]**
2. In "Crossing the Bar," what do you think the speaker is really talking about? In other words, what does the crossing symbolize, or represent? Who is the Pilot? **[Interpret]**
3. In "Break, Break, Break," how does the meter—the pattern of stressed and unstressed syllables—in line 1 (repeated in 13) reinforce the meaning of the words? **[Analyze]**
4. (a) How would you describe the speaker's mood in "Break, Break, Break"? (b) Why is breaking an apt word to use? **[Analyze; Interpret]**
5. In "Lines," why do you think the speaker's response to this setting has changed so dramatically? **[Speculate]**

COMPARE LITERARY WORKS

6. Compare and contrast the images of the sea in "Break, Break, Break" and "Crossing the Bar." **[Compare; Contrast]**

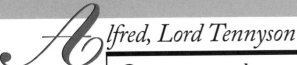

Alfred, Lord Tennyson

Correspondence With Queen Victoria

This introduction was written by the son of Alfred, Lord Tennyson.

These letters, which I have the Queen's gracious permission to publish, will, I am sure, be read with heartfelt interest: giving as they do fresh proof of Her majesty's deep sympathy with her subjects, and of my father's earnest and chivalrous devotion to her.

Father's letter to the Queen, accepting the Peerage.

Sept. 1883

MADAM,

I have learned from Mr. Gladstone[1] your Majesty's gracious intention[2] toward myself, and I ask to be allowed to express to your Majesty herself my grateful acknowledgments.

You, Madam, who are so full of sympathy for your subjects, will, I am sure, understand me when I say that the knowledge of your Majesty's approval of what I have been enabled to do, is, as far as I myself am concerned, all that I desire.

This public mark of your Majesty's esteem, which recognizes in my person the power of literature in this age of the world, cannot, however, fail to be gratifying to my nearest and dearest.

Believe me, dear Madam,

Your Majesty's loyal

and affectionate servant,

A. TENNYSON.

---

1. **Mr Gladstone:** William Gladstone, who was prime minister of Great Britain at the time.
2. **intention:** That is, to make him a peer, or baron (Lord Tennyson).

From the Queen

BALMORAL CASTLE,
Oct. 9th, 1883

DEAR MR TENNYSON,

I thank you sincerely for your two last kind letters.

It affords me much pleasure to confer on my Poet Laureate,[3] who is so universally admired and respected, a mark of my recognition of the great services he has rendered to literature, which has so great an influence on the world at large.

How I wish you could suggest means of crushing those horrible publications whose object is to promulgate scandal and calumny which they invent themselves!

Hoping to see you in the course of the next few months,

Believe me always yours most sincerely,

V. R. I.[4]

---

3. Poet Laureate (lôr′ ē it)**:** The official poet of Great Britain, appointed for life by the king or queen and called upon to write poems for national occasions, ceremonies, deaths of important people, and so on. Tennyson had become poet laureate in 1850, after William Wordsworth.

4. V. R. I.: Initials that stand for "Victoria Regina et Imperatrix," meaning "Victoria, Queen and Empress" (she had been given the title "Empress of India" in 1876).

The following lines on the Duke of Albany (who died in March 1884) were sent by my father to the Queen.

PRINCE LEOPOLD.[5]

An Epitaph.

Early-wise, and pure, and true,
Prince, whose Father lived in you,
If you could speak, would you not say:
"I seem, but am not, far away;
Wherefore should your eyes be dim?
I am here again with him.
O Mother-Queen, and weeping Wife,
The Death from which you mourn is Life."

---

5. Prince Leopold: In his capacity as poet laureate, Tennyson sent this poem to Queen Victoria following the death of her third and youngest son, Prince Leopold, the Duke of Albany. At the age of thirty, two years after his marriage, Leopold died of a burst blood vessel in his head (the same thing that killed Arthur Hallam).

From the Queen. (After the death of the Duke of Albany)

WINDSOR CASTLE

March 31st, 1884.

DEAR LORD TENNYSON,

I truly value your very kind words. My sorrows are many and great!

Almost all I needed most to lean on—and who helped and comforted—are taken from me! But tho' *all happiness* is at an end for me in *this* world, I am ready to fight on, praying that I may be supported in bearing my heavy cross—and in trying to be of use and help to this poor, dear young widow of my darling child, whose life, which was so bright and happy for barely two years, has been utterly crushed! But she bears it admirably, with the most gentle patience and courageous unmurmuring resignation.

All these terrible sorrows show us however, truly and really, that here is not our abiding home.

Still it is very hard to see such a young life, so full of talent, so gifted, and so useful, cut off so soon, and to feel that all the care and anxiety, which under Providence[6] enabled him to attain full manhood, was unavailing at last.

I am well, and while I live shall devote myself to the good of my dear Country, which has on all occasions of sorrow or joy, but especially the former, shown such sympathy with me!

Ever yours truly,

V. R. I.

---

6. **Providence** (präv´ ə dəns): God's guidance.

☑ Check Your Comprehension

1. Tennyson turned down the title of "Lord" twice before he finally accepted it in 1883. In his letter to Queen Victoria, Tennyson says that the Queen's "approval" is all that he, personally, desires. What, then, is his explanation for why he is willing to accept "[t]his public mark" of her esteem?

2. In her reply to Tennyson, what does Queen Victoria say is her reason for offering him the title?

◆ Critical Thinking

INTERPRET

1. (a) Tennyson was certainly well-acquainted with grief. How does his poem "Prince Leopold" (written in his official role as poet laureate) relate thematically to "Crossing the Bar?" (b) Do you think "Prince Leopold" is as good a poem as "Crossing the Bar"? Why or why not? **[Compare/Contrast]**

APPLY

2. In her October 9, 1883, letter to Tennyson, Queen Victoria refers to "the great services he has rendered to literature, which has so great an influence on the world at large." Do you think poets today, or writers in general, are viewed as having this kind of influence on the world? Explain your opinion. **[Relate]**

Alfred, Lord Tennyson
Comparing and Connecting the Author's Works

◆ Literary Focus: Musical Devices

Tennyson has always been much admired for his "ear"—his control over the musical qualities of poetic language. In particular, he is considered a master of the melodious effects of alliteration, assonance, and onomatopoeia.

Alliteration is the repetition of the first consonant sound in a series of words. For example, in "The Splendor Falls," notice the repetition of b sounds in the refrain of "Blow, bugle, blow."
Assonance is the repetition of similar vowel sounds. In "Break, Break, Break," notice the repeated long o sounds in "On thy cold gray stone, O Sea!" (line 2).
Onomatopoeia is the use of a word that sounds like what it means. The word moaning (line 3) in "Crossing the Bar" is onomatopoetic because the sound of the word resembles a real moan.

Tennyson is famous for using alliteration and assonance to create overall onomatopoetic effects. In this classic example from *The Princess*, the sounds themselves imitate what the poet is describing: "The moan of doves in immemorial elms, / And murmuring of innumerable bees."

1. (a) Point out several examples of alliteration and one example of assonance in "In Love, If Love Be Love." (b) What is the dominant sound in this poem?
2. (a) In stanzas 1 and 2 of "The Splendor Falls," what consonant sounds are alliterated? (b) In stanza 3, what repeated vowel sound do you hear?
3. Can you find an example of onomatopoeia in "The Splendor Falls"?
4. (a) What is the main sound repetition in "Lines"? (b) How does this sound reinforce the speaker's mood?
5. Find two examples of assonance in "Crossing the Bar."

◆ Drawing Conclusions About Tennyson's Work

One critic wrote the following comment on the effect of Arthur Hallam's death on Tennyson's work:

The memory of Hallam remained a haunting, obsessive presence for the remainder of Tennyson's life, a focal point for all his . . . feelings of yearning, desolation, and loss, the emotional experiences at the heart of his finest work.

—Brian Southam

Sometimes a poem's connection to grief is not that obvious. For example, according to another critic, "Tithonus" embodies Tennyson's *own sense of life's intolerable burden . . . . Tithonus . . . yearning for escape from a cruel immortality, represents the despair of continuing an existence now void of purpose.*

— Jerome Hamilton Buckley

In a brief essay, analyze one or more of the poems you have just read in light of these critical comments.

◆ Idea Bank

Writing

1. **Poem** Write a poem answering the speaker in "In Love, If Love Be Love." In your poem, try to use a metaphor—an imaginative comparison—to clarify your response or argument. Write from the point of view of the distrustful lover.
2. **Description** Many of Tennyson's speakers express a powerful emotional response to a particular landscape. Write a description of a setting that evokes strong feelings in you—either

positive or negative. Use images that describe how the setting sounds as well as how it looks.

3. **Compare and Contrast Poems** The speakers in "Tithonus," "Lines," and "Break, Break, Break" are all different from their former selves. Pick two of these poems and write an essay comparing and contrasting how each speaker's transformation reveals itself in the poem. Before you begin writing, use a chart like this one to organize your ideas.

Lines	Tithonus
Response to setting has changed	Has grown old and withered
"here again I come, and only find" (line 5)	"if I be he that watched" (line 54)

Speaking and Listening

4. **Oral Interpretation** Choose your favorite Tennyson poem, and read it aloud to the class. As you practice your reading, pay close attention to the poem's musical devices, such as rhyme, alliteration, and assonance. Also think about the poem's meter— its pattern of stressed and unstressed syllables—but try not to sound too mechanical or unnatural. **[Performing Arts Link]**

Researching and Representing

5. **Research Report** "In Love, If Love Be Love" is part of the "Merlin and Vivien" idyll in *Idylls of the King*. In it, Vivien speaks to Merlin after she has tricked him into revealing his magic. Research this Arthurian legend and present your findings to the class. (Does knowing the poem's context change your interpretation at all?) If

you prefer, research the Greek myth of Tithonus.

6. **Song** Many of Tennyson's poems have been set to music (see Further Reading, Listening, and Viewing). Listen to some of these works and then try composing your own song, using one of the poems as the lyrics. Record your song or perform it live for the class. **[Performing Arts Link]**

◆ Further Reading, Listening, and Viewing

- *Poems of Tennyson,* edited and introduced by Jerome H. Buckley (1958) An excellent selection

- Norman Page: *Tennyson: An Illustrated Life* (1992) A gracefully written biography full of photographs, drawings, manuscript pages, and other rich visual material

- *Scott, Tennyson & Kipling: The Heroic Tradition* (1976, 1998) Video including readings of "The Splendor Falls" and "Crossing the Bar"

- *Idylls of the King* (1967) Audiocassettes read by Basil Rathbone

- Richard Strauss: *Enoch Arden* (1999, 1994) CDs (two versions) of the composer's Op. 38, based on Tennyson's poem

- Benjamin Britten: *Serenade, Nocturne, Sinfonietta* (1992) CD of several compositions by Britten, including songs based on two Tennyson poems, "The Kraken" (Nocturne, Op. 60) and "Now Sleeps the Crimson Petal"

- *Princess Ida* (1982). Movie of the Gilbert and Sullivan opera based on Tennyson's *The Princess*

On the Web:

http://www.phschool.com/atschool/literature
Go to the student edition *Platinum*. Proceed to Unit 9. Then, click Hot Links to find Web sites featuring Tennyson.

Miguel de Cervantes In Depth

"Each man is the child of his own works."

—*Cervantes*

MIGUEL DE CERVANTES never experienced the rewards of his achievements during his lifetime. The disabled war hero returned home to poverty and unemployment. He wrote plays, poetry, and romances, but had to eke out a meager living as a tax collector.

Cervantes was nearly sixty when *Don Quixote* appeared in print. It was an immediate popular success, but it brought him neither a literary reputation nor financial security, and Cervantes died in poverty. Nevertheless, for nearly four hundred years *Don Quixote* has remained the most popular book in Spain, and, after the Bible, the most frequently published book in the world.

Youth Miguel de Cervantes, one of seven children of a poor barber-surgeon, was born September 29, 1547, in Alcalá de Henares, a small university town in the center of Spain. Cervantes did not receive much formal schooling, but he managed to acquire a good education in classical and Spanish literatures. When he was twenty-one, his verses commemorating the death of the queen, Isabel de Valois, were included in a book by the educator Lopez de Hoyos.

The Soldier A duel forced Cervantes to leave Spain in 1569. He went to Italy, where he joined a Spanish army regiment. The Muslim Turks of the Ottoman Empire had become a threat to the Christian countries in Eastern Europe.

In 1571, a fleet of ships sailed from Sicily to the Gulf of Patrai in Greece. There, in the naval battle of Lepanto on October 7, 1571, the forces of Christian Europe fought and defeated the Turks,

preventing the expansion of the Ottoman Empire into Europe. Cervantes was wounded three times, and permanently disabled his left arm, but he remained in the army for four more years. On his voyage home to Spain in 1575, Barbary pirates captured his ship and he was held as an enemy prisoner in Algiers for five years until finally he was ransomed.

Homecoming When Cervantes returned to Spain in 1580 at the age of thirty-three, the heroic soldier and defiant prisoner-of-war found his family poorer than before and himself unemployed. He scrambled for a living writing for the theater in Madrid. During this time he had an affair with an actress by whom he had his only child, a daughter, Isabel. In 1584, he married Catalina de Salazar from Esquivias in La Mancha.

Success In 1585 Cervantes' first book, *Galatea*, was published, a pastoral romance told in elegant prose and verse of refined countryfolk. This literary success did not greatly improve his financial status. Cervantes got a civil service job and traveled throughout Spain as a purchasing officer for the Spanish Armada, the huge fleet the Spanish were assembling to attack England.

The Armada was defeated in 1588, and Cervantes then became a tax collector. State employment did not necessarily mean regular pay. By 1590, Cervantes had not been paid for two years. He was so poor that he tried to get a job in the Spanish territories in the Americas, but failed. In 1597, irregularities in his tax records landed Cervantes in jail in Seville for four months. It is believed Cervantes began his masterpiece, *Don Quixote*, during this time.

The first part of *Don Quixote* was published in 1605 and was an immediate success all over Spain and across the Atlantic as well. Don Quixote and Sancho Panza became famous, but their creator did not profit from their popularity. In 1606 Cervantes abandoned itinerant life moved back to Madrid.

Cervantes continued to write. In 1613, *Exemplary Novels*, a collection of a dozen long short stories, and *Eight Plays and Eight Interludes* appeared. Every year brought forth a new work. Cervantes' comic verses were successful. *Voyage to Parnassus*, published in 1614, relates the misfortunes and sufferings of poets which Cervantes knew firsthand.

For ten years, since the publication of the first part of *Don Quixote*, Cervantes had been working on a sequel. So had Alonso Fernández de Avellaneda, who published his own version a few months before Cervantes finished his. Cervantes' fury drove him to finish and publish part two of *Don Quixote* in 1615.

Cervantes was sixty-nine and suffered from dropsy, a disease of the lymphatic system. In April of 1616, religious rites were performed, and Cervantes died on April 23. Too poor to afford a headstone, Cervantes was buried in an unmarked grave in the Trinitarian convent in Lope de Vega Street in Madrid.

◆ The Golden Age in Spain

The unification of Spain and retaking of the Muslim kingdom of Granada was accomplished by King Ferdinand of Aragon and Queen Isabella of Castile, in 1492, the same year Columbus discovered America for them. The marriage of their daughter Joanna to Archduke Philip of Austria eventually made their grandson Charles King of Spain and its territories in Italy, the Netherlands, and the New World, and Holy Roman Emperor in Eastern Europe. Spain was constantly at war to defend this empire, and the enormous treasure in silver that poured into Spain from America gushed out to pay for soldiers and warfare in Europe. Inflation climbed in Spain, and money lost three-quarters of its value between 1500 and 1600. The Spanish crown declared bankruptcy twice. Poverty created beggars, vagrants, and crime.

The literature of the Golden Age, like that of the contemporary Elizabethan period in England, boasted a profusion of lyric poets, both secular and religious. Theater, too, flourished along with prose fiction of various genres—the pastoral novel and the picaresque novel. All were surpassed by Cervantes' incomparable comedy *Don Quixote*, the crowning achievement of Spanish literature.

◆ Literary Works

Cervantes' romances and drama found favor in his day, but are a type of stylized literature which no longer appeals to the general public.

Galatea (1585)
Voyage to Parnassus (1614)
Eight Plays and Eight Interludes (1616)
The Trial of Persiles and Sigismunda (1617; published posthumously)

His Greatest Works Cervantes' *Don Quixote* and *Exemplary Novels* are the works that hold our interest today. In these the wildly imaginative element is joined to a realistic view of life.

Don Quixote, Part One (1605);
Part Two (1615);
Exemplary Novels (1613)

TIMELINE

Cervantes' Life

1547	Miguel de Cervantes Saavedra is born on September 29 at Alcalá de Henares
1568	Verses on the death of Queen Isabel published
1571	Wounded at Battle of Lepanto; left arm and hand permanently disabled
1575	Honorable discharge from the army; captured by Barbary pirates and held for ransom in Algiers
1580	Ransomed by Trinitarian friars; returns to Spain; writes for the theater in Madrid
1584	Marries Catalina de Salazar from Esquivias in La Mancha
1585	Pastoral romance *Galatea* published; begins career as a civil servant
1597	Jailed in Seville
1605	Part One of *Don Quixote* published
1606	Moves to Madrid
1613	*Exemplary Novels* published
1614	*Voyage to Parnassus* published
1615	Part Two of *Don Quixote* appears
1616	*Eight Plays and Eight Interludes*
1616	Dies of dropsy in Madrid on April 23
1617	*The Trials of Persiles and Sigismunda* is published posthumously

World Events

1550	Spain at the height of political and economic power
1554	Mary I of England marries Philip of Spain, novel *Lazarillo de Tormes* appears
1555	Tobacco brought from America to Spain
1556	Emperor Charles V abdicates; his son Philip becomes King of Spain; his brother Ferdinand becomes Holy Roman Emperor
1559	Elizabeth I crowned Queen of England; *La Diana*, by Jorge de Montemayor published
1564	Spanish occupy the Philippines and build Manilla; William Shakespeare born in England
1568	First public theater presentation in Madrid
1572	Dutch begin War of Independence against Spain.
1574	Spain loses Tunis to Turks
1582	Gregorian Calendar adopted
1585	Shakespeare leaves Stratford for London
1588	Spanish Armada defeated by English
1590	Shakespeare's *Henry VI*, Parts 2, 3 performed
1597	Second Spanish Armada destroyed in a storm
1598	Philip III becomes king
1599	Globe theater built in London
1600	Hamlet performed
1604	Peace between England and Spain; Lope de Vega's *Comedias* are published in twenty-five volumes
1608	Galileo constructs telescope
1614	Part two of *Don Quixote* by Alonso Fernandez de Avellaneda appears; Spanish painter El Greco dies
1615	Galileo faces the Inquisition
1616	Shakespeare dies on April 23

Miguel de Cervantes

Prologue to Part I from Don Quixote
translated by J. M. Cohen

Idle reader, you can believe without any oath of mine that I would wish this book, as the child of my brain, to be the most beautiful, the liveliest and the cleverest imaginable. But I have been unable to transgress the order of nature, by which like gives birth to like. And so, what could my sterile and ill-cultivated genius beget but the story of a lean, shriveled, whimsical child, full of varied fancies that no one else has ever imagined—much like one engendered in prison, where every discomfort has its seat and every dismal sound its habitation? Calm, a quiet place, the pleasantness of the fields, the serenity of the skies, the murmuring of streams and the tranquility of the spirit, play a great part in making the most barren muses bear fruit and offer to the world a progeny to fill it with wonder and delight. It may happen that a father has an ugly and ill-favored child, and that his love for it so blinds his eyes that he cannot see its faults, but takes them rather for talents and beauties, and describes them to his friends as wit and elegance. But I, though in appearance Don Quixote's father, am really his step-father, and so will not drift with the current of custom, nor implore you, almost with tears in my eyes, as others do, dearest reader, to pardon or ignore the faults you see in this child of mine. For you are no relation or friend of his. Your soul is in your own body, and you have free will with the best of them, and are as much a lord in your own house as the King is over his taxes. For you know the old saying: under my cloak a fig for the king—all of which exempts and frees you from every respect and obligation; and so you can say anything you think fit about this story, without fear of being abused for a bad opinion, or rewarded for a good one.

I would have wished to present it to you naked and unadorned, without the ornament of a prologue or the countless train of customary sonnets, epigrams and eulogies it is the fashion to place at the beginnings of books. For I can tell you that, much toil though it cost me to compose, I found none greater than the making of this preface you are reading. Many times I took up my pen to write it, and many times I put it down, not knowing what to say. And once when I was in this quandary, with the paper before me, my pen in my ear, my elbow on the desk and my hand on my cheek, thinking what to write, a lively and very intelligent friend of mine came in unexpectedly and, seeing me so deep in thought, asked me the reason. I did not conceal it, but said that I was thinking about the prologue I had to make for the history of Don Quixote, and that it so troubled me that I was inclined not to write one, and even not to publish the exploits of that noble knight; "For how could you expect me not to be worried," I went on, "at what that ancient lawgiver they call the public will say when it sees me now, after all these years I have been sleeping in the silence of oblivion, come out with all my years on my back, with a tale as dry as a rush, barren of invention, devoid of style, poor in wit and lacking in all learning and instruction, without quotations in the margins or notes at the end of the book; whereas I see other works, never mind how fabulous and profane, so full of sentences from Aristotle, Plato and the whole herd of philosophers, as to impress their readers and get their authors a reputation for wide reading, erudition and eloquence? And when they quote Holy Scripture! You will be bound to say that they are so many St. Thomases[1] or other doctors of the church, observing such an ingenious solemnity in it all that in one line they will depict a distracted lover and in the next preach a little Christian homily, that is a treat and a pleasure to hear or read. My book will lack all this; for I have nothing to quote in the margin or to note at the end. Nor do I even know what authors I am following in it; and so I cannot set their names at the beginning in alphabetical order, as they all do, starting with Aristotle and ending with Xenophon—and Zoilus or Zeuxis, although one of them was a libeler and the other a painter. My book must go without introductory sonnets as well—or at least sonnets, by dukes, marquises, counts, bishops, great ladies or famous poets; although were I to ask two or three friends in the trade, I know that they would give me them; and such good ones as would be unequalled by the productions of the most highly renowned poets in this Spain of ours. In fact, my dear friend," I continued, "I have decided that Don Quixote shall stay buried in the archives of La Mancha till Heaven provides someone to adorn him with all the jewels he lacks; for I find myself incapable of supplying them because of my inadequacy and scanty learning, and because I am too spiritless and lazy by nature to go about looking for authors to say for me what I can say myself without them. That is the cause of the perplexity and abstraction you found me in, for there is reason enough for my mood in what I have just told you."

When my friend had heard me to the end he slapped his forehead and broke into a loud laugh, saying: "Good Lord, brother, you have just relieved my mind of an error I have been in ever since I have known you, for I have always thought you were sensible and judicious in all your actions. But I see now that you are as far from being so as the sky is from the earth. How is it possible for matters of so little importance and so easily put right to have the power to perplex and preoccupy as ripe an intelligence as yours, so

---

1. **St. Thomases:** St. Thomas Aquinas (1225–1274), medieval scholar and philosopher, author of the *Summa Theologica*.

fitted to break down even greater difficulties and trample them underfoot? This does not spring from any lack of ability, I promise you, but from excess of laziness and poverty of resource. Would you like to be convinced that what I say is true? Then listen to me and you will see me confute all your difficulties in the twinkling of an eye, and set right all the defects which, you say, perplex and frighten you into giving up the publication of the history of your famous Don Quixote, light and mirror of all knight errantry."

"Tell me," I replied. "By what means do you propose to fill the void of my fear and reduce the chaos of my confusion to clarity?"

"Your first stumbling block," he replied, "the sonnets, epigrams and eulogies which you lack for your introduction, and which should be by important and titled persons, can be got over by I taking a little trouble and writing them yourself. . . ."

"As to quoting in the margins the books and authors from whom you gathered the sentences and sayings you have put in your history, all you have to do is to work in some pat phrases or bits of Latin that you know by heart, or at least that cost you small pains to look out. . . ."

"With these little bits of Latin and such like, they may even take you for a scholar; and it is no small honor and profit to be one nowadays. As to putting notes at the end of the book, you may safely follow this method: if you mention a giant in the text, see that it is the giant Goliath. And by that alone, which will cost you almost nothing, you have a grand note, since you can write: *The giant Goliath or Golias was a Philistine, whom the shepherd David killed with a sling-shot in the Vale of Terebinth, as is recounted in the Book of Kings*—whatever chapter you find it is. After that, to show that you are learned in the humanities and in cosmography, contrive to work some mention of the river Tagus into your story, and you will find yourself at once with another famous note: *The river Tagus was so called by a king of Spain; it has its source in such a place and flows into the Ocean, kissing the walls of the famous City of Lisbon. It is reported to have sands of gold etc. . . .*

"Let us come now to references to authors, which other books contain and yours lacks. The remedy for that is very simple; for you have nothing else to do but look for a book which quotes them all from A to Z, as you say. Then you put this same alphabet into yours. For, granted that the very small need you have to employ them will make your deception transparent, it does not matter a bit; and perhaps there will even be someone silly enough to believe that you have made use of them all in your simple and straightforward story. And if it serves for no other purpose, at least that long catalogue of authors will be useful to lend authority to your book at the outset. Besides, nobody will take the trouble to examine whether you follow your authorities or not, having nothing to gain by it. What is more, if I understand you rightly, this book has no need of any of the things that you say it lacks, for the whole of it is an invective against books of chivalry, which Aristotle never dreamed of, Saint Basil never mentioned, and Cicero never ran across. Nor do the niceties of truth or the calculations of astrology come within the scope of its fabulous narrative; nor is it concerned with geometrical measurements; nor with arguments which can be confuted by rhetoric; nor does it set out to preach to anyone. . . . In what you are writing you have only to make use of imitation, and the more perfect the imitation the better your writing will be. And since this book of yours aims at no more than destroying the authority and influence which books of chivalry have in the world and among the common people, you have no reason to go begging sentences from philosophers, counsel from Holy Writ, fables from poets, speeches from orators, or miracles from saints. You have only to see that your sentences shall come out plain, in expressive, sober and well-ordered language, harmonious and gay, expressing your purpose to the best of your ability, and setting out your ideas without intricacies and obscurities. Be careful too that the reading of your story makes the melancholy laugh and the merry laugh louder; that the simpleton is not confused; that the intelligent admire your invention, the serious do not despise it, nor the prudent withhold their praise. In short, keep your aim steadily fixed on overthrowing the ill-based fabric of these books of chivalry, abhorred by so many yet praised by so many more; for if you achieve that, you will have achieved no small thing."

I listened in complete silence to my friend's words, and his arguments so impressed themselves on my mind that I accepted them as good without question, and out of them set about framing my prologue. By which, kind reader, you will see his wisdom, and my own good fortune in finding such a counselor in a time of such need; and yourself be relieved at the straightforward and uncomplicated nature of the history of the famous Don Quixote de la Mancha; who, in the opinion of all the inhabitants of the district around the plain of Montiel, was the chastest lover and the most valiant knight seen in those parts for many a year. I do not want to exaggerate the service I am doing you by introducing to you so notable and honored a knight. But I do want your thanks for making you acquainted with the famous Sancho Panza, his squire, in whom I think I present to you an epitome of all those squirely humors scattered through the swarm of vain books of chivalry.

And so, God give you health, and may He not forget me.

Farewell.

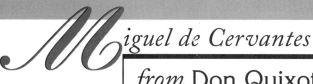

Miguel de Cervantes

from Don Quixote, Part II

translated by J. M. Cohen

Chapter XXIX. *Of the Famous Adventure of the Enchanted Boat.*

Two days, by their reckoning, after they left the poplar grove Don Quixote and Sancho came to the river Ebro, the sight of which was a great delight to Don Quixote, as he contemplated and gazed upon the charms of its shores, the clearness of its waters, the smoothness of its stream, and the abundance of its liquid crystal. In fact this cheering sight recalled a thousand amorous thoughts to his mind. . . . Well, as they were riding along in this way, there hove in sight a little boat without oars or any sort of gear, made fast to the trunk of a tree which grew on the bank. Don Quixote looked in all directions, but could see no one. So without more ado he dismounted from Rocinante, and bade Sancho get down from Dapple and tie the two beasts close together to the trunk of a poplar or willow growing there. And on Sancho's enquiring the reason for this sudden dismounting and tethering, Don Quixote answered:

"I must tell you, Sancho, that this boat, deliberately and beyond all possibility of error, summons me to embark, and travel in it to succor some knight or other person of rank in distress; and he must be in very great trouble. For this, as we read in histories of chivalry, is the practice of the enchanters whose actions and speeches they describe. When a knight is placed in some peril from which he can only be delivered by the hand of another knight, though they may be six or eight thousand, or even more, miles apart, they either snatch the second knight up in a cloud or provide him with a boat to board, and in less than the twinkling of an eye, they take him, through the air or over the sea, where they will and where his aid is needed. So, Sancho, this boat is put here for that very purpose, and that is as true as it is now day. But, before this happens, tie Dapple and Rocinante together, and may God's hand guide us, for I would not fail to embark were barefoot friars to entreat me."

"Well, as it's like that," replied Sancho, "and your worship will run at every step into these follies—I don't know what else to call them—there's nothing for it but to obey and bow my head, according to the proverb: Do what your master orders and sit down with him at his table. But for all that, for my conscience's sake I must warn your worship, that I don't think this said boat belongs to any of your enchanted folk, but to some fishermen of this river, for they catch the best shad[1] in the world here."

This Sancho said as he was tying up the beasts, leaving them to the care and protection of the enchanters. with great grief in his heart. But Don Quixote bade him not to worry about abandoning the animals, for He who was to lead them through such longinquous ways and regions would take care to provide for them.

"I don't understand this logiquous of yours," said Sancho. "I have never heard such a word in all the days of my life."

"*Longinquous*," replied Don Quixote, "means remote; and, it is wonder you do not understand it, for you are not obliged to know Latin, like some who claim to know it and do not."

"Now they're tied up," said Sancho, "what have we to do next?"

"What?" answered Don Quixote, "Cross ourselves and weigh anchor. I mean embark and cut the ropes by which this boat is fastened." Then, jumping in, with Sancho after him, he cut the boat adrift, and it was carried little by little from the bank. When Sancho found himself some two yards off shore he began to tremble, fearing that he was lost; and nothing caused him more pain than to hear Dapple braying and to see Rocinante struggling to break loose.

"The ass is braying," he said to his master, "for grief at being deserted, and Rocinantes trying to get free to rush after us. 0 my dearest friends, stay there in peace, and may the madness that takes us from you turn to disappointment and bring us back to your company!"

At this he began to weep so bitterly that Don Quixote asked peevishly and testily: "What are you afraid of, cowardly beast? What are you weeping at, butter-heart? Who is pursuing you or harassing you, soul of a town mouse? What do you lack, always in need amidst the bowels of abundance? Are you perchance traveling barefoot over the Riphaean mountains? No, you are sitting on a bench, like an archduke, on the calm current of this delightful river, from which we shall emerge in a short while into the wide sea. But we must have come out already and have traveled at least two thousand miles—or more. If I had only an astrolabe[2] here with which I could take the height of the pole, I would tell you how far we have gone; though if I know anything we have passed, or soon shall pass, the equinoctial[3] line which divides and cuts the opposing poles at equal distance."

1. **shad:** A type of fish.
2. **astrolabe:** An instrument to measure the altitude of the sun or other heavenly bodies used in navigation.
3. **equinoctial:** The celestial equator.

"And when we get to this noxious[4] line your worship speaks of," asked Sancho, "how far shall we have gone?"

"A long way," replied Don Quixote, "for we shall have covered the half of the three hundred and sixty degrees of earth and water the globe contains according to the computation of Ptolemy, who was the best cosmographer[5] known, when we come to the line I mentioned."

"By God," said Sancho, "but your worship has got me a pretty fellow for a witness of what you say, this same Tolmy or whatever you call him, with his amputation."

Don Quixote burst out laughing at the interpretation Sancho had on the name, the computation and the reckoning of the cosmographer Ptolemy, and said:,

"You must learn, Sancho, that according to the Spaniards and those who embark at Cadiz to go to the East Indies, one of the signs by which they know that they have passed the equinoctial line I mentioned is that the lice die on everyone aboard ship. Not one remains alive, and you could not find one in the whole vessel if you were to be paid its weight in gold. So, you might pass a hand over your thigh; if you catch anything living, we shall have no doubts on that score; and if not, then we have passed."

"I don't believe a word of that," answered Sancho, "but I'll do what your worship orders all the same, though I don't know why we need to make these experiments, for I can see with my own eyes that we haven't moved more than five yards from the bank. We haven't drawn two yards off from where the animals are, for there are Rocinante and Dapple in the very place we left them; and, taking our bearings as I do now, I swear we aren't stirring or moving at an ant's pace."

"Make the investigation I asked of you, Sancho, and do not worry about any others, for you know nothing about the colures, lines, parallels, zodiacs, ecliptics, poles, solstices, equinoxes, planets, signs of the zodiac and points, which are the measures of which the celestial and terrestrial spheres are composed. But if you had that knowledge, or part of it, you would clearly see how many parallels we have cut, how many signs seen, and what constellations we have left behind and are now leaving. Once more I ask you, feel and fish, for I believe you are as clean as a sheet of smooth white paper."

Sancho felt himself and, reaching his hand gently and cautiously behind his left knee, raised his head and looked at his master, saying: "Either the test's false or we haven't got where your worship says, not by many a long mile."

---

4. **noxious:** Harmful.
5. **cosmographer:** A person who describes the universe; Ptolemy, a second-century Greek, described a system in which the sun and planets revolved around the earth.

"Well, why?" asked Don Quixote. "Have you found anything?"

"More than somewhat," answered Sancho. And shaking his fingers he washed his whole hand in the river, down which the boat was softly gliding in midstream, without any occult[6] intelligence to move it or any hidden enchanter, but only the current of the water, which was calm there and smooth.

At that moment they caught sight of two great watermills in the middle of the river, and no sooner did Don Quixote view them than he exclaimed to Sancho in a loud voice: "Do you see? There, my friend, stands the city, castle, or fortress. In it must lie the persecuted knight, or the Queen or Princess in distress, for whose succor I have been brought here."

"What the devil does your worship mean by city, fortress, or castle?" asked Sancho. "Can't you see that those buildings in the river are watermills, where they grind the corn?"

"Hush, Sancho!" said Don Quixote. "They may seem to be watermills, but they are not. I have already told you that spells transform all things and change them from their natural shapes. I do not mean that they actually change them, but they appear to, as we learnt by experience in the transformation of Dulcinea,[7] sole refuge of my hopes."

By this time the boat had got into the middle of the stream and had begun to travel rather less slowly than before. And when the millers saw it drifting down the river and on the point of being dragged under by the millstream, a number of them rushed hurriedly out with long poles to stop it. And when they came, all floury, with their faces and clothes covered with meal, they presented an ugly appearance, as they shouted out: "Where are you going, you devils? Are you out of your senses? What are you after? Do you want to drown or be dashed to pieces on these wheels?"

"Did I not tell you, Sancho," exclaimed Don Quixote at this, "that we had reached a place where I have to show the strength of my arm? Look what scoundrelly villians have come out to encounter me! Look what fiends are opposing me! Look at those ugly faces grimacing at us! Now then, you shall see, rogues!"

And standing up in the boat he began to threaten the millers, crying out loudly: "Ugly and ill-advised rabble, set free and deliver him whom you keep under duress in this fortress or prison of yours, be he of high or low or of whatever degree! For I am Don Quixote de la Mancha, otherwise called *the Knight of the Lions,* for whom by Heaven's high destiny the happy accomplishment of this adventure is reserved."

---

6. **occult:** Supernatural.
7. **the transformation of Dulcinea:** Dulcinea is Don Quixote's imaginary girl-friend; previously Sancho Panza introduced a peasant girl to Don Quixote as Dulcinea, but Don Quixote saw only a peasant girl, not his ideal beloved, and assumed that his lady had been transformed by a magician.

As he spoke he grasped his sword and began to make passes in the air against the millers who, hearing but not understanding these ravings, wielded their poles to stop the boat, which was now entering into the rapids of the millrace.[8] Sancho went down on his knees, devoutly praying Heaven to rescue him from his imminent peril, which it did, thanks to the prompt efforts of the millers, who planted their poles against the boat and stopped it, but not so skillfully as to prevent its overturning and throwing Don Quixote and Sancho head over heels into the water. Fortunately for the knight, he could swim like a duck, though the weight of his armor took him twice to the bottom; and if it had not been for the millers, who plunged into the water and dragged them both out bodily, it would have been good-bye to the pair of them. Then, when they were brought to land, drenched and far from dying of thirst, Sancho went down on his knees and, with hands joined and eyes fixed to Heaven, implored God in a long and devout prayer to deliver him from all his master's rash plans and enterprises in future.

By this time the fishermen had arrived, who owned the boat, which had been broken to pieces by the millwheels; and when they saw it smashed, they set about stripping Sancho and demanding payment of Don Quixote, who told the millers and the fishermen very calmly, as if nothing had happened, that he would pay for the boat with the best will in the world, providing they would set free the person or persons who were oppressed in that castle, without ransom.

"What persons and what castle are you talking of, madman?" asked one of the millers. "Can it be the people who come to this mill to have their corn ground that you want to carry off?"

"Enough," said Don Quixote to himself. "It would be preaching in the wilderness to try and induce this rabble by prayers to do any virtuous act. Two powerful enchanters must have met in opposition in this adventure, the one frustrating the other's designs. One provided me with the boat, and the other threw me out. God help us, but this whole world is tricks and devices, one against the other. I can do no more." And raising his voice, he went on, gazing all the while at the watermills: "Friends, whoever you are, who lie locked up in this prison, pardon me. For unfortunately for myself and for you, I cannot deliver you from your affliction. This adventure must remain reserved for another knight."

Saying this, he compounded with the fishermen and paid them fifty *reals*[9] for the boat, and Sancho handed the money over with very ill grace, saying:

---

8. millrace: The stream that diverts water in a river towards the water wheel of a mill.

9. *real*: (rā äl′) Spanish silver coin.

"Two boat trips like this will sink our whole fortune to the bottom."

The fishermen and the millers gazed in astonishment at those two figures, so unlike other men, and were quite unable to make out what Don Quixote was driving at. But, concluding that both knight and squire were mad, they left them, the millers returning to their mill and the fishermen to their huts. Don Quixote and Sancho went back to their beasts, and to their beast-like existence; and such was the end of the adventure of the enchanted boat.

Chapter XXX. *Don Quixote's Meeting With a Fair Huntress.*

Knight and squire were sufficiently depressed and out of humor when they reached their animals—especially Sancho. Indeed it grieved him to the soul to have touched their stock of money, for with every penny taken he seemed to be robbed of his very eyeballs. At length they mounted in silence and left the famous river, Don Quixote deep in thoughts of his love, and Sancho of his preferment,[10] which at that time seemed to him very far from his grasp. For, fool though he was, he was well enough aware that all, or most, of the knight's actions were extravagant, and he was looking for an opportunity of escaping and going home without entering into any reckonings or farewells with his master. But Fortune was kinder to him than he had feared.

It fell out, then, that the next day at sunset, as they were emerging from a wood, Don Quixote cast his eyes about a green meadow, and saw some people on the farther side, whom, when he drew near, he recognized to be a hawking party. He rode closer, and saw among them a gallant lady on a palfrey or milk-white hack[11] decked with green trappings and with a silver sidesaddle. The lady herself was in green, so bravely and richly attired that she looked the very soul of bravery. On her left wrist she bore a hawk, from which Don Quixote concluded that she was a great lady, and probably the mistress of all the hunters, as was the fact; and so he said to Sancho:

"Run, Sancho my son, and tell that lady with a hawk on the palfrey that I, the *Knight of the Lions,* salute her great beauty, and that if Her Magnificence gives me leave, I will go and kiss her hands, and serve her to the uttermost of my strength in all that her Highness may command me. And mind, Sancho, how you speak. Take care not to mix any of your proverbs into your embassage.[12]

---

10. **preferment:** Promotion, advancement.
11. **palfrey or milk-white hack:** A lady's riding horse.
12. **embassage:** The mission of an ambassador.

"What sort of mixer do you take me for!" answered Sancho. "To tell me that! As if this was the first time in my life I've taken messages to high and mighty ladies."

"Except for the one you took to the lady Dulcinea," replied Don Quixote, "I do not know of any you have ever carried, at least in my service."

"That's right," answered Sancho, "but a good paymaster doesn't worry about sureties, and in a well-stocked house the supper's soon cooked. I mean that there's no need to tell me anything or give me any sort of advice, for I'm ready for anything and I can manage a bit of everything."

"Indeed I believe you,' said Don Quixote. "Go then and God guide you!"

Sancho went off at a trot, urging Dapple out of his usual pace and, coming up to the fair huntress, dismounted and went down on his knees before her, saying: "Beautiful lady, that knight you see yonder, the *Knight of the Lions* by name, is my master, and I am one of his squires, called at home Sancho Panza. This same *Knight of the Lions*, who was known not long ago as the *Knight of the Sad Countenance*,[13] sends by me to ask for your Highness's permission to come, with your approval, goodwill and consent, and put his desire into effect; which is no other, as he says and I confirm, than to serve your lofty haughtiness and beauty. In giving your permission your ladyship will be doing something which will redound[14] to your fame, and he will receive a most signal favor and happiness."

"Indeed, good squire," answered the lady, "you have delivered your message with all the ceremony that such messages demand. Rise from the ground; for it is not right for the squire of so great a knight as he of the *Sad Countenance,* of whom we have already heard a great deal here, to remain on his knees. Rise, friend, and tell your master that he is most welcome to come and serve me and the Duke my husband, in a country house of ours near here."

Sancho got up, impressed alike by the great lady's beauty and by her good breeding and courtesy, but even more so by her saying that she had knowledge of his master, the *Knight of the Sad Countenance*—and if she did not call him the *Knight of the Lions* it could only be owing to his having taken the name so recently. The Duchess—whose title is unknown—then asked him:

"Tell me, brother squire, about this master of yours. Is he not one about whom a history has been printed called *The Ingenious Gentleman Don Quixote de la Mancha,* and has he not for the lady of his heart a certain Dulcinea del Toboso?"

---

13. **countenance:** Appearance, facial expression.
14. **redound:** Have an effect on; contribute to.

"That's the man, my lady," answered Sancho, "and his squire, Sancho Panza by name, who is, or should be in that history, is myself, unless I was changed in my cradle—I mean changed in the press."

"All this is most delightful," said the Duchess. "Go, brother Panza, and tell your master that he is heartily welcome on my estates, and that nothing would give me greater pleasure than his visit."

Sancho returned to his master, overjoyed at this most agreeable answer, and repeated all that the fine lady had said to him, lauding her great beauty, her charm and her courtesy to the skies in his country language. Don Quixote preened himself in his saddle, set his feet firmly in the stirrups, adjusted his visor, gave the spur to Rocinante, and advanced with a graceful bearing to kiss the Duchess's hands. And she meanwhile called the Duke, her husband, and repeated the whole of Sancho's message to him while Don Quixote was on the way. The pair of them had read the first part of this history, and consequently knew of Don Quixote's extravagances. So they awaited him with the greatest delight and were most anxious to make his acquaintance, their intention being to fall in with his whimsies, to agree with him in all he said, and to treat him like a knight errant for so long as he would stay with them, observing toward him all the ceremonies usual in books of knight errantry, which they had read and were very fond of.

Now Don Quixote rode up with his visor raised and made as if to dismount, whereat Sancho hurried to hold his stirrup. But the squire was so unlucky as to catch one foot on a cord of the pack-saddle as he was dismounting from Dapple, and was unable to disentangle himself; so that he remained dangling, with his face and his chest on the ground. Don Quixote was not accustomed to dismounting without someone to hold his stirrup, and thinking that Sancho had already caught hold of it, threw his body off with a jerk, carrying Rocinante's saddle, which must have been badly girthed,[15] after him, so that he and the saddle fell to the ground together, to his no small discomfiture,[16] and to the accompaniment of a volley of curses which he uttered between his teeth at the unfortunate Sancho, who still had his foot in the noose. The Duke ordered his huntsmen to go to the assistance of the knight and the squire, and they raised Don Quixote, who was in an ill plight from his fall and went limping to kneel as best he could before the Duke and Duchess. But the Duke would on no account permit this; instead he dismounted from his horse and went to embrace Don Quixote, saying:

---

15. **girthed:** Encircled, belted.
16. **discomfiture:** Embarrassment.

"I am grieved, Sir Knight of the Sad Countenance, that the first step your worship has taken upon my land has been as unlucky as we have seen; but the carelessness of squires is often the cause of even worse accidents."

"The moment of my first meeting with you, valorous Prince," answered Don Quixote, "could not possibly be unlucky, even had my fall been to the center of the deep abyss; for even from there the glory of seeing you would have raised and rescued me. My squire—God's curse on him—is better at loosening his tongue to utter malice than at securing a saddle firmly. But wherever I may be, prostrate or upright, on foot or horse, I shall always be at the service of yourself and of my lady the Duchess, your worthy consort,[17] the sovereign mistress of beauty and universal princess of courtesy."

"Gently, my dear Don Quixote de la Mancha," said the Duke, "for where my lady Doña Dulcinea del Toboso is no other beauties should be praised."

By this time Sancho Panza was free from the noose and, being close at hand, anticipated his master's reply by saying: "It cannot be denied—in fact it must be declared that my lady Dulcinea del Toboso is very beautiful. But the hare starts up when least you expect it, and I've heard say that what's called Nature is like a potter who makes vessels of clay, and if a man makes one fine pot he can also make two, three or a hundred. This I say because my Lady the Duchess is every bit as fine as the lady Dulcinea del Toboso, I swear."

Don Quixote turned to the Duchess and said: "Your Highness can imagine that never in the world has knight errant had a more garrulous[18] or a droller squire than mine, and he will prove my words if your great Sublimity will accept my service for a few days."

To which the Duchess replied: "I am most heartily glad that Sancho is droll, for it is a sign that he is wise. Since jokes and humor, Don Quixote, as you very well know, do not go with sluggish wits. So, as the good Sancho is droll and humorous, from now on I'll affirm he is wise."

"And garrulous," added Don Quixote.

"So much the better," said the Duke. "For much humor cannot be expressed in few words. But let us not waste our time in talk. Come, great Knight of the Sad Countenance . . ."

"Of the Lions, your Highness, should say," interrupted Sancho, "for there's no *Sad Countenance* now."

"*Of the Lions*, be it," continued the Duke, "Come, Sir Knight of the Lions, I say, to a castle of mine not far from here. There you will be entertained as so exalted a personage should be, and as the Duchess and I are accustomed to entertain all knights errant who come here."

---

17. **consort:** Spouse, mate, or partner.
18. **garrulous:** Overly talkative, longwinded.

While they were speaking Sancho had adjusted and girthed Rocinante's saddle. So, Don Quixote mounting on him, and the Duke on a fine horse, they put the Duchess between them and took the road for the castle, the Duchess commanding that Sancho should ride beside her, for she found infinite delight in listening to his wise sayings. Sancho did not require pressing, and working his way in among the three of them, made a fourth in the conversation, to the great pleasure of the Duke and Duchess, who counted it great good fortune to receive in their castle such a knight errant[19] and so itinerant[20] a squire.

---

19. **knight errant:** A free-lance knight, not permanently attached to any master.
20. **itinerant:** Wandering.

☑ Check Your Comprehension

1. In the prologue the author fears that the public will judge his book harshly. List three features that the author thinks his book should have, but lacks.

2. What does the author's friend tell him to do about references to authors?

3. Summarize Chapter XXIX, The Famous Adventure of the Enchanted Boat.

4. Identify and give an example of one good and one bad character trait that Sancho Panza reveals in The Famous Adventure of the Enchanted Boat.

5. In Chapter XXX how do the Duke and Duchess know about Don Quixote?

6. What kind of impression do Don Quixote and Sancho Panza make when they present themselves to the Duke and Duchess? And how do the Duke and Duchess treat them?

◆ Critical Thinking Questions

INTERPRET

1. What advice about writing does the author's friend give him at the end of the prologue? Find an example of this kind of writing in *Don Quixote*. **[Analyze; Evaluate]**

2. In Chapter XXIX, Don Quixote uses three words that Sancho Panza misunderstands. What are they? Could this misunderstanding have been avoided? How? **[Interpret]**

3. In Chapter XXX, why does Don Quixote tell Sancho Panza not to mix any proverbs into his address to the Duchess? Why does Sancho Panza take offense at this advice? **[Interpret]**

4. Sancho Panza compares himself to a well-stocked house in Chapter XXX. What is he trying to say about himself by this comparison? **[Interpret]**

5. Don Quixote calls Sancho Panza "garrulous" at the end of Chapter XXX. Compare Don Quixote's attitude toward this characteristic with that of the Duke and Duchess. **[Evaluate]**

Dale Wasserman and Joe Darion

from Man of La Mancha

ALDONZA: What does it mean—quest?
DON QUIXOTE: The mission of each true knight . . . his
duty—nay, his privilege! *(He sings)*

> To dream the impossible dream,
> To fight the unbeatable foe,
> To bear with unbearable sorrow,
> To run where the brave dare not go.
>
> To right the unrightable wrong,
> To love, pure and chaste, from afar,
> To try, when your arms are too weary,
> To reach the unreachable star!
>
> This is my Quest, to follow that star,
> No matter how hopeless, no matter how far,
> To fight for the right without question or pause,
> To be willing to march into hell for a heavenly
>   cause!
>
> And I know, if I'll only be true to this glorious
>   quest,
> That my heart will lie peaceful and calm when
>   I'm laid to my rest.
> And the world will be better for this,
> That one man, scorned and covered with scars,
> Still strove, with his last ounce of courage,
> To reach the unreachable stars!

Miguel de Cervantes
Comparing and Connecting the Author's Works

◆ Literary Focus: Levels of Style

Cervantes' main characters perceive the world differently: Where Sancho Panza sees an empty fishing boat floating in the river, Don Quixote sees an enchanted vessel sent to transport him to a chivalric adventure. They have corresponding differences in style: they express themselves differently, too.

Sancho Panza uses the low style, the simple, down-to-earth language of ordinary folk; Don Quixote uses the high style, a type of language appropriate to the educated and upper classes. **Style** is not <u>what</u> you express, but the combination of distinctive features of expression: in other words, <u>how</u> you express it.

In Chapter XXIX, Sancho Panza and Don Quixote disagree about how to determine how far they have traveled in their borrowed boat. Sancho Panza says: "I don't believe a word of that, but I'll do what your worship orders all the same though I don't know why we need make these experiments, for I can see with my own eyes that we haven't moved more than five yards from the bank." Don Quixote replies: "Make the investigation I asked of you Sancho and do not worry about the colures, lines, parallels, zodiacs. eclilptics, poles, solstices, equinoxes, planets, signs of the zodiac and points which are the measures of which the celestial and terrestrial spheres are composed."

1. Compare the message communicated by each speaker's statement; compare the vocabulary used by each speaker.
2. What information do you infer about the education and social background of each speaker from his style?

3. What does the speaker's style tell you about his tone, or attitude towards his subject or his audience? The grid shows some of the features of high and low styles. Use it to analyze speeches in Chapters XXIX and XXX.

	High Style	**Low Style**
Speaker:	educated upper class equal or superior to audience	uneducated lower class equal or inferior to audience
Purpose:	show respect flatter, impress	show familiarity
Language:	formal language foreign or archaic long complex sentences literary references	informal language contractions, dialect, slang simple/ compound sentences popular general knowledge

4. In Chapter XXIX, Don Quixote scolds Sancho Panza for cowardice. What features of the high style do you find there?
5. What style does Sancho Panza use when he first introduces himself to the Duchess in Chapter XXX? What features of this style do you recognize?

◆ Idea Bank

Writing

1. Write a short letter to a great-aunt announcing the death of a beloved relative. Write another letter to this same aunt informing her the super-

market is out of bananas. What style do you use in each and why?

2. Rewrite Don Quixote's speech to Sancho Panza accusing him of cowardice in the low style.

3. Write a brief letter asking for a job in both the high style and the low style. What determines which style you will use?

Listening and Speaking

4. Carry on a conversation with a classmate in which one of you uses the high style and the other uses the low style. **[Performing Arts Link]**

5. Discuss your plans for the weekend in the high style.

6. In a small group, decide what the appropriate style would be for: a letter asking for a job; a notice on a supermarket bulletin board about a lost cat; a love letter; a wedding announcement. What features from the grid count most in making the decision for each one? **[Communications Link]**

Research and Representing

7. Shakespeare was an exact contemporary of Cervantes. Find a character in a Shakespeare play who uses the low style and another in the same play that uses the high style. **[Drama Link]**

◆ Further Reading, Listening and Viewing

- Dale Wasserman (book): *Man of La Mancha*. Music by Mitch Lee and Lyrics by Joe Darion. The stage musical of Cervantes' novel also filmed for the cinema

- Anthony Mann (director): *El Cid* (1960). A Castilian knight tries to keep his country from civil war in the year 1060

- William Byron: *Cervantes: A Biography* (1979). A lively, detailed and colorful account of Cervantes' life

- Manuel de Falla: *Master Peter's Puppet Show* (1959). An opera based on Chapter XXVI of Cervantes' novel

- Jules Masssenet: *Don Quichotte* (1910). French opera in five-acts based on Don Quixote

On the Web:

http://www.phschool.com/atschool/literature
Go to the student edition *Platinum*. Proceed to Unit 10. Then, click Hot Links to find Web sites featuring Miguel de Cervantes Saavedra.

HarperCollins Publishers
From *Pilgrim at Tinker Creek* by Annie Dillard, Copyright © 1974 by Annie Dillard: "Untying the Knot" and "Intricacy." Excerpt from *An American Childhood* by Annie Dillard. Copyright © 1987 by Annie Dillard. Excerpt from *The Writing Life* by Annie Dillard. Copyright © 1989 by Annie Dillard. "Living Like Weasels" and "Sojourner" from *Teaching a Stone to Talk* by Annie Dillard, Copyright © 1982 by Annie Dillard.

Harvard University Press
"The Pit and the Pendulum" from *Collected Works of Edgar Allan Poe.* Copyright © 1969 and 1978 by The President and Fellows of Harvard College.

Alfred A. Knopf
From *Collected Poems* by Langston Hughes. Copyright © 1994 by the Estate of Langston Hughes: "I Dream a World," "Boogie: 1 a.m.," "Juke Box Love Song," "Good Morning," "My People," "Me and My Song," "Afro-American Fragment," "We're All in the Telephone Book," "Luck," "Stars," and "Bouquet." Reprinted by permission of Alfred A. Knopf Inc.

Oxford University Press UK
From *The Poems of Emily Brontë,* edited by Derek Roper with Edward Chitham, © Derek Roper 1995: "Song," "Hope," "To Imagination," "Stanzas," "High waveing heather . . . ," "The day is done—the winter sun," and "My heart is not enraptur'd now . . . "

Penguin Books Ltd.
Excerpts from the First Part Prologue and the text of *The Adventures of Don Quixote* by Miguel de Cervantes Saavedra, translated by J. M. Cohen, first published 1950.

Random House, Inc.
Excerpt from *Man of La Mancha* written by Dale Wasserman. Copyright © 1966 by Dale Wasserman; Copyright © 1965 Andrew Scott, Inc.; Copyright © 1968 by Dell Publishing Co., Inc.

University of Chicago Press
From Sophocles, "Oedipus the King," translated by David Grene, from *The Complete Greek Tragedies,* edited by David Grene and Richmond Lattimore. Copyright 1954 by The University of Chicago. Reprinted by permission of the publisher, the University of Chicago.

University of Iowa Press
Excerpt from *The Brontës: Interviews and Recollections,* edited by Harold Orel. Copyright © 1997 by Harold Orel. Reprinted by permission of University of Iowa Press.

University of New Mexico Press
"Remembering Lobo" from *Nepantla: Essays from the Land of the Middle* by Pat Mora. Copyright © 1993 by University of New Mexico Press. Reprinted by permission of University of New Mexico Press.

A. P. Watt
"The Bet" from *Selected Tales of Tchehov,* translated from the Russian by Constance Garnett. Copyright 1949. "Difficult People" from *The Essential Tales of Chekhov,* translated by Constance Garnett. Copyright © 1919, 1972 by Macmillan Company.

Note: Every effort has been made to locate the copyright owner of material reprinted in this book. Omissions brought to our attention will be corrected in subsequent editions.

Photo Credits

Cover photos clockwise from upper left:
Edgar Allan Poe: Corbis-Bettmann; Miguel de Cervantes: The Granger Collection, New York; Langston Hughes: New York Public Library; Pat Mora: ARTE PUBLICO PRESS; Sophocles: Vatican Museum/Scala/Art Resource, NY; Annie Dillard: Thomas Victor; Alfred, Lord Tennyson: c.1840, S. Laurence, By courtesy of the National Portrait Gallery, London; Gwendolyn Brooks: Corbis-Bettmann; Anton Chekhov: Corbis-Bettmann; Emily Brontë: The Granger Collection, New York.

• • • •